TREATING SELF-DESTRUCTIVE BEHAVIORS IN TRAUMA SURVIVORS

Treating Self-Destructive Behaviors in Trauma Survivors, Second Edition, is a book for clinicians who specialize in helping trauma survivors and, during the course of treatment, find themselves unexpectedly confronted with client disclosures of self-destructive behaviors, including self-mutilation and other manifestations of deliberately "hurting the body" such as bingeing, purging, starving, substance abuse, and other addictive behaviors. Arguing that standard safety contracts are not effective, renowned clinician Lisa Ferentz introduces viable treatment alternatives, assessment tools, and new ways of understanding self-destructive behaviors using a strengths-based approach that distinguishes between the "experimental" non-suicidal self-injury (NSSI) that some teenagers occasionally engage in and the self-destructive behaviors that are repetitive and chronic. In the new edition, many of the treatment strategies are cross referenced to a useful workbook, giving therapists and clients concrete ways to integrate theory into practice. In addition, Ferentz emphasizes the importance of assessing and strengthening clients' self-compassion, and explains how nurturing this idea cognitively, emotionally, and somatically can become the catalyst for motivation and change. The book also explores a cycle of behavior that clinicians can personalize and use as a template for treatment. In its final sections, the book focuses on counter-transferential responses and the different ways in which therapists can work with self-destructive behaviors and avoid vicarious traumatization by adopting tools and strategies for self-care.

Treating Self-Destructive Behaviors in Trauma Survivors, Second Edition, can be used on its own or in conjunction with the accompanying client-focused workbook, *Letting Go of Self-Destructive Behaviors: A Workbook of Hope and Healing*.

Lisa Ferentz, LCSW-C, is the president and founder of the Institute for Advanced Psychotherapy Training and Education, which provides continuing education to mental health professionals. She is an internationally acclaimed speaker and highly sought after clinical consultant. She has been in solo private practice specializing in trauma for more than thirty years, and in 2009 was named social worker of the year by the Maryland Society for Clinical Social Work.

TREATING SELF-DESTRUCTIVE BEHAVIORS IN TRAUMA SURVIVORS

A Clinician's Guide, Second Edition

Lisa Ferentz

Routledge
Taylor & Francis Group

NEW YORK AND LONDON

Second edition published 2015
by Routledge
711 Third Avenue, New York, NY 10017

and by Routledge
2 Park Square, Milton Park, Abingdon, Oxon OX14 4RN

Routledge is an imprint of the Taylor & Francis Group, an informa business

First edition published by Routledge 2012

Library of Congress Cataloging in Publication Data
Lisa Ferentz, author.
Treating Self-destructive behavior in Trauma survivors:
a clinician's guide/by Lisa Ferentz.—Second edition.
p.; cm.
Includes bibliographic references and index.

ISBN: 978-1-138-80074-8 (hbk)
ISBN: 978-1-138-80075-5 (pbk)
ISBN: 978-1-315-75529-8 (ebk)

Typeset in New Baskerville and Stone Sans
by Swales & Willis Ltd, Exeter, Devon, UK

DEDICATIONS

This book is dedicated, with much love, to my parents, siblings, husband, and children. Everything I am grateful for "makes sense" given where I've come from, and the immeasurable love, support, and joy you bring to my life.

And to all of my clients—past and present teachers—for the countless ways in which you have educated me with your wisdom and inspired me with your courage, resiliency, and grace.

CONTENTS

PREFACE

I am delighted that this book has piqued your curiosity! I know you will find the clinical philosophy and creative treatment approaches genuinely helpful as you strive to effectively and compassionately work with the very challenging issue of treating your clients' self-destructive behaviors. One of the new components to this second edition is the cross referencing that links many of the treatment strategies to exercises from my second book, *Letting Go of Self-Destructive Behaviors: A Workbook of Hope and Healing.*

The workbook is written for people who struggle with eating disorders, addictions, and acts of self-mutilation and self-harm. It can be used as a companion piece as you integrate the treatment philosophy and techniques described in this second edition. As you read about various strategies that can be used, you'll be given the coinciding pages in the workbook where clients can put the techniques into practice. You can use these exercises as homework assignments to be processed in subsequent sessions, or you can incorporate the writing, drawing, collaging, and visualization prompts to create content for an actual therapy session.

The great advantage to this approach is that you and your clients will be "on the same page" in terms of the way you think about and treat self-destructive behaviors. Your open-hearted and open-minded willingness to read this book means you will bring a strengths-based approach to a presenting problem that is often frightening or confusing. As your clients identify, explore, and process the workbook material, their insights will also be rooted in this strengths-based approach.

In the workbook, those who are struggling are encouraged to do their work with the guidance, wisdom, and support of therapists who can address their symptoms with compassion and creativity. This book will enhance your ability to do just that! One of the most powerful byproducts will be a strengthened trusting therapeutic alliance, which can create a context for safe and non-judgmental healing.

Publishing a second edition of this book provides a great opportunity to highlight a component of this work that is crucial for clinicians to focus on and for clients to eventually embrace and integrate in their healing journeys. Clinicians should pay close attention to the issue of *self-compassion* when working with traumatized clients who use self-destructive behaviors to cope. As you'll see in future chapters, many of these clients don't come into therapy with the ability to see themselves through a compassionate lens. They usually hold feelings of guilt, anger, disappointment, frustration, and shame, and those emotions are typically directed at themselves. Keep in mind that if your clients struggle at times with the strategies presented in this book, it might be because you haven't adequately addressed their inability to access and hold self-compassion.

You've probably noticed that these clients are often able to feel and express compassion towards other people: engaging in acts of kindness, forgiving others when they make mistakes, hurt them, or let them down. When they see people "beating themselves up" they might try to be encouraging or offer a more realistic perspective. They can gently say, "You're human, we all make mistakes, don't worry about it, you can let it go." Ironically, being empathic comes so easily and naturally, as long as they are directing those words of kindness and encouragement *to someone else.*

It's interesting that people who find it relatively easy to be kind, supportive, and understanding to others actually score fairly low on self-compassion tests (Neff, 2011). They are more likely to chastise themselves for shortcomings or for poor choices made in the past. They may also berate themselves for an inability to integrate new behaviors. Many clients actually believe the best way to motivate themselves is by evoking feelings of guilt. They think that being hard on themselves is a way to make changes or succeed in life. If they are too easy on themselves everything will eventually fall apart. I frequently see this in clients who have abuse or pain narratives. They attempt to move ahead in life by listening to an inner voice that is bullying, embarrassing, or shaming.

Unfortunately, this mindset is probably reinforced by our culture which still sees positive self-talk as too "touchy feely." People are afraid they won't get things done, won't be competitive or successful enough unless they are relentlessly driven (Seppala, 2011; Neff, 2013). Our society supports the notion of motivating through constant reminders of flaws and deficits, rather than through words of encouragement. We think this will get us to try harder. Or we keep comparing ourselves to others, focusing on how we fall short, so we don't become complacent and get left behind. As you teach your clients the strategies in this book, pay attention to the extent to which they are using shame as a source of motivation, and recognize that this will inevitably backfire and never create sustained changes. Since some of this book is also focused on you, the helping professional, notice the ways in which you internally use shaming words in an effort to push or chastise yourself when treatment isn't progressing fast enough.

Additionally, clients shy away from self-compassion because they equate positive self-talk with being self-indulgent (Neff, 2004). They may come into therapy believing they are inherently crazy or out of control, and if they coddle themselves with kindness, they won't be able to stay in check or prevent their "true" negative selves from surfacing. So, they constantly berate themselves, pointing out their inadequacies and focusing on what they haven't accomplished, rather than giving themselves credit for what they have accomplished. I call this the "yeah, but" syndrome. I'll say, "Wow you did this great thing" and they'll say, "Yeah, but I haven't done this other thing yet!" As a result, positive accomplishments get minimized and even discounted, trumped by the fact that they haven't realized some other goal yet. And usually this becomes a bottomless well of "something else," so it never really feels acceptable to cel-ebrate. Often this is a mindset taught to them by a harsh or abusive caretaker.

If your clients have this attitude, then it might resonate for them to feel defeated, give up, or label a challenge as overwhelm-ing and not doable. The more self-criticism, the more fearful cli-ents become about the possibility of failing. This fear of failure can be crippling, leading clients to the conclusion that it's not worth trying because failing is too devastating an outcome. If your clients seem hesitant to move forward in their work con-sider the possibility that they are being held back, in part, by this fear of failure. When clients focus on all of their shortcomings, often exaggerating them, it will never motivate them to succeed. It just creates the self-fulfilling prophecy of doing less, which, sadly, generates new "evidence" and perpetuates the idea that they can't measure up. As the helping professional and guide in their healing journey, it's important to point out this paradox. The reality is, clients are *more* motivated when they talk to them-selves with self-compassion, rather than bullying or shaming themselves into doing a desired behavior or making an impor-tant change. The more they beat themselves up and self-criticize the *less* likely they are to feel motivated to change.

When your clients frequently criticize themselves they begin to lose an accurate sense of self. Struggling with self-destructive behaviors means there are arenas ripe for growth and change. But these clients "can't see the forest for the trees" so their objective, realistic view of their strengths and weaknesses overlap, become blurred and indecipherable. Research shows that self-critics are more likely to be anxious and depressed, and have less self-confidence in their abilities (Neff, 2011).

Conversely, people who feel higher degrees of self-compassion statistically have lower rates of stress, anxiety, and depression, are more likely to gravitate towards healthier behaviors, seek medical attention when they need it, report greater levels of happiness, and ultimately, accomplish more in their lives (Neff, 2011). Additionally, people who are self-compassionate are less likely to feel incompetent or humiliated, or take things too personally (Neff, 2011). This is critically important for those who struggle with self-destructive acts. When they can talk about their behaviors with empathy or de-personalize their triggers, this goes a long way towards mitigating and reducing the anxiety and shame that perpetuates the self-harm cycle.

I also believe that people who are kind to themselves are less likely to be in emotionally unavailable or abusive relationships and more likely to leave a toxic, unfulfilling workplace. They tend to be more patient with their children, less haunted by shame, better able to handle challenges in life, and overall feel a greater sense of inner peace.

Neff (2011) talks about compassion being associated with the alleviation of suffering. This is critical for clients who hurt themselves as a way to cope and survive. When they can feel a sense of compassion and empathy for the pain that comes from self-destructive acts, poor choices, inadvertent mistakes, falling short in some way, dysfunctional coping strategies, or unresolved trauma, they are motivated to want to heal that pain. This can be an important step in finding the courage to try the new behaviors offered in this book. *Self-compassion becomes the catalyst for motivation and change.* It motivates through a desire to be healthy, rather than motivating through guilt, shame, or the fear of self-punishment.

When clients operate from self-compassion it also helps them recognize that failure is an inevitable part of life (Emel, 2013; Neff, 2011). That's important because some of the resistance to self-compassion is the idea that it sugarcoats everything. Being self-compassionate doesn't mean being in denial about what a client has done or what they need to start doing differently. It's just a better, gentler way of processing those things and coming to new insights about how to move forward.

When clients can look at "failure" through a lens of self-compassion they can see that "failing" at something actually creates an opportunity to learn and grow (Seppala, 2011.) It's not something they need to run from or bully themselves into avoiding. It's actually something they can embrace when they see it as an opportunity for growth. Helping clients to assess their disappointing actions in a compassionate way can motivate them to make positive changes because they want to be happier and believe they deserve that happiness.

You will see how important it is to incorporate self-compassion into the work when we look at the cycle of self-destructive behaviors and talk about re-framing "failures" and other negative thoughts. The notion of "failing" is replaced with the idea of a "teaching moment." Rather than getting stuck on the "hamster wheel" of self-blame, we move clients forward by teaching them to nonjudgmentally ask, "What could I have done differently? If I could 're-wind the tape' what would I see that could help me make different choices next time?" "Did I have an option other than hurting myself?" One of the things that will help your clients get off that hamster wheel and move forward will be the conscious awareness of incorporating self-compassion when answering those questions.

When assessing for your clients' levels of self-compassion look for how they react when faced with challenging life experiences, and how they view themselves when they do any form of self-inventory. Since most clients chronically engage in self-destructive acts even when they don't want to, you will have many opportunities to track their reactions and assess for self-compassion.

If they handle a situation poorly, repeat an unwanted behavior, or react in ways that are not effective, notice if they become judgmental or self-critical. How do they respond when they focus on qualities they don't particularly like about themselves? When they identify a personal flaw notice if they get stuck in obsessive thinking rather than addressing it in a pro-active way. Can they find ways to be patient and understanding about their shortcomings and self-harming acts or do they become angry or intolerant of them?

Clients' self-perceptions and self-talk will go beyond their reactions to destructive behaviors. Listen closely as they process their experiences at work, their inter-personal dynamics, the challenges they face as parents, the narratives they hold about family-of-origin experiences, and prior trauma or abuse. Clients who are lacking in self-compassion will always home in on their mistakes. And they tend to beat themselves up more after identifying them. When you point out their suffering notice if they minimize their pain, engage in self-blame, or seem unwilling to self-soothe with words of comfort or hope. Assess for the extent to which they exhibit any empathy for their struggles.

Let me give you a few examples from my work as I think this will bring these issues to light for you. A 23-year-old client recently had her first baby. She still had some of her pregnancy weight on and every time she looked in the mirror she heard herself saying, "I am so fat. I can't believe I gained all of this weight and I still can't get it off. I hate my body and I'm going to starve it until I lose the extra pounds." A 17-year-old boy missed a goal in soccer and re-lived it over and over in his mind saying, "I let down the entire team. I totally embarrassed myself in front of everyone. No one is going to want me on their team next season. I'm a loser and I'm just gonna cut myself." Or the 55-year-old client suffering from panic who berated himself after every episode saying, "I'm crazy. No one else suffers from these attacks the way I do. I'll never be able to get them under control. The only thing left to do is drink."

You can hear how their self-talk is unfair, critical, judgmental, and detrimental to their sense of self. In all three cases, guilt and shame are the prevailing emotions rather than kindness and empathy, and as a result, these clients are primed to hurt themselves. The total lack of self-compassion sets them up to actually perpetuate a self-destructive behavior, which, in turn, will continue to fuel feelings of failure and self-loathing.

If instead, these clients learned to approach their struggles with kindness, understanding, patience, and a higher level of tolerance for the inevitable difficulties that everyone encounters in life, self-compassion would begin to emerge. Recognizing that countless people grapple with the same issues helps to engender self-compassion and empathy (Emel, 2013; Seppala, 2011). If these clients could bring a more balanced perspective to their experiences it would begin to diminish the intensity and power of their shortcomings. This includes the ability to recognize that what's happening is not the end of the world, is typically time-limited, and can be addressed and resolved with a forward thinking action plan.

Staying with those same examples, notice the profound shift in thinking after clients integrate the concept of self-compassion. These are exciting examples to share because these clients did not start out from a place of self-compassion, yet they all landed there in time. And I can tell you that it has made a huge, positive difference in their lives.

The 23-year-old new mother was able to eventually say, "It's amazing that my body created, carried, and birthed a baby! My baby is only nine months old so it makes sense that I wouldn't be at my pre-pregnancy weight yet. It's probably unfair to beat myself up about it. I know, in time, I'll lose the weight and starving myself would be a mean thing to do."

The 17-year-old soccer player changed his internal tape, too. He was able to start telling himself that *everyone*, even professional players, occasionally misses goals. He realized that everyone on his team had missed goals throughout the season, and no one else was worried about being kicked off the team so he probably shouldn't worry either. He was even able to focus on the goals he *had* made during the season and realized he never really celebrated those before. He also recognized how much soccer meant to him and if he began cutting again it would jeopardize his position on the team.

The 55-year-old client with panic attacks actually figured out the more he beat himself up for the attacks and abused alcohol the more his panic increased and the longer his episodes lasted. He said, "When I breath and accept what I'm feeling it actually shortens the attacks. So I figured out I *can* manage them without drinking, and actually it's kind of moving that I have suffered for so long and been alone in my pain for much of my life."

So, how can we help our clients move forward in this quest for increased self-compassion? As I discuss in a later chapter, there is nothing more powerful than the way clients talk to themselves about themselves. I absolutely believe this to be true. Clients often think that their level of happiness and sense of well-being is contingent upon how other people talk to them and treat them, but the honest truth is, they are most affected by the way they talk to and treat themselves. This is actually great news because it is the one thing in life they can control and change! It's not possible to get other people to always say and do things that are validating or positively reinforcing. Ultimately, a healthy, loving sense of self has to be internally based.

I often say that other people may try to give them "tickets" for a guilt trip. They may wave those tickets in their faces and beg them to take the trip. But ultimately each person decides if they are going to take the tickets, get on the bus, and take that ride. When it comes to a lack of self-compassion, they are not only grabbing the tickets, they are actually driving the bus! They can choose to crash it into a tree or choose to move on a path towards inner peace, self-acceptance, and positive change. Many of the strategies in this book will give you and your clients opportunities to re-frame negative and self-effacing thoughts and feelings. Let your clients know that the intention is to build self-compassion. This is a key that unlocks many doors for them.

Obviously, the opposite of self-compassion is self-criticism. Help your clients to identify, without judgment, the way or ways in which they do their inner criticism. Teach them to notice when they start to go to that place and help them to realize that, in the end, it won't be helpful. This is a powerful first step. They might be amazed by how often that destructive voice kicks in throughout the day. Many of my clients discover certain words or phrases they internalize when they become self-critical. Some of the more common thoughts include:

"I can't do this," "I shouldn't do this," or "I should do this."

"I can't believe I screwed up again."

"I'm stupid."

"I need to be like everyone else."

"This is not good enough."

"I am being lazy."

"I don't deserve to be loved."

"What the hell is wrong with me?" "Everyone is better than me."

"Everyone knows there is something wrong with me."

"I made a horrible mistake."

"I am so disgusting."

In addition to recognizing the words, help your clients pay attention to their tone of voice. Is it harsh, mean, cold, enraged? Is it reminiscent of someone from their past who was relentlessly critical of them, too? Once they have an awareness of their own process, you can begin to help them shift that voice and those messages. In the chapter that addresses negative thoughts you will learn about helping clients to create a healthier "inner tape." Again, the key idea is to soften criticism and eliminate a feeling of shame. Help your clients to approach this task, as well as other strategies designed to re-frame negative thoughts and feelings, with *kindness*. Help them to recognize that the intention—to motivate, protect, or move forward—is actually being hampered by a self-critical approach. Again, they are back on the hamster wheel and not moving forward!

As you embark on this journey with your clients, keep in mind that when they notice their negative, critical inner messages, and learn to shift them to thoughts that are kinder and more supportive, they actually increase the likelihood that they *will* be motivated to try harder, be happier, and experience more inner peace and self-confidence. Focusing on self-compassion can help change a long-standing cultural belief that the way to promote change and growth is through bullying and intense criticism. Letting go of this mindset will have a positive effect on our clients, making the idea of engaging in self-destructive behaviors more and more dissonant. Sometimes therapy may feel stalled. This is an inevitable and normal part of the journey. Help your clients to have compassion about that, too. Continue to revisit the concept of self-compassion. You will discover that it is a great way to jumpstart the process and inspire a genuine desire to heal. And continue to tap into your own feelings of self-compassion. This work is very rewarding, and at times, very challenging. Your clients are fortunate to have your wisdom, encouragement, guidance, and sense of hope. You don't have to have all of the answers all of the time. One of your most important contributions will be modeling self-compassion!

ACKNOWLEDGMENT

There isn't a day that goes by when I am not profoundly grateful for my two amazing parents, Sasha and Burt, my remarkable 99 year old grandmother Fay, and my incredible siblings, Steven, Beth, and David. You have always been a source of such love and support. I deeply treasure the memories we share, the new ones we create, and the laughter and warmth they evoke. Thank you all for the precious gift of having you in my life.

Throughout my career, I have been blessed with the support and encouragement of many talented colleagues and dear friends. They were unwavering cheerleaders for the first edition, and continue to give such generous support and feedback about my work. I am deeply grateful to Michael Kermin, Sabrina N'Diaye, Susan and Jerry Osofsky, Patricia Mullen, Dr. Patricia Papernow, Dr. Joy Silberg, Amy Weintraub, Denise Tordella, Robyn Brickel, Maria Hadjiyane, Joan Kristall, Susan Kachur, Nancy Napier, Dr. Daniel Lerner, Elaine Witman, Suzanne Ricklin, Peggy Kolodny, Debbie Marks, and Meg Wolitzer.

I am also grateful to all of the exceptional faculty and wonderful participants at my Institute for their enthusiasm about the book, and their ongoing loyalty. To my three incredibly creative and energetic assistants, Gerri Baum, Kim Brandwin, and Renee Moore, I really couldn't do what I do without you. Thank you for being as passionate about the work as I am.

An extra special thank you to my editor and dear friend, Anna Moore, for everything you do to encourage and support me. It is a blessing having you in my corner. I also want to thank

Kate Reeves, Elizabeth Graber, Julie Willis, Sarah Hudson, Julia Gardiner, and Paris West, for their great attention to detail and their diligent behind-the-scenes efforts to bring this second edition to print.

I continue to be indebted to the clinical work of Tracy Alderman, whose "cycle of addiction" was the inspiration for my paradigm, and to Dusty Miller, whose Trauma-Re-enactment Syndrome model offers a brilliant way to understand and treat self-harm and has deeply influenced my work. I am also very grateful to the giants in our field, particularly Milton Erickson, Eric Erickson, John Bowlby, Mary Ainsworth, Bessel van der Kok, Judith Herman, Babette Rothschild, Pat Ogden, Peter Levine, and Daniel Siegel, whose research and clinical acumen continue to inform my clinical practice.

I am forever grateful for the guidance, wisdom, friendship, and support that I receive from Richard Schwartz, the brilliant creator of the Internal Family Systems paradigm. Throughout this book, any references that are made to identifying and working with clients' "parts" have been directly inspired by Dick's model. I am also deeply grateful for the love, encouragement, clinical wisdom, and enthusiastic cheerleading and feedback that my dear friend and "co-mentor" Dr. Janina Fisher is always on hand to supply.

And most of all, my deepest gratitude goes to Kevin, my amazing husband, best friend, and gifted editor. I could not ask for a more loving, generous, supportive, encouraging life partner. You understand my mission and my passion, and you have helped me, every step of the way, to achieve my goals. Thank you for making this a much better book. And thank you for inspiring me to be a better me. And to our beautiful three grown sons, Jacob, Zachary, and Noah, no matter what I accomplish or achieve in my lifetime, you will always be the three best gifts I'll ever have.

PART I

IT MAKES SENSE
GIVEN WHERE THEY'VE
COME FROM

1

TOWARD A NEW UNDERSTANDING OF SELF-DESTRUCTIVE BEHAVIORS

See if you can relate to the following clinical scenario: There are 5 minutes to go at the end of a seemingly calm and productive therapy session with a trauma survivor. Suddenly, the client rolls up her sleeve, exposes her wrist and forearm, and reveals five deep, angry-looking scratches and a cigarette burn. Her affect is a combination of intense shame and pride. She says she spent the whole session internally debating about whether to show you what she had done the night before. She discloses that she has been hurting her body off and on for years. She is worried that you will be angry, disgusted, or afraid. She is even more terrified about the possibility of you wanting to put her in the hospital. You are trying to maintain an outwardly calm facade, yet your heart is racing, and you are unsure of how to proceed. Although you have been working competently and comfortably with trauma survivors and their issues, when faced with client disclosures of chronic self-destructive behaviors, you are on less confident ground.

Those of us who work with trauma have many tools in our toolbox. We understand the importance of building a therapeutic alliance, incorporating mind–body approaches, addressing cognitive distortions, creating safety, assessing for attachment, focusing on affect regulation, and offering clients reparative experiences. However, much of this sound clinical knowledge can be overshadowed by anxiety and other countertransferential responses that get activated when challenging and tenacious self-destructive behaviors such as eating disorders, addictions, and acts of self-mutilation (cutting, burning, inserting objects into the body, etc.) are brought into the therapy room. As a result, we are put into a state of emotional disequilibrium, trying to balance genuine compassion and concern for the client with our own fears and hyperarousal. Walking this tightrope can deplete our energy and focus and potentially compromise our clinical efficacy.

Much of the time, self-destructive acts are not articulated as the presenting problem or revealed to us in the early stages of treatment. In fact, many clients who have experienced significant traumatic events do not initially identify themselves as trauma survivors. When these issues surface in treatment, they can catch well-meaning and well-qualified clinicians off guard. This book offers guidance to therapists who may feel blindsided or understandably overwhelmed by disclosures of childhood abuse and subsequent behaviors that harm the body.

It would be inaccurate to state that all clients who engage in self-destructive behaviors have prior histories of trauma, abuse, or neglect. However, this book is designed to specifically explore the connections between trauma and self-destructive behaviors, offering creative ways to work with the large cohort of people who chronically harm or injure their bodies and who do come from significantly dysfunctional and abusive backgrounds. The correlation between abuse, neglect, and self-destructive behaviors has been well documented in the literature and is worthy of our attention (Briere & Jordan, 2009; Cozolino, 2006; Gladstone et al., 2004; Glassman, Weierich, Hooley, Deliberto, & Nock, 2007; Goulding & Schwartz, 2002; Gratz, 2003; Hollander, 2008; Miller, 1994; Najavits, 2001; Nock & Prinstein, 2005; Sansone, Gaither, & Songer, 2001; van der Kolk, McFarlane, & Weisaeth, 2006; van der Kolk, Perry, & Herman, 1991; Yates, 2004).

We will focus on male and female adolescent and adult clients who engage in self-destructive acts that are repetitive, chronic, and diversified and who, on closer inspection, come from backgrounds where abuse, neglect, and traumatic experiences were the norm. In these cases, acts that compromise the body can be attributed to severe affect dysregulation, loss of attachment, feelings of worthlessness, distorted self-blame that evokes the need to self-punish, and the profoundly debilitating effects of a breach of caretaker trust and protection. In later chapters we will explore these issues in greater detail. Their identification and resolution become an important part of the treatment process.

Regarding acts of self-mutilation (cutting, burning, etc.), some well-respected researchers and clinicians emphasize the importance of focusing on and treating the function of the behavior (Hollander, 2008; Mikolajczak, Petrides, & Hurry, 2009; Nock and Prinstein, 2005). Yates (2004) also supported a more in-depth understanding of the functionality and treatment needs of this population when he said, "[A] negative response to self-injurious behavior has fueled a multitude of treatment paradigms that endeavor to eliminate the behavior, but place comparatively little emphasis on understanding its developmental origins and adaptational functions." (p. 63). Klonsky (2007) echoed this concept as well when he said, "Understanding the function of self-injury, or in other words, the variables that motivate and reinforce the behavior, could greatly improve prevention and treatment." (p. 228).

I feel it is equally essential to process the meaning of the behavior, particularly as it relates to unresolved trauma. Yates (2004) echoed this sentiment, suggesting that the treatment of self-injurious behavior (SIB) should integrate behavioral methods with "psychodynamic techniques to foster a greater understanding within the individual of the meaning of SIB" (p. 64). Swales (2008) also acknowledged that "some therapists advocate addressing the underlying problems in the past (and also in the present) that lead to the behavior, rather than focusing on the behavior itself. They argue that when these problems are resolved the behavior will cease" (p. 6). Glassman et al. (2007) theorized that if treatment focused on family interventions designed to eliminate the maltreatment of children, this would translate into a reduction of nonsuicidal self-injury in that population.

The treatment debate between addressing the function of the behavior versus addressing the meaning of the behavior can be confusing. I suggest it is equally valid to work on both pieces of this puzzle: What do clients "get" from their actions, and what is the underlying communication that is nonverbally articulated through the behavior? This invites an understanding and discussion of the "metacommunication" of these behaviors as they serve to either reenact or restory prior pain narratives. We will explore how to psychoeducationally present these issues to clients and then how to weave them into treatment strategies. In this way, we help clients gain the most insight and decrease the likelihood that they will sublimate the behavior into other self-destructive behaviors.

Despite the fact that self-destructive behaviors are often seen in adolescents, and it seems to be the population most often studied and written about by researchers and clinicians, if you are a therapist working in the trauma field, you know from firsthand experience that these behaviors continue well into adulthood. Many of my clients carved into their skin and were sexually promiscuous as teenagers, and in adulthood they grapple with bingeing and a sexual addiction that has left them with an STD or HIV.

Consider the possibility that many clients who began hurting their bodies as teenagers are still doing versions of self-destructive behaviors in their 40s, 50s, and 60s because their treatment remained solidly planted in present-tense cognitive behavioral work that simply attempted to extinguish the behavior. I believe one of the critical missing pieces for these clients is assessing for and healing their unresolved trauma. Symptomatic adults often carry "pain narratives" that have not been identified or decoded. Present-day parenting, relationships, and workplace challenges can rekindle anxiety, grief, fear, and rage that have their roots in unmetabolized past traumas. Clients regress back to the self-destructive behaviors of their adolescence when these unresolved emotions reemerge. If we don't address underlying causes and meaning, we may be trying to put a Band-Aid on something that actually requires surgery to extinguish the behavior and promote true healing.

In the past, attempts have been made by researchers such as Ross and McKay (1979) to compartmentalize self-destructive behaviors by classifying acts of self-mutilation such as cutting and burning as "direct" and other behaviors such as substance abuse and eating disorders as "indirect." Some current authors in the field focus predominately on acts of self-mutilation, suggesting that when those behaviors are thwarted, clients then develop other diagnoses including eating disorders and substance abuse.

I invite you to view all self-imposed, self-directed behaviors as self-destructive. Starving or purging; getting drunk or high; shopping or gambling compulsively; engaging in unsafe, unprotected sex; or taking a razor blade or lighter fluid to one's body can all serve the same purpose. For this reason, throughout the book the term *self-destructive behavior* represents this full range of addictive, destructive acts that are punitive, are harmful, hurt the body, or compromise physical safety.

So why do our clients engage in these behaviors? They manage affect through distraction, numbing, or endorphin release; short-circuit bad thoughts and feelings; punish or reclaim control over the body; evoke dissociative or regrounding responses; reenact pain; and communicate or restory prior abuse. All self-destructive acts are, ultimately, creative attempts to cope with untenable thoughts, feelings, and memories. They are cries for help, and ones that should be heeded, not ignored. Ironically, provocative behaviors that scare or disgust us are actually attempts to engage us and connect with significant others. They tell us that our clients are in pain; they need something that they are not getting.

Clients who engage in these behaviors often get the pathological label of being "manipulative," yet self-destructive acts represent the only language trauma survivors know how to speak. Taking amorphous, invisible, internal pain and making it visible through a cut, burn, drunken state, or obese or dramatically underweight body gives us something to bear witness to, and this, in turn, validates experiences that were never acknowledged before. In addition to punishing their own bodies, clients sometimes engage in destructive behaviors to punish others, evoking fear, helplessness, anger, and anxiety. For clients with no self-worth and no sense of self, being floridly symptomatic can be a way to reclaim a sense of identity.

When we put all of these behaviors on a level playing field rather than hierarchically categorize cutting as "self-harm" and eating disorders and addictions as "something else," it allows us to define self-harm in a more inclusive way. With this broader mind-set, the metadialogues and deeper meanings we uncover, as well as the treatment modalities we use, can be applied to a much wider range of presenting problems. The fact that so many clients give up one manifestation of self-destructive behavior (cutting) and move on to another (anorexia, substance abuse, gambling addiction) suggests they all serve the same purpose and are rooted in the same unmet needs and unresolved pain narratives.

Hollander (2008) supported the notion that teens tend to not engage in self-injury under the influence of drugs or alcohol because they all serve similar functions. Therefore, I believe we can look at the functionality, metacommunication, and reinforcing components of these different behaviors somewhat interchangeably. Briere and Jordan (2009) corroborated this idea, defining trauma-related behaviors as "external activities that are used in an attempt to reduce negative internal states, typically through distraction, self-soothing, or induction of a distress-incompatible positive state. Examples of such behaviors are compulsive sexual behaviors, binge/purge eating, impulsive aggression, suicidality, and self-mutilation" (p. 378). Najavits (2001) also recognized the universal dynamics of the aforementioned impulsive behaviors and suggested that a treatment paradigm can successfully address more than one kind of self-destructive behavior.

In recent years, issues including cutting, burning, eating disordered behaviors, substance abuse, and sexual addiction have been paraded out in the open. Made-for-TV movies, talk shows, Web sites, chat rooms, and books (for both profession-als and the general public) disseminate information, universal-ize the dynamics, and attach real people—even celebrities—to the behaviors. In some ways this has been positive: our clients

no longer have to suffer in silence as their struggles are identified and validated. It is hoped that clients are inspired by the
courage of others who talk openly about these behaviors and
feel encouraged to seek out help for themselves. Unfortunately,
there can be a downside to this public processing. The issues can
be minimized, even romanticized, on a talk show or in a movie.
Vulnerable viewers who are in pain and feel bereft of resources
can be lured into trying self-destructive behaviors after viewing
glamorized versions of it depicted by popular actors. Seventeen-
year-old Tiffany, struggling in a toxic family rife with domestic
violence and poverty, turned to cutting after learning about it
on TV.

> I guess I was sad and angry all the time, but I couldn't show it
> 'cause it would hurt my parents or make things get worse at
> home. When I saw this girl cutting her arms on a TV movie, it
> seemed to make everything better, so I found a box cutter and
> tried it.

The pain and struggles associated with self-destructive behaviors can be significantly exploited on television and in film.
This exploitation is usually followed by the intimation that these
behaviors can be resolved within the quick fix of a half-hour talk
show or 2-hour movie. This is dangerous and insulting to those
who have grappled with these behaviors for many years.

The challenge for us as helping professionals is to accept that
until the behavior is translated, understood, and put into the
context of a chronic cycle, and until our clients have successfully
integrated alternative coping strategies and self-soothing techniques, the behavior will continue (Alderman, 1997; Hollander,
2008). To expect anything else is unreasonable. I explain to clients that they understandably cling to self-destructive behaviors
as if they were clinging to tiny life jackets in the middle of the
ocean (Ferentz, 2002). It's all they have, and it's all they know.
As far as they are concerned, it keeps them afloat. The instinct
to have and hold on to a life jacket is actually appropriate and
necessary. It is a primitive survival response that is a part of our

hardwiring. No one could manage being out in the ocean without one. It doesn't matter to them that this seemingly helpful resource is too small, has lots of holes in it, and may get them into trouble later on. When they are out there struggling, that tiny jacket is the only thing that feels accessible to them. And they hold on to it for dear life.

Many well-meaning helping professionals demand that clients relinquish their destructive behaviors either through standard safety contracts that make clients promise not to hurt themselves or by making the continuation of treatment, and even the therapeutic alliance, contingent on stopping the behavior. Some inpatient programs feel strongly about the role contracting plays in treatment, advocating that sessions, and even treatment, be terminated if clients injure or relapse after promising not to engage in the behavior. This is framed as being in the clients' best interests.

From the perspective of clients, it's like the helping professional is leaning over the side of a cruise ship, insisting that they turn over the life jacket they've been using because it's not good for them and will make things worse. Clients understandably believe that being out in the ocean with no life jacket at all is far worse. Clients will often resent this cavalier approach and reconcile the helping professional's stance by saying, "What does she know? She's not out in the ocean where I am—she's safe on a cruise ship! She doesn't understand how much I need this!"

Although it can seem counterintuitive, it is unfair to ask clients to relinquish the only life jacket that has kept them afloat. Self-destructive acts can be reduced and eventually extinguished only when we can offer our clients alternative strategies that work just as well. Simply telling clients to stop hurting themselves leaves them with no other way to cope. In fact, pressuring clients to stop because it is triggering and uncomfortable for the therapist or because a loved one wants them to will often backfire and end in failure (Alderman, 1997; Goulding & Schwartz, 2002). At best, clients will sublimate their urges into other self-destructive acts: eating disorders, substance abuse, unsafe sex, and so on (Levenkron, 1998; Yates, 2004).

In this book, we will discuss safer alternative life jackets that can be swapped with clients' more complicated and less effective ones. These additional life jackets expand the repertoire of potential coping strategies and introduce the critical notion of choice into the equation. Research conducted by Mikolajczak et al. (2009) supports the notion that "increasing the use of alternative, adaptive coping skills could lead to a decrease and, ideally, a cessation of self-harm" (p. 191).

Gratz and Chapman (2009) articulated an understanding of this concept when they said, "Taking self-harm away without giving you a substitute that meets your needs is a recipe for failure" (p. 86). Goulding and Schwartz (2002) and Judith Herman (1992) supported this idea when they described clients' paradoxical take on self-injury as a form of self-preservation and self-protection that cannot simply be taken from them. Conterio and Lader (1998) and Tracy Alderman (1997) echoed this sentiment, describing self-injury as a life-sustaining act: a behavior designed to help clients cope while alleviating distress. Yates (2004) addressed the relationship between what he called self-injury and childhood trauma, theorizing that self-injury is an adaptational "self-cure" when no other viable coping strategies have been integrated.

However, many clinicians working with self-destructive behaviors don't look at it through this lens, and this perceived lack of understanding and support often triggers clients, resulting in an increase in their behaviors. Clients hurting their bodies while in ongoing therapy with us is a way for them to reclaim a sense of power and control, externalize anger about not being adequately understood, and, perhaps, illustrate the sense of futility they feel about the treatment approach and their ability to heal.

Goulding and Schwartz (2002) believe that clients may continue to hurt themselves in an attempt to test their therapist's fortitude, to punish them for inadvertent missteps in treatment, and to evoke empathic responses. In addition, I believe that clients hurt themselves to evoke worried or angry responses in significant others, and this may be the only way they know how to feel connected or attached in relationships. This can certainly play out in their relationships with us. Stewart, a 43-year-old male client struggling with a sexual addiction, illustrated this when he said in session:

> One of the embarrassing things about my sexual addiction is that I actually like to imagine you are worried about me during and after sessions. I sometimes imagine that you are thinking about me, wondering if I will act out, maybe even considering picking up the phone and calling to check on me. Sometimes it crosses my mind to act out again, so that maybe you will worry about me. I know that sounds kinda crazy and probably egotistical, but I think it's a way for me to feel like you're still with me and care about me when I'm not in your office.

As we move toward a new understanding of the meaning and treatment of self-destructive behaviors, we have to be willing to question and reevaluate some of the ways in which our professional culture currently views this issue. There are popular clinical books that continue to pathologize these behaviors, especially acts of self-inflicted violence, attributing it to mental illness and labeling it "abnormal" or part of a disturbed psychiatric disorder.

The literature is rife with articles and research that make connections between self-destructive behavior, borderline personality disorder (BPD), and other psychiatric illnesses (Gerson & Stanley, 2008; Linehan, 1993). Many respected current works on self-destructive behavior make a point of putting the behavior into the clinical context of a personality disorder (Brodsky, Cliotre, & Dulit, 1995; Haw, Hawton, Houston, & Townsend, 2001; Zanarini, Gunderson, & Marino, 1989). There is such a strong correlation between BPD and acts such as cutting and burning because "one of the diagnostic criteria for BPD is self-harm [so] it's not surprising that there is so much overlap between BPD and self-harm" (Gratz & Chapman, 2009, p. 61). Many clinicians who specialize in trauma work continue to look at self-injury through the lens of a personality disorder.

On close examination of the individuals studied in much of the research on what is typically called "self-injury," one discovers that they are identified as having BPD. Although a large percentage of research participants also have a history of trauma, abuse, and neglect, the focus seems to remain on their personality disorder diagnosis. Klonsky (2007) cautioned, "Limiting the scope of investigations to patient and prison populations precludes a complete understanding of self-injury and may obscure the phenomenology, functions, and treatment implications of self-injury" (p. 237).

The association between these behaviors and BPD is further solidified by a paradigm most frequently cited as effective in the treatment of self-mutilation: dialectical behavioral therapy (DBT) (Gerson, 2008; Gratz & Chapman, 2009; Hollander, 2006; Klonsky, 2007; Levenkron, 1998; Linehan, 2006; Low, Jones, & Duggan, 2001; Sansone et al., 2001). Although this is a well-studied, highly regarded, and often effective treatment modality, it was originally created for the express purpose of treating BPD. My concern is that an exclusive focus on this treatment strategy intrinsically reinforces the notion that clients who hurt themselves are all "borderlines." In addition, Klonsky (2007) reported that despite the effectiveness of the modality, "many patients treated with DBT continue to self-injure even if less frequently" (p. 229).

I would argue that the diagnosis of BPD puts a "glass ceiling" on the extent to which clients can actually get better. In the mental health world, BPD is often code for "hopeless." I see it as a death sentence for clients and a diagnosis that evokes some of the strongest countertransferential responses in us. Try this exercise: imagine a colleague has left a voice mail message asking you to please make time in your busy practice to take on a new client. "I know you can help her. She really needs you," implores your colleague. "Please agree to see her. She's borderline." Now take a moment and notice your most honest cognitive, emotional, and visceral responses. If you are like most capable and compassionate clinicians, you'll notice your stomach drop; a tightening or tensing of your body; feelings of anxiety, fear, or distaste; and the words "Sorry, my practice is full, and I can't take on anyone else" quickly forming in your mind. This is not unusual. Borderline clients have a terrible reputation, and many professionals avoid them at all costs.

Now, rewind your answering machine, and let's try again. This time, your colleague implores you to make room in your practice for a client who "desperately needs your help. She's a trauma survivor." What is your knee-jerk response? In all likelihood, the phrase "trauma survivor" evokes a softening of your body, an exhalation, a nod or a knowing smile, and an automatic feeling of empathy and compassion. In all likelihood, you will find a way to welcome that client into your practice. This speaks to the power of diagnostic labels and to the assumptions and preconceived notions that we all bring to our work.

And here's the most important point: BPD really means "trauma survivor." The cardinal features of clients with BPD include ambivalence around attachment and intimacy issues, affect dysregulation, and an inability to handle emotional distress. They grapple with these issues because they weren't allowed to resolve trust versus mistrust, and they had to negotiate insecure or ambivalent attachment patterns. Or even worse, there were disorganized attachments with totally emotionally unavailable, volatile, or abusive caretakers. These unpredictable primary relationships have left them with an interpersonal template that says, "Getting close equals getting hurt." No wonder they vacillate between an intense desire for intimacy and overwhelming anxiety about the inevitably traumatic repercussions of closeness.

These kinds of dysfunctional and unpredictable relationships also leave trauma survivors hypervigilant. They quickly read mental health professionals' subtle defeatist and futile attitudes regarding a borderline diagnosis, which elicits anxiety in clients and, ironically, increases their acting out and self-destructive behaviors. When clients see themselves through our pathologizing lens, it can exacerbate their sense of shame, decrease the likelihood of disclosure, and infuse the treatment with a kind of resigned hopelessness.

It also minimizes a key issue that must be unpacked in therapy: *Self-destructive acts are creative coping strategies, designed to alleviate distress, communicate a pain narrative, and provide critical information to helping professionals while offering a modicum of short-term self-soothing for the client* (Ferentz, 2001). Michael Hollander (2008) echoed this reframe when he described how clients gain short-term relief by using what he called self-injury to shift out of emotionally painful and overwhelming states.

I understand that moving away from a BPD diagnosis can be troubling for some clinicians. After all, self-injury is a part of the diagnostic criteria for this disorder. However, because of the intensely negative countertransferential responses the label evokes in us, my hope is that borderlines can be reframed and talked about as trauma survivors, which yields more empathic and hopeful responses from us. At the very least, consider *borderline* an adjective rather than a noun. Gratz and Chapman (2009) spent a lot of time discussing the correlation between BDP and what they called self-harm, but to their credit they also added, "The knee-jerk diagnosis of BPD for anyone who self-harms is illogical and potentially harmful" (p. 62).

Another important paradigm shift to consider is that effective treatment for self-destructive behavior requires a willingness on our part to avoid engaging in power struggles or strong-arming our clients into giving up what they are doing. It therefore follows that standard safety contracts that force clients to agree to not engage in harmful acts for a specific period of time are seen as inherently disempowering and are not encouraged. Walsh (2008) also discouraged the use of standard safety contracts, recognizing that they do more harm than good. He maintained that contracting fosters dishonesty in clients: they will deny that they are engaging in the behavior in order to sustain approval from the therapist. Michael, a 27-year-old man, was seriously physically and emotionally abused in childhood and had a long-standing history of self-mutilating acts. He was hospitalized as a teenager and shared this insight:

In the hospital, I had to sign a safety contract. Whenever my therapist asked me about hurting myself, I lied and told him I wasn't. I mostly lied because I didn't want him to be disappointed or mad at me. He was the first man who was ever nice to me, and I didn't want to blow it by telling him I was still cutting. The sad part is, as long as I lied, I wasn't getting the help I needed. To make things even worse, I felt bad about lying to someone who was nice to me, but it seemed like the only option.

I believe that trauma survivors often focus on the need to maintain approval from authority figures. Knowing how to please, even if it means being dishonest, is a well-honed coping strategy from childhood: if the powerful adult is accommodated, the child remains safe.

Perpetrators certainly leave victims feeling like they will be secure and loved only if they are compliant. We never want our clients thinking that our acceptance and availability is contingent on their acquiescence. We should also avoid engaging in any subtly or overtly manipulative interventions as we attempt to help our clients extinguish destructive behaviors. Trauma survivors have exquisite radar to such manipulations, and they experience this as the reenactment of a perpetrator–victim dynamic. Seasoned clinicians have begun to realize that treatment techniques are rendered ineffective without first accepting and validating the clients' experiences (Hollander, 2008).

Instead, we can promote true healing by allowing our clients to retain a sense of dignity and control in the process. Giving our clients options and empowering them to find wisdom and healthy answers within themselves helps us avoid that recapitulation of prior abuse. Therefore, we must always communicate to our clients that the decision to engage in any kind of self-destructive behavior—or not—is truly theirs to make.

Of course, the notion of letting go of standard safety contracts as a treatment philosophy can feel counterintuitive and be understandably anxiety producing for us as helping professionals. However, in this book, you will be encouraged to reject standard safety contracts and, instead, incorporate CARESS

(Communicate Alternatively, Release Endorphins, and Self-Soothe), a unique and effective behavioral model that enables clients to work through their destructive urges. This model gives our clients an alternative way to achieve what self-destructive behaviors accomplish for them: a creative way to communicate their trauma/pain narratives, a way to manage or short-circuit bad thoughts and feelings, and a way to self-soothe and comfort (Ferentz, 2002).

CARESS allows clients to experience the positive outcomes they were getting from their self-destructive behaviors by offering alternative behaviors that avoid the injurious and revictimizing outcomes. It resonates for clients because they maintain control, and it resonates for clinicians because it gives us a concrete, effective way to address the problem. In addition, unlike contracts that make contacting the clinician a part of treatment, this book discourages that directive. Other internal and external resources are promoted instead, and these alternative resources enable us to hold appropriate boundaries with our clients while discouraging the codependency that often emerges when treating this symptom.

Incorporating CARESS and helping our clients find alternative ways to accomplish what their self-destructive acts accomplish illustrates another fundamental premise of this book: *self-destructive behaviors are not arbitrary and meaningless acts.* Clients get something positive and reinforcing out of the behaviors (Alderman, 1997). This is part of why they are such difficult behaviors to give up. Seventeen-year-old Tiffany supported this idea when she said:

> Even though I was scared and felt stupid using the box cutter like the girl did on TV, it worked! I felt better for a while. I stopped thinking about my parents fighting. Now, I am more confused because even though it's weird to cut myself, it really helps me.

In many ways, these destructive behaviors can be enigmatic to work with in therapy. As stated earlier, for most clients it is a shame-based behavior and, therefore, not something they will readily bring up in treatment. Although clients find relief in the positive reinforcements they experience from self-destructive acts, they don't like the fact that they hurt themselves and often consider it another reason why they are "weird" or "crazy." It may be several years before clients feel comfortable enough to disclose their behaviors. Most clients are quite discerning and selective in their disclosures (Walsh, 2008). When they do admit to physically hurting themselves, eating disordered behaviors, or addictions, they will often minimize the behavior, fearful that we will be overwhelmed, angry, frightened, or disgusted.

Clients also fear that we will insist on referring them to an expert in self-harm, thus ending a trusting and deeply meaningful relationship. When we are initially confronted with these behaviors, it often makes sense that we think about referring them out. If we don't have expertise in dealing with various self-destructive behaviors, it is important and ethical to disclose this to our clients. However, in my opinion, transferring to another therapist is rarely necessary and often counterproductive. It may be useful to process the option of adjunctively consulting with an expert. Unless clients insist on being transferred (which in my experience rarely happens), it makes the most sense to continue working together.

Ogden, Minton, and Pain (2006) described our fundamental need for social engagement as a primary resource for attachment and safety. When clients are doing emotionally charged work that activates either the sympathetic system (hyperarousal) or the dorsal vagal system (hypoarousal), they are more likely to productively address the issue when they are simultaneously connected to our grounding presence. A well-established therapeutic relationship provides that emotional safety net and makes a strong case for not referring clients out.

In addition, self-destructive acts are only one piece of the puzzle and shouldn't be the sole focus of treatment. Our clients' larger issues shouldn't be obscured by the seemingly provocative dynamic of self-destructive behaviors. This is particularly true for trauma survivors, who need to safely reclaim their past narratives and, with the help of a trusting therapeutic witness, heal on a deeper level. Otherwise, unresolved pain will manifest in other destructive behaviors.

When well-meaning therapists suggest referring out, clients' cognitive distortions such as "I will never get better," "I am too sick for my therapist to help me," or "When I show people my pain, they abandon me" get inadvertently reinforced. Fifteen-year-old Cathy expressed this sentiment when she said:

> You are the third therapist I'm seeing. I liked the first therapist, but when I told him about my cutting and burning and bingeing, he said he had to refer me to someone else. The second one was okay, but I think she freaked out when I showed her some of my scars. She said that I needed an expert in cutting. I figured if they both couldn't handle it, then I must be pretty far gone. I guess I'm waiting for you to fire me, too.

In truth, the existence of a consistent, trusting therapeutic alliance is one of the most important ingredients in this work (Alderman, 1997). It is my hope that as you read this book, it will increase your understanding of how to work with these behaviors while having your own inevitable countertransferential responses validated and addressed. This, in turn, will reduce anxiety and enhance a sense of efficacy, making referral unnecessary. The third part of this book offers support and guidance to clinicians who find themselves triggered and vulnerable as they attempt to help clients with these issues. Ultimately, this book celebrates our clients' capacities to transcend and heal from trauma, reclaiming a more accurate and positive view of the self. It also supports the notion that clients want safer, healthier ways to communicate, short-circuit bad thoughts and feelings, and engage in self-care.

If you are reading this book, you obviously have a vested interest in the topic. You are probably working with enigmatic clients who either jump from one self-destructive behavior to another, relapse with regularity, or repeatedly engage in scary acts of self-inflicted violence. These are the clients we lose sleep over, go to conferences for, and buy more clinical books to figure out. And yet despite your best efforts and unwavering commitment to your clients, you may still be feeling frustrated by their lack of progress or the chronicity of their relapses. Reading this book with an open mind and an open heart can enable you to discover potential missing pieces in your treatment approaches. This, in turn, will allow you to integrate additional ideas and, perhaps, create a fundamental shift in your thinking.

In our new understanding of treatment, one of the goals of therapy is to work with trauma survivors to decode the communication and meaning behind their self-destructive behaviors. Again, this means *working with* the behavior rather than engaging in a client–therapist power struggle and aggressively trying to extinguish it. As we will discuss, inviting our clients to be curious about their behaviors, and seeing them through a compassionate lens rather than feeling ashamed of them, is the first step in this process. In the workbook, the exercise entitled IDENTIFYING MY SELF-DESTRUCTIVE BEHAVIORS on page 25 is a good way to gently invite clients to begin acknowledging their self-destructive acts. For the work to move forward, the clinical underpinning must be a depathologized, strengths-based perspective. Rather than focusing on what's wrong with clients, we must focus on their resiliency, strength, and innate ability to heal. You will discover that this mind-set is a far more effective framework than one that views self-destructive clients as sick.

Even if it seems counterintuitive, you will be reminded to reframe cutting, starving, purging, abusing substances, or engaging in sexually addictive behaviors as inevitable, creative coping strategies that evolve from a history of trauma, pain, neglect, and abuse. Although the behavior is certainly not condoned or encouraged, we must respect the idea that there is a repetitive and cyclical nature to these acts (Alderman, 1997) that makes sense, given clients' prior repetitive traumas. This mind-set strengthens the therapeutic alliance and allows us to approach the work with newfound hope.

The centerpiece of our work with these clients will be the integration of a specific cycle of self-destructive acts into treatment. This offers a template for clients and clinicians to better understand the repetitive, chronic, and cyclical nature of these behaviors. This is a key dynamic that is not adequately explored in other treatment modalities. It provides the road map for creative work that empowers clients to short-circuit their destructive behavior at many different intervention sites. This increases the likelihood that clients will feel a sense of success and control. These interventions work for clients *regardless* of where they are in the cycle of self-destructive acts, which broadens its application. You will appreciate the fact that the cycle can be used as a didactic tool and a treatment guide.

Although this cycle of self-destructive acts is almost universally experienced by clients who engage in these behaviors, the specific ways in which it is experienced is uncovered and personalized during the therapy process. Keep in mind that this cycle is applicable to a wide variety of self-destructive behaviors and can be quite useful in addressing eating disorders, substance abuse and other addictions, sexual promiscuity, and so on.

As we incorporate the cycle into treatment, it allows us to work collaboratively with clients to identify many possible intervention sites. These are windows of opportunity for change, as they offer clients new cognitive, emotional, and behavioral responses that move them beyond their trauma-informed conditioned responses. These new options will emphasize ego strengthening, the identification and management of triggers, reframes for cognitive distortions, healthy affect management and containment, regrounding, the creation of internal and external safety, and satisfying alternatives to self-destructive behavior. This model infuses the work with hope and moves clients toward decreasing and eventually extinguishing the behavior.

As trauma therapists, we must be willing to bear witness to and validate our clients' painful narratives and incorporate creative treatment modalities that often go beyond talk therapy. We must also be willing to let go of the need to control the pacing

of treatment. Most of all, we must inherently believe in the resiliency of the human spirit to survive and thrive. When our clients
are assessed and treated from this mind-set, destructive, harmful behaviors can be truly understood and, in time, become no
longer necessary. Clients can begin to embrace a more positive and accurate sense of themselves when we normalize and
depathologize symptoms and struggles, reframing them as necessary, creative coping strategies.

Finally, this book is uniquely sensitive to the fact that as a
clinician working with self-destructive behaviors and trauma,
you may be a trauma survivor yourself. And even if you aren't,
this is inherently difficult and triggering work, and we are all at
increased risk for secondary traumatization and burnout. Texts
often ignore this pivotal issue. In response to this, the case studies
presented in this book provide a concrete way to bring to life the
didactic material presented, without being gratuitously graphic.
In fact, if descriptions of self-destructive behaviors become too
vivid, our own fight–flight response gets activated, and the reasoning, analytical part of our brain goes off-line. Once stuck
in the more primitive parts of our brain, our ability to take in,
process, and integrate new information becomes compromised
(Taylor, 2006). The goal is for us to work with the dynamics of
trauma and self-destructive behaviors grounded in both the left
and the right brain hemispheres.

In addition, the third part of this book uses therapist vignettes
to addresses our specific vulnerabilities toward vicarious traumatization and depathologizes and normalizes typical countertransferential responses and common clinical pitfalls when
working with these clients. Each section offers you specific action
steps to enhance self-care and emotional safety, increase physical grounding during sessions, and recoup after difficult ones.
Although you will find that the self-help strategies are equally
useful for your clients and can certainly be taught to them as
well, give yourself permission to personally try them on, as they
will go a long way toward ensuring that your own efficacy is not
compromised.

2
WORKING WITH TRAUMA SURVIVORS
The strengths-based approach

I've always considered it an extraordinary privilege to work with survivors of trauma. Their capacity to be resilient, courageous, creative, loyal, and accomplished in the face of devastating life experiences continues to amaze me. What is equally amazing is how they often see themselves through an antithetical lens: inadequate, damaged, weak, helpless, and hopeless.

Over the years I have noticed this disparity between my perception of clients who have been abused and their subjective sense of self. Unresolved traumatic pasts often create cognitive distortions, pervasive negative affect, and profoundly compromised self-esteem. Yet it is ironic that so many clients do not consciously attribute their poor self-image to their trauma. In fact, if you ask clients why they are symptomatic or struggle in the world, the typical response is "I'm crazy" or "I'm abnormal." Trauma survivors believe they are inherently flawed, bad, and incompetent. Glassman, Weierich, Hooley, Deliberto, and Nock (2007) and Conterio and Lader (1998) theorized that children are made to feel responsible, dirty, and bad through messages conveyed by abusive or neglectful parents. It stands to reason that once these critical messages are internalized and solidified, they become truths for our clients. Children don't question or challenge the messages that come from a trusted caretaker. Operating from this distorted mind-set of self-blame, our clients are unable to attribute abusive family-of-origin or traumatic childhood experiences to their subsequent thoughts, feelings, and behaviors. Instead, they hold themselves solely responsible for the way they are in the world, believing they have problems because there is something intrinsically wrong with them.

As a result, who they are, how they interact with others, the myriad ways in which they get triggered, their destructive coping strategies, their labile emotions, and their poor behavioral choices don't make sense to them. They rationalize every symptom with a core belief that says, "There is something defective about me." This inability to put themselves in a historic traumatic context or to recognize the reverberating effects of neglect or abuse sustains their distorted sense of self.

When they come into the treatment process, it is as if they are carrying a large box filled with individual jigsaw puzzle pieces. If you've ever done a puzzle, you know that the completed picture is on the box lid. In essence, we know ahead of time what the final product will look like once the pieces are put together. In our work with traumatized clients, there is a box with a lot of pieces but no lid: no one is privy to the whole picture ahead of time. We painstakingly look for and join pieces that seem to fit, but it can take years before a coherent image or narrative emerges. As daunting as this is, we can assist clients in this process when we connect the family-of-origin pieces with long-standing symptoms and struggles. Although this correlation makes sense to us, our clients will often balk at the suggestion that this connection exists. Yet clients need some way to make sense out of their issues. They often need someone to blame. The safest and easiest target is the "flawed self."

One of the reasons why so many clients don't initially frame their experiences as traumatic or their caretakers as abusive or neglectful is their need to maintain a sense of allegiance and connection to family. It is not acceptable for them to think about losing this connection. Therefore, a logical coping strategy is to minimize, rationalize, or deny traumatic interactions. Shawna, a 50-year-old recovering alcoholic, illustrated this in a therapy session:

Where I come from, you didn't bad-mouth your family members. Everything had to look good, especially to the outside world. If you wanted even a little bit of acceptance, you didn't rock the boat. Throughout my childhood, and even as an adult, I wanted my alcoholic mother to love me and approve of me. That meant ignoring all the things she did to hurt me. It also meant not getting angry at my father for never protecting me when my mother hurt me. I told myself I was getting hurt because I did something wrong. I made the abuse my fault.

When faced with choosing between attributing their pain to "being crazy" and having had abusive parents, clients will choose "crazy" most of the time. Dora, a 38-year-old, was profoundly abused by multiple family perpetrators and has grappled with cutting and eating disordered behaviors for most of her life. She poignantly echoed this dilemma in her therapy:

I hate it when we talk about my family as "dysfunctional" or "abusive." Think about what you are asking me to accept—that my parents didn't love me, care about me, or protect me. If I have to choose between "being abused" or "being sick and crazy," it's less painful to see myself as nuts than to imagine my parents as evil.

In the course of therapy, we often witness clients' capacities to report abuse stories with intellectualized, detached demeanors. And they are quick to add disclaimers that minimize their experiences such as "It wasn't so bad," "I probably deserved it anyway," "I know my parents did the best they could," "It didn't have any negative effect on me," or "That was a long time ago, and it can't be relevant to my life now."

Many clients expend tremendous amounts of energy disavowing traumatic or abusive histories, believing that revisiting old feelings and thoughts will keep them stuck or are irrelevant to who they are today. Jim, a 32-year-old very successful business owner who struggles with a sexual addiction, expressed this belief whenever therapy veered in the direction of his childhood:

Why would I want to talk about growing up on the West Coast with parents who were compulsive gamblers? The days of not having enough to eat and moving from house to house and school to school are dead and buried. Today, I can afford whatever I want. I don't want to go back there in my mind. It's depressing. And anyway, who says living with parents who gamble is "abusive"? I

know kids who had it a whole lot worse than I did! Besides, it has
nothing to do with my life now. The difficulties I'm having in my
marriage won't be fixed by going back to the past.

We can experience a powerful tug-of-war with clients who "don't
want to go back there," believing, instead, that disowning the
past is the best way to be healed. I explain to clients that, metaphorically, it is as if traumatic experience was represented by their
injured left arm and they go through life saying, "If I could only
cut off this damaged left arm and get rid of that part of my life,
then I would be whole again." Ironically, "getting rid" of this critical part of their life experience can never make them whole, just
as a human body without a left arm can never be whole. It is only
through the process of accepting and embracing that hurting
and painful left arm that clients can achieve genuine wholeness.
Much of the therapy journey, therefore, is about helping clients to
reconnect with earlier, painful experiences in a way that promotes
healing rather than self-blame or shame.

Oftentimes, the impulse to get rid of the damaged part of
oneself is manifest through self-destructive behaviors. Judith
Herman (1992) suggested that the self-loathing created by self-
blame increases a client's vulnerability toward self-aggression.
If one sees oneself as damaged, it resonates to hurt the body.
Dusty Miller (1994) concurred that these messages manifest
as an internalized, abusive voice, which sets the stage for self-
destructive behaviors. Feeling guilt and shame and holding
oneself responsible for childhood abuse can be one of the cata-
lysts for self-inflicted violence (Alderman, 1997). Many studies
support the notion that hurting the body is a way to punish
it for being bad (Briere & Gil, 1998; Swales, 2008). Klonsky
(2007) cited six studies corroborating the notion that self-
punishment is a motivator for self-destructive behaviors, particularly in adolescents.

When our clients ignore, invalidate, or dismiss their traumatic
past experiences, they deny themselves the critical context that
actually helps them to make sense out of who they are and why they

think, feel, and behave in the ways that they do. We can provide invaluable assistance when we help clients connect the dots between prior abuse or historical "pain narratives" and current struggles.

Conterio and Lader (1998) said that clients who engage in self-destructive behaviors have grown up in family systems that are rigid, critical, intrusive, lacking in emotional expressiveness, inappropriate in parenting styles and boundaries, and often alcoholic. Miller (1994) placed tremendous emphasis on the relationship between what she called self-injurious behavior and a prior childhood history of abuse and neglect. Her brilliant paradigm reframes self-destructive acts as a reenactment of that earlier abuse, which supports the notion that there is high communicative value in these behaviors. Noll, Horowitz, Bonanno, Trickett, and Putnam (2003) concurred, saying, "Individuals who self-injure may be re-enacting the abuse perpetuated on them" (p. 1467). Najavits (2001) supported the idea that behaviors like cutting and substance abuse are "self-destructive behaviors that reenact trauma, particularly for victims of childhood abuse" (p. 5). These researchers, and others, understand that adolescent and adult struggles have their roots in a painful and often hidden traumatic past.

In many ways, this has become the central focus of my work with trauma survivors, particularly the ones who engage in self-destructive behaviors. Everything about them makes sense given where they've come from. And unless they can acknowledge and address where they've come from, what has happened to them, and the impact it's had, nothing about them makes sense. Their distorted core beliefs, depression and anxiety, difficulty with intimacy, ambivalence about relationships, need for drama and crisis, need to self-medicate, destructive coping strategies, somatic symptoms, distorted self-perceptions, struggles to feel normal in the world, hypervigilance, and vulnerability to triggering all make sense when they are able to see themselves through the lens of prior traumatic experience.

The idea of depathologizing these issues by framing them as the inevitable by-products of trauma was echoed by Aphrodite

Matsakis (1996) when she stated, "Many of the emotional and cognitive changes that trauma survivors experience are appropriate to the situation of trauma. Often these changes hold survival value; they may even have saved lives during the traumatic episode" (p. 3).

Clients who are raised in emotionally unhealthy families are more likely to be impulsive, and that impulsivity manifests through acts of self-mutilation such as cutting and burning, substance abuse, and dysfunctional adolescent and adult relationships. Hollander (2008), Glassman et al. (2007), and Conterio and Lader (1998) connected the rigid, dichotomous thinking and pervasive low self-esteem exhibited in many trauma survivors with an inevitable increased need to harm oneself. In their research and clinical work, van der Kolk, Perry, and Herman (1991) repeatedly found a powerful relationship between self-mutilating behaviors and childhood abuse and neglect.

Romans, Martin, Anderson, Herbison, and Mullen (1995) described "a clear statistical association between sexual abuse in childhood and self-harm that was most marked in those subjected to more intrusive and more frequent abuse" (p. 1336). Other researchers and clinicians agree that children who were sexually abused have a greater predilection toward self-harm later in life (Briere and Jordan, 2009; Gladstone et al., 2004; Glassman et al., 2007; Sansone, Gaither, & Songer, 2001; van der Kolk, McFarlane, & Weisaeth, 2006). Survivors of chronic childhood abuse do not know how to engage in self-care, and they often rely on self-destructive behaviors in the absence of healthier self-soothing strategies (Ferentz, 2001; Herman, 1992).

As we put self-destructive behaviors in a context of trauma, abuse, and neglect, we can easily see the profound adverse effects that these experiences have on developing children. Families using toxic or dysfunctional communication skills such as yelling, blaming, verbal abuse, the "silent treatment," or triangulating take a toll on children's sense of self-worth, burden them with shame, and deprive them of gaining mastery over the essential life skill of effective expression.

When boundaries are either disengaged or enmeshed, children are left feeling neglected and invisible, suffocated, or violated. When you add into the mix undiagnosed and untreated parental substance abuse, anxiety, depression, or trauma, the odds are greatly increased that children are left with emotionally unavailable, hyper or hypoaroused parents who cannot provide healthy role modeling, protection, informed guidance, consistent or predictable nurturance, or attachment. These are the parents who cannot do their own healthy affect regulation or model it and provide it for their children.

Growing up with dysfunction makes it hard enough for trauma survivors to get by in the world. This is exacerbated by the fact that they view themselves as damaged or bad. But imagine how much more difficult and shaming it is for clients who engage in self-destructive acts. In their minds, this ups the ante and provides even more compelling evidence for their self-diagnosed "craziness." Herman (1992) concurred that clients who self-injure grapple with feelings of shame and disgust and expend a lot of energy attempting to hide the behavior from others. Favazza (1996) also discussed the level of self-consciousness and guilt experienced by self-harmers and the extreme measures they go to keep their wounds concealed. The shame experienced by clients who self-harm often prevents them from pursuing intimate relationships, which perpetuates their sense of isolation (Turner, 2002).

The approach

By the time clients come to us for treatment, they have often exhausted other, less formal, options for guidance and support. Or it may be that you are their tenth therapist. In either case, their perception of themselves as failures or irreparably damaged intensifies as they struggle with the inability to modify or extinguish unwanted behavior, despite repeated attempts in therapy and well-meaning advice from others. For trauma survivors, this can exacerbate preexisting feelings of worthlessness and profoundly influences the negative stories they have about themselves when they finally, courageously, land in our office. Clients see themselves and their behaviors through a pathologized lens and expect that we will view them in a similar way. They therefore place a tremendous emphasis on what is "wrong with them," including the fact that they do self-destructive things, and assume we want information and "behavioral evidence" that supports only a self-effacing diagnosis.

The philosophy behind a strengths-based perspective encourages you to view your traumatized clients in positive ways and to redefine their symptoms as necessary coping strategies that are the inevitable consequences of trauma, abuse, and chronic psychic pain. When assessment and treatment are organized around this paradigm, four fundamental precepts emerge: normalizing, universalizing, depathologizing, and reframing.

When we work with clients who engage in self-destructive behaviors, it's useful to remember that their self-reporting operates from a deep-seated belief that they are abnormal. All of the confusing thoughts, feelings, and behavioral choices related to self-destructive acts fuel this mind-set and shroud it in guilt and shame. As previously stated, one of the most valuable interventions we can offer is to introduce the notion that everything about the client makes sense given what they've experienced and where they've come from. When clients can look at their emotions and behaviors from a historical context of trauma, the pieces begin to fit together. In addition to the ongoing reassurance we should provide throughout the treatment process, our clients can be encouraged to internalize this mantra of normalizing symptoms and experiences, so it can be incorporated into positive self-talk and used as a new internal resource for self-soothing. Thirty-two-year-old Marci articulated the value of this resource when she said:

> Out of all the things I've learned in treatment, by far the most valuable and comforting is the idea that who I am and what I struggle with actually makes sense and is inevitable given my family background and the things I've endured. Whenever I start to panic about my thoughts, feelings, or behaviors, I remind myself that I'm not crazy—that it all makes sense—and this always seems to calm me down.

Many of the symptomatic behaviors that our clients struggle with have their roots in a desire to tell a suppressed trauma story, dissociate from painful feelings, and self-soothe. Schiraldi (2009) elucidated this concept when he stated, "When trauma material cannot be processed and verbally expressed, the pain is often expressed physically, frequently around body areas that were physically traumatized. Often the physical pain is a distraction from the emotional pain" (p. 31).

It is completely normal and healthy to want to avoid pain and find a way to express one's life narrative. The ways in which trauma survivors attempt to achieve these outcomes are often detrimental to their self-esteem and destructive to their minds and bodies. Yet it is often all they know and all that has been modeled for them. Choosing to engage in self-destructive behaviors becomes a reenactment of prior abuse and corroboration that self-care was severely disrupted or unavailable in childhood (Herman, 1992; Miller, 1994; Noll et al., 2003). Our clients don't make bad choices because there is something wrong with them. They make bad choices because no one ever showed them how to make good choices or made them feel worthy of good choices. *True healing can begin when clients learn to separate out who they are from what happened to them.*

Although every trauma survivor's story is unique, the sad truth is that countless people have experienced some form of sexual, physical, emotional, verbal, or psychological abuse or neglect. Despite this reality, many survivors feel completely alone in their trauma experiences. When we universalize the dynamics of abuse and neglect, our clients can actually feel reconnected to others and the world at large. The feeling of being uniquely and negatively different, and therefore ostracized and misunderstood, can begin to abate for survivors who learn that they are not alone in their suffering. Stan is a 62-year-old who was emotionally neglected by his family. For most of his life, he coped by drinking. He didn't seek out treatment until he was much older:

Until I started talking to you about my life and the pain I experienced growing up, I didn't realize that other people felt the way I did. I always thought that I was different, and I never wanted anyone to know about my past. I was embarrassed and ashamed of my family. I thought everyone else had great parents. I also didn't realize that I was drinking to numb out my pain—and that I'm not the only one who does that, either.

It is equally important to universalize human responses to trauma, including the biologically hardwired responses to either fight, flee, freeze, or feign death in the face of subjective danger or threat (Ogden, Minton, & Pain, 2006). Many survivors, particularly those who were abused in childhood, rely most heavily on the freeze or dissociative response. This makes sense given the fact that it would be nearly impossible and extremely unsafe for a child to either fight off a perpetrator or physically extricate himself or herself from abuse. Mentally escaping what they cannot physically escape is therefore a logical and universal response. Unfortunately, clients can chastise themselves, holding on to significant self-blame and shame for not doing enough in response to threat.

The necessary freeze or feigned death responses also lead to subsequent struggles, including, ironically, a state of disempowerment and helplessness. The idea that the survival skills that save victims in childhood are the same ones that perpetuate victimization in adulthood is a hard concept for our clients to embrace and integrate. The idea of letting go of a strategy like dissociation is counterintuitive to many survivors. It is therefore important to normalize their initial resistance and ambivalence about addressing it in treatment. Creating a nonjudgmental and safe therapeutic context to openly discuss the dissociative process becomes essential, because dissociation plays such a pivotal role in the cycle of self-destructive acts (Alderman, 1997; Conterio & Lader, 1998; Herman, 1992; Yates, 2004).

In addition, as helping professionals, we should universalize the idea that unresolved traumatic experiences leave behind tangible and often debilitating cognitive, somatic, and psychological residue. When your clients are ready, the workbook exercise entitled HOW THESE BEHAVIORS MAY NOT HELP IN THE LONG TERM on page 28 can help them make connections between their actions and their potentially traumatic side effects. Although it is certainly true that 10 people can experience the same trauma and respond in 10 different ways, it is equally true that people who have been traumatized can think, feel, and behave in very similar ways. Universalizing some of the reverberating effects of trauma and self-destructive behaviors can provide validation and corroboration, reassuring clients that their experiences are real and worthy of attention.

The notion of depathologizing harmful and injurious behaviors is central to effective treatment, as it goes a long way toward reducing guilt and shame. We should frequently remind our clients that it's not about being crazy, damaged, or bad—it's about trauma. When clients pathologize their issues and symptoms, they operate from a mind-set of internal attribution, which often manifests in cognitions such as "I'm bad" or "the abuse was my fault." Shifting into a depathologized mind-set allows clients to look at their experiences through the lens of external attribution, embracing the idea that "Something bad happened to me" or "The abuse was the fault of my perpetrator."

As stated earlier, when we work to help clients see themselves in a depathologized light, it is equally important that we view them through that same lens. Focusing on resilience, character strengths, and accomplishments allows us to move beyond a tunnel-vision approach to diagnosis and treatment.

The concept of reframing is crucial to the treatment of trauma and self-destructive behaviors. Reframing doesn't change the reality of an external experience. It does, however, enable clients to think and feel differently about that experience. And the good news is when clients can shift their cognitions about past abuse, how they feel about their bodies, or why they were mistreated by a trusted caretaker, the impact of those experiences shifts as well. This is a tremendous relief to clients who often believe that they can't stop their destructive acts unless something changes externally first. Mary, age 40 years, had endured a childhood of profound sexual and emotional abuse. She had tried, repeatedly, to get her father to take responsibility for abusing her. Early in therapy she said:

> I've been abusing my body, in many ways, for years. I always believed that until my father admitted what he did to me and understood the impact that it had on me, I would have to keep hurting myself, and I would forever be depressed. I'm starting to realize that if I keep waiting for him to "get it" or apologize, that I'm still giving him power and control over my life. Maybe I can get better and stop hurting my body even if my father doesn't cooperate.

One of the most profound reframes is the notion that a perpetrator doesn't need to apologize, cooperate in therapy, own the abuse, or express remorse and compassion toward the victim in order for a survivor to heal. All that matters is the survivors' ability to think and feel differently about their traumatic experiences: undoing the cognitive distortions that left them feeling responsible and damaged. This, in turn, increases an internally felt sense of self-worth (Levenkron, 1998). All destructive behaviors can be extinguished when clients are able to see their narratives in a more accurate and compassionate way. Since doing this work with a trained therapist is often the first step towards this less judgmental mind-set, using the workbook exercise entitled UNDERSTANDING YOUR FEELINGS ABOUT THERAPY on page 9 can help clients process their views and their family's views about seeking out professional help.

3

THE ROLE OF ATTACHMENT

I believe that it is impossible to effectively work with the issue of self-destructive behaviors without an understanding of attachment and its impact on affect regulation. Seeking out and maintaining safe, healthy attachment is a universally hardwired need. Attachment fulfills our desires for protection, safety, physical contact, belonging, soothing, emotional regrounding, and affiliation with and connection to others (Ogden, Minton, & Pain, 2006).

When we come into the world, our first task is to successfully attach to our primary caretakers: our literal survival is contingent on it. If the family system we are born into is a loving, predictable, safe, and emotionally available one, then the process of attaching is easy to accomplish. An infant is born with a woefully limited number of resources for self-soothing. He has a sucking reflex, he can avert his gaze when confronted with a noxious stimulus, and he can "zone out" or dissociate. Everything else that he learns to do comes from experiences that get introjected from his caretakers.

A distressed infant cries as a form of social engagement and communicates his desire for fundamental needs: physical and emotional comfort and connection. When he is spoken to in a soothing singsong voice, rocked, stroked, and gazed at lovingly, his immature and sensitive central nervous system is quickly reequilibrated. A responsive caretaker validates the infant's needs and teaches the baby to trust in the availability of others. "The primary ingredient of secure attachment experiences is the pattern of emotional communication between child and caregiver" (Siegel, 1999, p. 6). Babies are like "emotional light switches," in and out of hyperaroused states. Loving and comforting caretaking responses help them modulate these states more fluidly and with reduced distress. "It's as if they are 'borrowing' the stability of the parent's pre-frontal cortex" until their own capacity for self-regulation is solidified (Cozolino, 2006, p. 86).

Therefore, the attachment pattern that gets established for an infant is crucial, because it directly connects to the dynamic of affect regulation—the ability to self-soothe and manage one's emotional states. When there is secure attachment, the infant seeks out soothing and learns to trust that he will be accommodated. The infant can also easily receive comfort and, in time, learns to self-comfort when the attachment figure is temporarily unavailable. "Early successful attachments set the stage for the social regulation of biological processes throughout life" (Cozolino, 2006, p. 115). Ogden et al. (2006) stated that attachment relationships "provide the context within which the infant develops lifelong tendencies for regulating arousal and affect" (p. 41).

This is a key concept to teach clients. Affect regulation begins with *interregulation*: soothing, consistent nurturance from caretakers. Through the experience of modeling, neurological imprinting, and learned behavior, this gets introjected by the child and leads to *auto-regulation*, a developing child's ability to call on his own internal resources for self-soothing. In essence, the way we are held and comforted in childhood sets up certain chemical systems and patterns in the reward system of our brain. We experience sensations of pleasure, calm, and safety and release hormones that regulate stress. The dynamics of early childhood attachment or "attunement" play a pivotal role in many arenas of the infant's ongoing cognitive and emotional development. "This attachment dynamic, which operates at levels beneath awareness, underlies the dyadic regulation of emotion" (Schore, 2003, p. 64).

Over time, the positive "learned" experiences of comforting get imprinted on the infant's body, and he can begin to self-regulate in ways that reenact what was modeled and normalized by his caretakers. Hence, healthy, loving attachment is equated with soothing responses that can eventually be internalized and self-directed.

Good attachment leads to good affect regulation, a mantra in the treatment of self-destructive behaviors. If a child can develop a repertoire of healthy self-soothing techniques, it means that as he faces the inevitable stressors of adolescence and adulthood, he will be able to cope effectively and not feel the need to turn to dysfunctional strategies such as cutting, bingeing, drinking, and so on. We can reduce the shame for clients who do rely on these behaviors by making the connection to earlier inadequate parenting experiences they had no control over. Briere & Jordan (2009) succinctly echoed this connection by stating, "Maltreatment-related affect regulation deficits have been implicated in the development of various maladaptive or self-endangering behaviors" (p. 377).

Even more profoundly, there are neurobiological processes at play in the developing relationship between infant and caretaker. Cozolino (2006) stated, "The connection between mother and child is a potent determinant of brain development and adaptation.... The mother's impact on her child's brain is widespread and profound; early interactions build neural networks and establish biological set points that can last a lifetime" (p. 82). Alan Schore agreed, saying, "The early social environment, mediated by the primary caretaker, directly influences the final wiring of the circuits of the brain that are responsible for the future social and emotional coping capacities of the individual" (2003, p. 271).

Daniel Siegel's groundbreaking work supports this idea. He wrote, "An individual's abilities to organize emotions—a product, in part, of earlier attachment relationships—directly shapes the ability of the mind to integrate experience and to adapt to future stressors" (Siegel, 1999, p. 4). Schore (2003) further elucidated this connection when he suggested that our "right-brain regulatory capacities" are contingent on the quality of the attachment relationship between primary caregivers and infants. Additionally, attachment behavior is important far beyond the provision of a fundamental sense of safety and security. In fact, it may carve a "permanent trace" into a still developing brain.

If, however, caretakers are unavailable, inconsistent, abusive, easily triggered, dysfunctional, volatile, or violent, then the developmental task of attaching is complicated and compromised. Infants will attempt to use attachment cries, accommodating smiles, reaching out gestures, vocalizing, and so forth to engage their disinterested or unresponsive caretakers.

The impact of disconnected caretakers on infants is powerfully expressed in Tronick's "Still Face" experiments. After a period of normal engagement and interaction with an infant, the caretaker was instructed to not move or speak and to hold a "still face." After repeated failed attempts to reengage the parent, the infant "looked away, withdrew and expressed sad and angry affect, and turned to self-organized regulatory behaviors such as thumb sucking, to maintain coherence" (Tronick, 2007, p. 273). Despite the fact that the adults remained unresponsive for only 3 minutes, all of the infants in the study were greatly disturbed by this rupture in connection. Tronick concluded, "Reciprocity and mutual achievement of the goals of social interaction form a necessary basis for the growth of affective well-being in early infancy." Schore (2003) echoed the idea that when the attachment is dysfunctional or traumatic, it leads to "inefficient right-brain regulatory function, and maladaptive infant mental health." (p. 130).

Sadly, many primary caretakers are emotionally unavailable or easily triggered by their child's need for close attachment. This may be due, in part, to untreated parental depression or debilitating anxiety, substance abuse, mental illness, a chronic medical condition, intense family stressors, or their own unresolved history of abuse or neglect. "Parents who have unresolved trauma or conflicts will communicate their inner emotional world to their children" (Cozolino, 2006, p. 112).

In these scenarios, caretakers often parent from a place of fight–flight or freeze. This means the infant's requests for comfort will be met with avoidance, withdrawal, aggression, or dissociation. Studies show that the sound of an infant crying is a primary cause of child abuse. And yet before the development of language, crying is the primary way an infant can communicate her need for parental attention. When trigging occurs, and parental responses operate from an activated sympathetic system, the result is inconsistent, dismissive, preoccupied, or disorganized parenting, which creates infant attachment styles that are avoidant, resistant, ambivalent, or disorganized (Cozolino, 2006; Schore, 2003; Siegel, 1999).

Growing up in a dysfunctional family and being raised by an abusive, neglectful, or disengaged adult profoundly challenges children's abilities to successfully attach to their caretakers. Briere (2009) cited several studies that substantiate the fact that child–caretaker relationships fraught with instability, threats of violence or abandonment, and a lack of parental attunement often produce "attachment insecurity." Children are deprived of consistent and appropriate soothing when this healthy attachment is compromised. Affect regulation can be introjected and mastered by children only if their adult caretakers model it. Rocking, holding, verbally comforting, and stroking must be experienced throughout the early stages of childhood so they can be internalized and utilized later in life. Van der Kolk, McFarlane, and Weisaeth (2006) reiterated this idea, stating, "Consistent, external support appears to be a necessary condition for most children to learn to comfort and soothe themselves, and later to derive comfort from the presence of others" (p. 185). You can help your clients identify their own family-of-origin dynamics with the workbook exercise entitled EXPLORING CARETAKER RESPONSES TO YOUR EMOTIONAL NEEDS on page 62.

In a dysfunctional family system, as the child grows, her legitimate emotional and physical needs continue to be minimized or ignored, and she learns to feel a sense of shame for wanting anything. In addition to the overtly abusive caretaker, children can be profoundly traumatized by parents who are "nonprotective bystanders." In this case, despite the fact that they are not directly inflicting harm or pain on the child, their inability or unwillingness to shield or extricate the child from abuse becomes a form of perpetration and caretaker betrayal in and of itself.

Overwhelmed parents who refuse to be held accountable for their deficits will shift the blame by labeling their child as needy, overly sensitive, demanding, or selfish. Whether the caretaker is neglectful, abusive, or nonprotective, the message to the child is the same: you are unworthy of love and my attention. This "childhood propaganda" is internalized by the child and accepted as a core truth. It may be one of the reasons why the child stops being emotionally expressive and loses the ability to effectively communicate her needs to others. It also deprives the child of the ability to model self-protection and self-care. Dusty Miller (1994) described "self-harming behaviors" as a way for clients to "reinforce their belief that they are incapable of protecting themselves because they were not protected as children." (p. 8). You can begin to offer a new perspective about the inherent goodness of your clients by introducing the workbook exercise entitled STRENGTHS THAT A LOVING RESOURCE WOULD IDENTIFY on page 57. In time, this can be followed by FIVE OF MY STRENGTHS INDENTIFIED BY ME on page 57.

As children grow, they must continue to find ways to attach to abusive caretakers. It is not acceptable for children to think of their parents as toxic, unloving, or bad; that cognitive reality would make it impossible to attach and bond with them. Instead, children can unconsciously make sense out of their parents' neglectful or abusive actions by taking ownership of the poor parenting, telling themselves they are not loved because they are unlovable. This reframe allows them to successfully attach: my parent isn't bad; the problem is me. Scaer (2001) corroborated this, stating, "The child really has no choice, and will use self-blame to justify re-attaching to the abuser, since some sort of attachment or bonding is the child's greatest unconscious need at this age" (p. 87). This adaptive strategy of self-blame may be at the core of the cognitive distortion that haunts trauma survivors and, in their minds, justifies the use of self-punishing behaviors later in life. Linehan (1993) concurred that early invalidating environments may not provide strategies for coping with emotional distress.

In the workbook, the exercise entitled EXPLORING SELF-BLAME on page 47 can help clients explore the cognitions they were forced to use to make sense out of their painful childhood experiences. The next workbook exercise entitled RE-THINKING THE WAY I DESCRIBE PAINFUL

EXPERIENCES on page 50 gives clients the opportunity to reframe those thoughts and begin to move beyond self-blame.

In addition, children who are in survival mode take on the behaviors, body postures, and movements that are most adaptive in their families. They will act, move, and speak in ways that keep them safe and are deemed acceptable by caretakers. In a 2011 Sensorimotor Psychotherapy training, Pat Ogden taught, "If our attachment figures don't want us to show ourselves, the body begins to constrict." In this state, children cannot gain mastery over healthy, proactive ways to communicate or advocate for themselves. Their body language communicates a sense of a shamed self and gives others information about how they expect to be treated in relationships. This can create a tragic self-fulfilling prophecy, as predators seem to have radar for detecting the more vulnerable children and adults and are able to exploit and revictimize them without consequences.

Clients do not come into the therapy process with an awareness of how early childhood attachment and relationship dynamics profoundly impact their current behavioral choices and their core sense of self. Fifty-year-old Brian spent much of his childhood in foster care and was repeatedly abused and neglected. Early in treatment he said:

> OK, I get that I had a really crappy childhood, and I even understand that I have the right to be angry about it. But that doesn't explain my addiction to porn and why I keep winding up with women who hurt me and cheat on me. I feel like despite my childhood, I am responsible for the mess I am making of my adulthood. There's no one to blame now but myself.

This is a common mind-set and needs to be addressed in the beginning stages of therapy. As we strive to help clients better understand their self-destructive behaviors, making a connection between the ways in which they hurt themselves, early attachment issues, and affect regulation is one of the linchpins of treatment and a critical psychoeducational intervention. It is worth taking the time to educate clients about the different kinds of attachment patterns that can be forged through the infant–caretaker dance: secure, insecure, ambivalent, avoidant, or disorganized. However, it is also important to reiterate that all infants inherently and appropriately want and crave an ideal attachment, one that is characterized by trust, security, and consistency. The extent to which this gets carried out has everything to do with the level of healthy, predictable, and loving responsiveness exhibited by the primary caretaker. "The early social environment, mediated by the primary caretaker, directly influences the final wiring of the circuits of the brain that are responsible for the future social and emotional coping capacities of the individual" (Schore, 2003, p. 73).

In this regard, it is the *adult's* parental obligation and responsibility to create a secure attachment, not the child's. This reframe is often another step toward alleviating the sense of shame and guilt survivors feel about the quality of their family-of-origin relationships. We should never underestimate the long-term effects of insecure, ambivalent, avoidant, or disorganized attachment patterns on children. The necessary experience of being consistently and unconditionally comforted by one's caretakers is what enables a child to eventually auto-regulate.

When attachment is problematic, sporadic, or unavailable, a child is left with affect dysregulation: the inability to modulate or manage his or her emotional states. This deficit follows children into adolescence and adulthood, leaving them vulnerable to a perpetual state of emotional overload with no internalized resources for comfort or self-soothing. When there is disorganized attachment, clients struggle with hypervigilance, distress that is disproportionate to the level of loss, intense proximity-seeking behaviors juxtaposed with withdrawal, a constant need for reassurance in relationships, and the use of crisis and self-destructive acts as a way to connect with others. The exciting news is that the therapeutic alliance can become an extraordinarily reparative context in which healthy, secure attachment can be safely experienced and integrated by your clients. When the work unfolds within that trusting relationship, it will resonate for clients to begin experimenting with healthier self-soothing strategies. It also allows them to tap into their own inner wisdom, and true healing can begin.

4

THE INHERENT STRUGGLES
OF ADOLESCENCE

It is important to distinguish the population of teens who harm themselves and come from a context of trauma from a different cohort of adolescents who superficially engage in nonsuicidal self-injury (NSSI). The dynamics associated with NSSI can be quite different from the underlying motives connected to abuse survivors who chronically hurt themselves. Adolescents who have "tried" NSSI may engage in the behavior for other reasons. They may be experimenting to fit in with other peers. When an increase in cutting occurs within a school or a residential treatment setting, some of the literature associates this with a "contagion factor" (Walsh, 2008). However, the research is mixed regarding the extent to which this, alone, is a way to explain an increase in the experimentation.

People who are engaging in self-destructive behaviors in a superficial way may be testing their courage or emulating popular media personalities who disclose—even parade—their eating disorders, addictions, and self-mutilating behaviors such as cutting and burning as a means to manage their emotional pain (Rasmussen, 2011). Or they may be acting out from a place of impulsivity, poor judgment, or aggression features strongly associated with the developing adolescent brain (Nixon, Cloutier, & Jansson, 2008; Nock & Prinstein, 2005; Smith, 2008; Whitlock, Power, & Eckenrode, 2006; Yates, 2004).

Some teenagers get anonymous support for their attempts at hurting themselves, as well as guidance about how to engage in self-destructive behaviors through a subculture of Web sites and online videos that normalize and romanticize cutting and starving behaviors. There are more than 400 Web sites containing this information, including many where self-injury is even glorified. Access to detailed information about how to "safely" cut or endure the physical pain of starvation may account for an increase in the behavior among certain curious teenagers. It may also provide a socially sanctioned way to connect with other adolescents. Interestingly, female adolescents make up the preponderance of Internet message board users on these sites. This may "reflect a tendency for females to solicit more formal and informal help and social support compared with males" (Whitlock et al., 2006, p. 9).

Much has been written about teenagers who experiment with cutting, burning, purging, and substance abuse. It is almost presented as a normal and inevitable rite of passage. Having worked with many teenagers who engage in these behaviors, I strongly believe that it is a mistake to frame these actions as typical experimentation. The aforementioned behaviors can all serve similar functions: They help teens regulate emotional states and self-soothe by distracting, numbing, or releasing endorphins. They are provocative behaviors that hurt the body while seeking attention and help from concerned peers or disengaged adults. When any adolescent experiments with these kinds of actions, we have an ethical responsibility to ask ourselves, "Why does this behavior resonate for this teenager?" and "What is going on in their life that would warrant the deliberate infliction of physical or emotional pain or discomfort?"

In this regard, I disagree with the notion that adolescents hurt themselves strictly because it is contagious behavior. This is not like mimicking the dress code or hairstyle of the "cool kids." These are provocative, dangerous, sometimes painful, and often scary behaviors that speak to certain adolescents for very specific reasons. We will explore ways to help our clients gain insight about why the behavior resonates for them, as this is a critical part of treatment.

Behaviors such as body piercings and tattoos are often categorized as manifestations of self-harm, when in fact they aren't.

The critical distinction is that teens often do these things for body beautification. They are motivated by a genuine belief that metal studs in their tongues, spikes in their lips and eyebrows, and all kinds of permanent images imprinted on their bodies make their bodies look *better*. Of course, this is when I really feel the generation gap between young clients and me, but it's critically important to listen to the motivation and meaning that they attach to these actions.

In addition, piercings and tattoos are generally done by someone else and often have an intrinsically social component to them: kids go in a group to the mall or the tattoo parlor—often inebriated—and share the experience. An important caveat to stay mindful of is that if clients allow piercings to get infected and then pick at those scabs, not letting them heal, you can arguably say they have found a socially mediated gateway into a self-destructive act (Ferentz, 2001). When adolescents are engaging in these behaviors, they are self-inflicted, often shame based, isolative, and certainly not about cosmetically enhancing the body.

I am not suggesting that all of the teenagers who engage in self-destructive behaviors are or were abuse survivors or have neglectful parents. I am suggesting that there is an untapped "pain narrative" that has not been articulated with words. This might connect to the inherent intrapsychic challenges of evolving identity or the interpersonal complications of stressful peer dynamics. What does seem clear is that instead of processing developmental challenges with words and overt affect, these teenagers are expressing themselves and trying to process their pain through self-destructive behaviors.

In your practice you will find a cohort of teenagers who grapple with self-destructive behaviors yet appear to have no explicit or specific trauma or neglect experiences. Consider the possibility that the developmental challenges of adolescence, in and of themselves, may be traumatic for these teens. You can help your clients begin to identify possible sources of teenage stress by encouraging them to do the workbook drawing prompt entitled EXPLORING ADOLESCENT STRESSORS on page 39. Even Marcia Brady in *The Brady Bunch* had days when she struggled with low self-worth, interpersonal angst and tension, and the inevitable disappointments of life. However, in Marcia's case, there were loving and available resources to help process her difficult experiences, challenge and undo the cognitive distortions, problem solve, console, and install a sense of hope and optimism by reminding her that the pain was time limited.

However, as we've already discussed, many teenagers have to deal with the vicissitudes of life alone, reconciled to the reality that their emotionally and/or physically unavailable caretakers will not be there to lend support, guidance, wisdom, or encouragement. Another major difference is that Marcia Brady grew up in simpler times: the kinds of conflicts and decisions she grappled with were relatively tame compared to the options, conflicts, and choices that teenagers currently face. Let's take a closer look at some of what teenagers have to juggle and reconcile in today's society.

Aside from our very first year of life, we experience the most physical and neurological changes during adolescence. Puberty is the biological process of turbulent change: the body is evolving in shape, size, and hormonal structure. For many adolescents, these changes are unwanted and confusing and can result in a phenomenon I call "body betrayal" (Ferentz, 2001). Rather than celebrating these newfound changes, male and female teenagers resent their bodies, connecting their lack of popularity, poor athletic prowess, or average academic performance to being too tall, overly developed, hairy or pimpled, underweight, or overweight. Many teenagers have experienced the embarrassment of having an unexpected menstrual cycle, being teased for their looks, or having an erection that wouldn't subside quickly enough.

Richard, who has struggled with intimacy issues, a dependence on marijuana, and sexual addiction, poignantly illustrated the concept of body betrayal when he recounted a devastatingly traumatic experience that began in eighth grade:

When I was in middle school, I had a young math teacher who was
a knockout. One day, at the end of class, the bell rang to dismiss
us for lunch. Almost all of the kids got up and ran out of the room.
I had a full-blown erection and couldn't move. I felt mortified and
terrified. I remember two of my friends trying to push me out of
my seat to get to the lunchroom. I was so embarrassed about
my erection, and I tried to make excuses about why I couldn't
get up. One of my friends saw it and started teasing me about it.
The teacher came over and saw it too. I wanted to die. I hated
myself, hated my body. Word spread, and I was taunted about
that through 12th grade. I never let go of those feelings of hating
my body. No wonder I abused my body for years afterward!

This corroborates a powerful notion: if clients hate their bodies,
then it resonates to hurt their bodies. And in today's culture,
the teasing is not limited to the high school hallway or the gym
locker room. Cyberbullying can be overwhelming, daunting, and
deeply traumatizing for many kids. It is impossible to take back
what is thrown out into cyberspace, and the speed with which
rumors and unkind taunts get disseminated is mind-boggling.
Rather than externalizing their anger or rage, many kids internalize these experiences, blaming the flaws and inadequacies of
their own bodies for the teasing and ostracizing they experience
from peers. Sadly, kids growing up in profoundly dysfunctional
families may endure additional teasing at the hands of uncaring
siblings or cruel parents who think it is acceptable or funny to
make crude comments about a teen's developing body.

According to Eric Erickson, the primary developmental task
of adolescence is "identity vs. role confusion," and this is accomplished, in large part, through peer affiliations. Therefore, it can be
devastating for adolescents to endure the unpredictable dynamics
of their best friends suddenly ignoring them or their peer groups
arbitrarily excommunicating them. Self-esteem and self-worth
become codependently mediated by fickle peer relationships.

And many teenagers feel they have to look a certain way to
be accepted. The idea that there is a right way and a wrong way
to look is promulgated by our culture in overt and covert ways.

Many teens are influenced by the images in fashion and gossip magazines, CD covers, 20- and 30-year-old movie stars who get plastic surgery and Botox, the buff actors on talk shows lamenting about how out of shape they are, and the teen Internet sites that award modeling contracts to girls who should be hospitalized for anorexia. We are a society that reveres the beautiful, young, and thin, and teenagers are very tuned in to this reality. If they already struggle with self-consciousness, low self-esteem, or fleeting feelings of worthlessness, the disparity between their body shapes and facial features and the images of perfection that bombard them can create the tipping point that makes self-destructive behaviors an option (Ferentz, 2001).

In addition to the almost obsessive emphasis that is placed on body image and the desperate need to fit in with other peers, adolescents in today's generation are faced with many other stressors. At ever-younger ages they are being asked to make difficult and complicated decisions about becoming sexually active, engaging in substance use, cheating in school, shoplifting, or driving with impaired drivers. They are pressured to excel academically, have clarity about their future careers at younger ages, juggle many extracurricular activities, build impressive résumés before graduating from high school, and even work part-time to help out with the family's troubled finances. Eleven-year-old Tammy illustrated how hard it is to navigate the world as a young teen when she spontaneously said at the end of a session:

> So a lot of my friends said it would be a good idea for me to "do it" with Jared at lunchtime in the bathroom. I mean not sex or anything, just like a blow job or a hand job so he knows I like him. I just don't want him to film it on his phone or anything 'cause I know my parents might see it. They also said if I did it, it would help me get in with the more popular group, and I really want to hang out with them. So, like, do you think I should? I kinda want to if it would get me invited to their parties.

How sad that an 11-year-old would even be contemplating this kind of behavior in order to fit in. Even when we are mindful of these adolescent stressors, in some cases this doesn't take into consideration the additional impact of undiagnosed learning differences, issues with organizational and executive functioning skills, attention deficit disorder, and the emotional or physical unavailability of parents and adult supervision. Many teenagers walk around with undiagnosed and untreated depression and anxiety, and this too increases their predilection toward engaging in self-destructive behaviors as a way to self-soothe and self-medicate (Ferentz, 2001).

If Marcia Brady was faced with these complications, it's possible she would go for advice to her housekeeper, Alice, if not a parent. Today, many successful parents are traveling, attending board meetings, working late, or spending after-hours on the Internet or, sadly, are oblivious to their teenagers' emotional needs.

The family dynamics in 15-year-old Tracie's home provide a painful cautionary tale regarding the consequences of being raised by emotionally or physically unavailable parents:

> At first it was fun to invite a bunch of kids over whenever my parents were away—which happened a lot. I got really popular—my house was known as the "party house." But then kids started having sex and bringing alcohol and heroin into the house, and I didn't know what to do. They didn't listen when I asked them to stop, so then I started drinking and snorting heroin too. Partly because it looked like fun, partly because I didn't want them to be mad at me or make fun of me if I didn't do it. There were times, though, that I wished my parents would come home sooner, even if it meant they would be angry at me. I just wanted them to take over, kick the kids out. Just handle it for me. Then I started to get high more so I wouldn't feel how angry I was at my parents.

I believe teenagers are also affected by an overexposure to violence and misogynistic sexuality on the Internet and in video games. Spending countless hours staring at the screens of electronic equipment can evoke a kind of hypnotic or dissociative state in almost anyone. Teens who zone out a lot may be at increased risk for self-destructive acts: the disconnect from their own bodies makes it easier to inflict physical pain. They have also become a generation with compromised social and communication skills because everything is texted or e-mailed. I wonder about the long-term effects of reduced "face-to-face time" and the impact that has on their fundamental need for social engagement, attachment, sustained intimacy in relationships, and safe touch.

Take notice of the fact that 11-year-old Tammy didn't think that a blow job or hand job was sex. And her concern about Jared filming the act on his phone was rooted in a fear of parental reprisal, not an awareness of his behavior as a gross violation of trust or privacy. All of these things take a toll, and we should consider the strong possibility that even in the absence of abuse, these are the issues that are creating pain narratives for many teenagers in today's world.

In early childhood, soothing strategies such as using a pacifier, sucking a thumb, holding a stuffed animal or blanket, or sitting in the lap of a safe caretaker would evoke the comfort and support a child needs. In adolescence, none of these strategies are viable, so teens need alternative ways to self-soothe. If there are no consistent, healthy, available resources, then self-destructive behaviors become an option. The irony is many parents believe that as their children get older, they require less and less supervision and hands-on parenting. Teens who are trying to individuate can certainly give their parents mixed messages about their desire for autonomy and privacy.

But in their most honest moments, adolescents typically confess that the world is a scary place, and for all their bravado, they don't really know what they're doing yet. They want and need guidance. What they are being asked to navigate requires wisdom, objectivity, the ability to do abstract thinking, and sophisticated cause-and-effect analyses. Those cognitive abilities are literally not yet fully wired in the adolescent brain, and as a result teens actually need a tremendous amount of guidance and support. When that safety net is in place, there is no need to self-soothe in destructive ways.

5

THE METACOMMUNICATION OF EATING DISORDERS, ADDICTIONS, AND SELF-MUTILATION

In this chapter and in those in Part II, we will explore specific stages in the cycle of self-destructive behaviors and then look at various treatment modalities within the context of each stage. In addition to the many cognitive, artistic, behavioral, and somatic interventions that you can employ, consider psychoeducation an essential intervention too. As we've already discussed, to put the disparate puzzle pieces together, clients need to be educated about the impact of attachment wounds, affect dysregulation, dysfunctional family-of-origin dynamics, and the developmental challenges of adolescents. In addition, they must come to understand the ways in which self-destructive behaviors communicate, recapitulate, and attempt to restory prior traumatic experiences and pain narratives. We will explore those dynamics in this section.

I have found the work of Virginia Satir and Dusty Miller to be of great help in elucidating these core issues. Satir's concept of "meta-communication" or the "message about the message" describes the nonverbal ways in which we send deeper information to others about our thoughts, feelings, and needs. We do this through body language, facial expressions, tone, pitch and speed of voice, the expression in our eyes, the avoidance of eye contact, and so on. It is a form of communication that transcends words and oftentimes appears to be incongruent with verbal statements (Satir, 1983). Parents can say to their child, "I love you," but the accompanying nonverbal gestures of arms folded in and the avoidance of eye contact belies and undermines the verbal message, creating confusion for the child.

We can see this same incongruence when clients tell us that nothing is wrong and they're not angry, yet they make aggressive behavioral choices that are hurtful and punitive to their bodies. Another example is the clients who verbally claim to be comfortable with intimacy yet continue to binge and gain weight or spend hours looking at pornography on the Internet, resulting in decreased sexual closeness with their partner. You can help clients explore this issue by using the workbook exercise entitled MY VERBAL AND NON-VERBAL MESSAGES on page 66.

In many ways metacommunication is a much more honest form of self-expression. We are all capable of manipulating or consciously selecting our words to please someone, avoid threat or conflict, obtain a desired outcome, and so on. But the body doesn't lie, and much of what we express nonverbally has a spontaneity and authenticity that seems beyond our conscious control. When we help clients find the courage to be curious about their metacommunication, it often opens the door to much deeper self-discovery.

Part of the psychoeducational process is suggesting to clients that there is metacommunication in their self-destructive behaviors: a deeper narrative of thoughts, feelings, and needs that, thus far, have not been put into words. Think of acts that are punitive and harmful as having high communicative value, something that inherently distinguishes them from suicide, which is not a behavior that is designed to address unmet needs or foster a greater sense of connectedness with others. Despite the fact that many trauma survivors are often unable or unwilling to verbally articulate these emotional needs or pain narratives, they still have an intrinsic hardwired desire to share them with empathic witnesses and to break the cycle of secrecy and denial. When words fail because they have been suppressed, feel futile, or are inaccessible, it makes sense that clients seek alternative ways to tell their stories (Ferentz, 2001, 2011).

One of the ways to help clients be curious about their narratives is to suggest that how and where they hurt themselves is not arbitrary, coincidental, or irrelevant. This perspective was brilliantly articulated by Dusty Miller and her paradigm TRS:

trauma reenactment syndrome. In this model the body is viewed as a battleground for the recapitulation and retelling of prior abuse. Eating disorders, addictions, and acts of self-mutilation such as cutting and burning become the vehicles through which sexual, emotional, and physical abuse are communicated. When we encourage clients to decode the hidden messages in their self-destructive acts, the pain narrative is revealed. Asking clients to assign meaning to the location and nature of their injuries, to theorize about why they gravitate toward one method over another, and to think about what the addiction, the injury, or that part of their body would say if it could talk are all inroads to a deeper understanding of the behavior.

As we invite clients to begin translating their actions, focusing on the metacommunication allows us to assess for two critical ingredients: reenacting a component of the pain narrative so it can be revealed and witnessed and/or restorying it so a sense of closure, power, or control can be reclaimed. Let's look at some of the more common dynamics associated with the reenactment and restorying of eating disordered behaviors, addiction, and self-mutilation. Of course, ultimately, we are interested in our clients' subjective interpretations, as those will resonate the most and are less tainted by the countertransferential narratives we might project onto our clients.

Eating disorders

The three most common manifestations of eating disordered behaviors are bingeing, bulimia, and anorexia. When working with clients with these behaviors, consider that the dynamics of binge eating, bulimia, and anorexia each uniquely reenact and restory specific aspects of abuse, trauma, or pain, and clients choose one behavior over another for conscious and unconscious reasons.

Binge eating

Binge eating is characterized by episodes of uncontrolled eating. Our clients quickly, and often in a dissociative state, consume large amounts of food. The food is not purged, and the binge continues until there is physical pain or exhaustion. Typically, our clients' eating is highly secretive and evokes intense guilt and shame. In regard to reenactment, when we think about *forcing* something into the body that is unwanted, we can connect the behavior to possible sexual trauma. Encourage clients to be curious about the physical pain that bingeing elicits. If they can visualize a binge and notice the sensations they feel on their body, they may connect with discomfort, fatigue, or pain in the throat, jaw, neck, or stomach or on the tongue. They may home in on the sensation of gagging, having trouble swallowing, or feeling nauseated.

Invite clients to stay with these somatic experiences within the context of a safe connection to you, noticing the cognitions, words, or images that surface. In addition, ask them, "When else and with whom else have you experienced these thoughts and feelings?" The physical pain they evoke through binges may be a reenactment of forced fellatio or nausea in response to some other sexual violation.

Another potential reenactment is the feeling of ambivalence that clients unconsciously evoke when something inherently nurturing (food) turns on them and becomes a source of pain (a caretaker who betrays them through perpetration). We can also consider the possibility that forcing food into the body reenacts a blatant disregard for what they need and feel: something that was modeled and normalized by an abusive caretaker. When our clients binge, they are often in a numb or dissociative state: standing outside of themselves and watching and not tasting what they are eating. Dissociation is often used as a way to cope with and survive sexual trauma, and clients' uncontrolled eating may be a way to reenact that part of their trauma narrative. Last, it's important to realize that bingeing is a secretive and shaming act for many clients, and this may be what they are reenacting as well.

Another traumatic experience that may be reenacted through bingeing is the family dynamic of "emotional incest." When this operates, children are co-opted to be a parent's emotional partner, providing him or her with the reassurance, listening ear, companionship, and comfort that should be supplied by the other adult partner. In this scenario, the boundaries become enmeshed, and children are made to feel guilty for and discouraged from individuating or wanting appropriate levels of privacy. Stuffing an overabundance of food into the body can be a metaphor for this dysfunctional family dynamic.

When we explore with our clients the possible ways in which binge eating restories sexual trauma, several possibilities emerge. Many sexual abuse survivors either hold themselves responsible for the abuse, believe they could have or should have done something to stop it, or, worse, think they liked it or participated in it because their bodies responded. Oftentimes, the perpetrator deliberately gives them pleasure or brings them to orgasm as a way to trick them into believing they wanted it to happen. The victims' confused state also decreases the likelihood that they will disclose the abuse to anyone. When clients hold this distorted sense of the experience, bingeing feels like a logical and necessary way to punish the body.

Another common phenomenon is using bingeing as a way to reclaim body control. The excessive weight gain can make clients feel empowered, as they take up more space. In their minds it also creates a protective shield around them, desexualizing their bodies and reducing the probability that they will be sexually attractive to others. Because many sexual abuse survivors get triggered somatically, go into flashback during sex, and don't know how to reground, becoming less desirable to their partner becomes a way to avoid that frightening experience.

Given the fact that bingeing can be a full-time job—buying the food, hiding it, planning the binge, and secretly engaging in it—there is an isolating component to it that increases a survivor's sense of safety in the short term. In addition, food can be used to self-medicate and evoke a sense of nurturance and comfort. For survivors who are bereft of healthy resources for affect regulation, this feels like a way to get those needs met.

It is also worth exploring the possibility that bingeing can help clients short-circuit their dissociative states. The sensation of pain or exhaustion can reconnect clients to their bodies, reminding them that they are alive and present, and this enhances their sense of control. In their most honest moments, clients will confess that food feels like a safe and trusted companion. They can count on the effects of bingeing and like the fact that it is predictable and consistent. This may be their most reliable relationship, and it gives them at least one thing they can count on in their lives. Last, the act of bingeing is distracting and a great way to literally swallow back down overwhelming and painful memories that spontaneously bubble up when these clients get triggered.

Bulimia

Bulimia is defined as clients quickly consuming large amounts of food and continuing to binge until they are exhausted or in physical pain. It differs from bingeing in that clients then try to get rid of the food through purging behaviors such as self-induced vomiting, laxatives, diuretics, enemas, or excessive exercise. Clients will often engage in restrictive eating in between binges. They do not feel in control of the behaviors and do them at least twice a week.

When we explore the connection between bulimia and sexual trauma, several reenactment and restorying scenarios can emerge. The physical act of forcing something into the body and then getting rid of it is a metaphor for many clients. Like bingeing, bulimia evokes physical pain and fatigue, although this is further compounded by the physical violence of purging behaviors that create stomach cramps, rectal pain or bleeding, burning sensations in the throat, and so on.

Ambivalence, disregard for the body, secrecy, and shame are intensely reenacted through the double-edged sword of a potentially nurturing source (food) that is then gotten rid of through the violence of the binge–purge cycle. Consider the possibility that the trauma narrative for these clients has a component of physical violence attached to it. Their perpetrators may have spent less time grooming and rewarding them and more time using threats to gain compliance and prevent disclosures.

We can also explore bulimia as a possible reenactment of verbal, psychological, or emotional trauma. Children who are abused in these ways are made to feel insignificant and bad. They often experience their caretakers as being disgusted with them. Interestingly enough, clients report that purging behaviors leave them feeling disgusting. This emotion is worth exploring cognitively, emotionally, and somatically, as it may connect back to these earlier experiences of being made to feel worthless.

The acts of bingeing and purging are also representative of not being in control. This is a very real and chronic feeling for sexual abuse survivors who were repeatedly violated and robbed of privacy, innocence, safety, or appropriate body boundaries. Last, consider the possibility that using self-induced vomiting to purge may be a more literal reenactment of either wanting to vomit or actually vomiting after a sexual violation or having to clean up the vomit of a perpetually drunk parent.

When we look at the possible restorying dynamics of bulimic behaviors, many clients describe them as a way to cleanse or rid the body of bad thoughts, internal feelings of being dirty, or intense feelings of guilt and shame. Purging is also a way to release unspoken memories and nonverbally articulate rage. Clients believe they are reclaiming a sense of control over their bodies when they can get rid of what has been forced inside.

Just as we discussed with bingeing, bulimia is a way to punish the body, only it's a double whammy: hurting it through forced eating and then again through the violent elimination of purging. Because clients often feel "weird" and "crazy" when they purge, the behavior reenacts and perpetuates a sense of "badness"—something that resonates with their core sense of self. The isolating dynamic of bulimia is also doubled, as energy is expended engaging in two secretive, time-consuming behaviors.

Anorexia

With a nearly 20% potential mortality rate, the highest for any mental disorder, anorexia is an extremely dangerous behavior.

It often appears with the onset of puberty and the development of secondary sex characteristics. Clients refuse to maintain body weight and experience a loss of least 15% of their total body weight. They have an intense fear of gaining weight and being fat, which leads to a preoccupation with food and calories, dieting despite having an emaciated body, and a distorted view of their body size and shape. Many girls who engage in restrictive eating refuse to take in fat. Because the hormone that is required to menstruate is stored in fat cells, these girls and women tend to stop menstruating.

Despite the fact that anorexia can feel like a particularly tenacious disorder to treat, if clients are not medically compromised, focusing on the metacommunication of the behavior, rather than food journals, weigh-ins, and calorie counting, can actually move clients forward and reduce the likelihood of relapses. Explore the possibility that anorexia is connected to emotional or physical neglect or abandonment. The literal act of starving is information about deprivation, a lack of nurturance, and loss. These clients are making themselves smaller and smaller in the world, evoking a state of invisibility and vulnerability. Working with this metaphorically can yield powerful information about a client's loss of control, feelings of being abandoned, and so on. The denial of food is a reenactment of a total disregard for the body, and this may have its roots in prior neglect and a lack of adequate nurturance (Ferentz, 2011).

When we put anorexia in the context of reenacting components of sexual trauma, we can explore the possibility that starving is a statement about the loss of ownership of one's body. Significantly underweight clients report that they no longer connect to or feel their bodies. Severely restricting calories can also reenact a dissociative state, as these clients begin to feel "spacey," light-headed, and dizzy when they don't eat. Most clients who exhibit anorectic behavior feel ashamed and are able to be quite secretive about it. Both of these emotions are reflective of sexual trauma. These clients are most likely to become medically compromised and wind up being hospitalized. Although they are deeply resistant to hospitalization, they may be unconsciously reenacting the loss of freedom, a sense of being perpetually watched, an obsessive focus on their bodies, and the loss of body control that comes from forced feedings.

Some of the restorying dynamics of anorexia parallel the other eating disordered behaviors. It is a way to punish the body for perceived participation in sexual acts or an inability to fight back or disclose the abuse. Anorexia can be viewed as an internalization of intense rage, as it is cruel to deprive oneself of food. Like bingeing, it desexualizes the body and protects it from sexual advances. Although in this case, clients lose their secondary sex characteristics and appear too physically fragile to participate in sexual activity.

Clients deciding what they do and don't put into their bodies is a powerful metaphor for the reclamation of body control. This loss of control may have been the consequence of a body violation, or it may be an emotional dynamic related to rigid, controlling parents who expect and demand perfection or discourage independence and individuation.

Conversely, when anorexia is not about restorying neglect, it may be about a counterbalance to invasive caretaking. Depriving the body of nurturance is a way to restory the fact that attachment dynamics were enmeshed and overbearing. This plays out with alcoholic parents who can't hold appropriate boundaries or promote emotional incest. In addition to the dissociation that starving creates, it can also evoke a sense of euphoria. For some clients this temporarily short-circuits negative affect and internal messages of self-loathing. It may feel like the only way they can temporarily achieve a more positive emotional state.

Another way traumatized clients can reclaim a sense of power and control is to use their destructive behavior to punish others, particularly family members. Starving behaviors and significant weight loss are genuinely frightening to parents and spouses. They often feel helpless and even held hostage by the behaviors. Ironically, the other side of that same coin is the fact that anorexia garners tremendous attention from significant others and may be a way for clients to lure them back in to being more socially engaged and concerned. Sadly, family members do react with increased connection when there is an exacerbation of symptoms but then disconnect again when the symptoms abate. Of course, the reinforcing message is connection can be maintained only when the client stays symptomatic. You can help your clients begin to identify and process the potential metacommunication of these self-destructive acts by using the workbook exercise entitled EXPLORING THE DEEPER MEANING OF AN EATING DISORDER on page 77.

Addictions

We can also invite our clients to look at the specific metacommunication of their addictions. Abusing drugs, alcohol, nicotine, and other substances; compulsive gambling and shopping; and sexual addictions are all designed to self-medicate, comfort, and create arousing distractions to keep unmetabolized pain suppressed. However, we want clients to be curious about why their self-destructive behavior of choice resonates for them. Having clients visualize doing their behavior and then notice the thoughts, feelings, images, body sensations, and movements that are elicited becomes a way for them to process the deeper meanings. Again, we will ultimately defer to the clients' interpretations and insights, but there are some possible messages that can be decoded when dealing with these behaviors.

In many cases, the numbing component of addictions can reenact a dissociative "state of being" that is familiar and comfortable for our clients. The desire to keep returning to a place of hypoarousal is worthy of further exploration. It may be information about a victim's implicit belief that the only way to be safe is in a "freeze" state. It is data about affect dysregulation and an unconscious belief that they lack the capacity to feel and deal with emotions. The disempowering facet of being numb may be metacommunication about learned helplessness. Some addicts

choose behaviors that mimic their alcoholic or drug-using caretaker as a way either to "connect" or join with them or to give
us potent information about their family-of-origin dynamics by
showing us what they lived with and endured growing up.

Over time, all addictions inevitably spiral out of control, and
this may be metacommunication about how out of control their
lives felt in the past. Like eating disordered behaviors, sexual
addictions and substance abuse reenact physical neglect, a
devaluing of self, and a total disregard for the body: a core
value that perpetrators normalize in their childhood. When
clients venture into dangerous neighborhoods to score their
drugs, have sexual encounters with strangers, drive drunk or
high, or make other poor decisions while under the influence,
this can be seen as a re-creation of being placed in physical or
sexual danger in the past.

Just as we discussed with eating disordered behaviors,
addictions are isolating and speak to a fundamental lack of
attachment and fear of subsequent connections. However, juxtaposed with this fear is the yearning for intimacy. Unfortunately,
clients' prior templates for relationships have taught them that
the only safe way to connect is superficially, either through the
temporary, forced camaraderie of the blackjack table or with
a sexual partner they don't really know. These behaviors may
also communicate a sense of invisibility or "feeling like a loser,"
a behavior that is both literally and metaphorically reenacted
through a gambling addiction. You can help your clients identify and process the metacommunication of these self-destructive acts by using the workbook exercise entitled EXPLORING
THE DEEPER MEANING OF AN ADDICTION on page 81.

The metacommunication of the injuries

When we explore the metacommunication of self-mutilating
behaviors, we often discover that clients are reenacting prior
abuse on their bodies. Clients cutting on the inner thigh might
represent where a perpetrator pulled out and ejaculated during a rape. Cutting on the upper forearm might reenact the

place on their body where clients were grabbed before abuse occurred. Clients who felt burned by parents' abusive words or a lack of protection might burn their bodies. Clients picking their lips until they are raw can be interpreted as metacommunication about having to keep secrets and not being allowed to speak.

In addition to clients' injuries giving us information about their actual physical, sexual, or emotional abuse experiences, clients may also be reenacting perpetrators' threats about what would be done to their bodies if they ever disclosed the abuse. When clients seem to be increasing their self-destructive behaviors after disclosing a part of their trauma narrative in session, we should be especially curious about this possibility. Clients who scratch across their throats may be telling us about a threat of having their throats slit. Clients who peel the skin around their fingers may be revealing the threat of having their hands burned in acid. In other cases, clients may be hurting their abusers in effigy by hurting their own bodies. One way to assess for this is to ask clients, "Whose hand are you cutting?" or "Whose body are you hurting?"

Clients may also be using the injuries as "event markers" to unconsciously validate and remember a prior unspeakable abuse experience that was forced underground because no one acknowledged it or it wasn't safe to tell anyone. Oftentimes clients' scars enable us to put the behavior into a historical context: where they were, who they were with, and what was happening when they got the impulse to hurt themselves. Although the verbal narrative may have become suppressed, the scar, bruise, burn, or other injury reassures clients that the event did indeed occur. It serves as a kind of reality check for clients who have had their realities repeatedly invalidated. The scars also allow someone to bear witness to their pain at a future time, when it is safer to feel and reveal it.

Modeling for clients our ongoing compassionate and nonjudgmental curiosity about the potentially deeper message embedded within their behaviors legitimizes their empathic curiosity about them as well. When clients come to realize that their behaviors serve this more profound function, it moves them through their shame. It also invites an exploration of how else they can begin to communicate and have someone bear witness to their pain narratives without perpetuating a sense of victimization and retraumatization. Use the following assessment tool to explore the possible functions of your clients' self-destructive behaviors. You can help your clients identify and process the metacommunication of these self-destructive acts by using the workbook exercise entitled EXPLORING THE DEEPER MEANING OF SELF-MUTILATION on page 85.

Understanding the function of self-destructive behaviors

People engage in self-destructive behaviors for many different reasons. Take a moment to read the following list of common reasons and circle Y (yes) if the statement applies to you and N (no) if it does not. Feel free to include additional reasons under "other."

Y   N   1. To stop feeling so bad or so tense

Y   N   2. To "take away" upsetting thoughts

Y   N   3. To feel more in control of my body

Y   N   4. To make invisible, inside wounds external and visible

Y   N   5. To create the opportunity and a reason to engage in self-care

Y   N   6. To "show" earlier trauma experiences

Y   N   7. To stop myself from telling something about my trauma story

Y   N   8. To get revenge

Y   N   9. To outwardly express anger that I hold inside

Y   N   10. To mark a certain occasion or event so I can remember that it happened

Y   N   11. To punish myself for behaviors I think are shameful, sinful, or bad

Y   N   12. To cry out for help

Y   N   13. To check out, dissociate, or feel numb

Y   N   14. To return to reality or stop feeling "out of it"

Y   N   15. To feel safer and more secure

Y   N   16. To feel unique, special, or different

Y   N   17. To feel a rush

Y   N   18. To achieve a sense of identity

Y   N   19. To reconnect with myself and feel whole or alive

Y   N   20. To stimulate myself

Y   N   21. To purify or cleanse my body

Y   N   22. To distract myself from something or someone threatening
Y   N   23. As a way for my alters to communicate
Y   N   24. To feel peaceful or calm
Y   N   25. To punish or control other people
Y   N   26. To get others to connect with me
Y   N   27. To show how much I hate myself
Y   N   28. To get attention from someone important in my life
Y   N   29. To leave a mark so people know my pain is real

Other reasons: _____

_____

_____

_____

PART II

UNDERSTANDING AND WORKING WITH SELF-DESTRUCTIVE BEHAVIORS

6

THE CYCLE OF SELF-
DESTRUCTIVE BEHAVIORS

The repetitive and cyclical nature of harmful and injurious behaviors can make them difficult to understand and treat. Ironically, these are inherently positively reinforcing behaviors, which is why so many clients are unable to stop on their own (Swales, 2008). Oftentimes a combination of shame, secrecy, and lack of insight prevents clients from making sense out of their actions. When we introduce clients to this cycle of self-destructive behaviors (Figure 6.1), it allows them to work collaboratively with us, identifying and understanding the internal and external dynamics that trigger and perpetuate the behavior.

We should use the context of therapy to explain, and simultaneously diagram, the cycle. Visualizing the process makes it more tangible and less overwhelming and often helps our clients achieve a fundamental understanding of their self-destructive actions. It also normalizes and universalizes the behavior, making it less secretive and shame based. With a concrete explanation that defines and describes behavior that seems weird, elusive, and bewildering, the cycle helps our clients feel validated, less anxious, and able to reclaim a sense of hope. Processing the cycle puts the behavior into a situational, cognitive, and emotional context. It illustrates how one experience naturally leads to another, and when those experiences are not adequately addressed or short-circuited, self-destructive behaviors become an inevitable response.

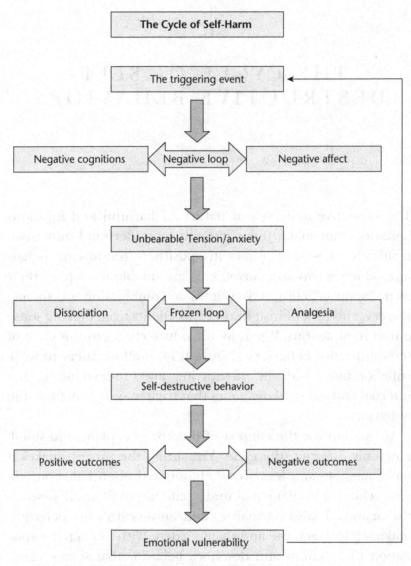

Figure 6.1 **The cycle of self-destructive behaviors**

Copyright August 1999 by Lisa R. Ferentz, LCSW-C. Adapted with permission from Alderman, Tracy, *The Scarred Soul: Understanding and Ending Self-Inflicted Violence—A Self-Help Guide,* New Harbinger, Oakland, CA, 1997.

An additional strength of the cycle is it makes sense when put into a family-of-origin context. We know that clients who are subjected to chronic dysfunction and abuse must evolve necessary coping skills to survive. Strategies such as hypervigilance, dissociation, and internal attribution, although lifesaving in childhood, leave behind a disempowering cognitive and emotional residue in adulthood. Having an extreme startle response, freezing or zoning out when threatened, and possessing a litany of self-blaming cognitions make these clients inherently vulnerable in the world and, therefore, easily triggered. Once the triggering takes hold, their inability to reframe negative thoughts or engage in affect regulation sets them up to hurt their bodies in some way.

Once clients understand this cycle, the opportunity is created for them to reclaim control by identifying potential "intervention sites" that will disrupt the cycle and short-circuit the self-destructive behavior. The hopefulness and efficacy of the model is rooted in the fact that our clients are given many opportunities to intervene, even after harmful acts have occurred. Although disabling the cycle after the fact will not spare clients an injury or the pain of their destructive behavior, it can reduce its severity and greatly decrease the likelihood of their engaging in that behavior the next time the cycle is reactivated.

As we process the sequence of events that unfold in the cycle, we will apply three different case examples. This will help the model come to life and will illustrate how the template should be personalized with each client. As these cases are presented, notice the depathologized frame that is used to explain clients' symptoms and struggles. In addition, focus on the ways in which specific harmful acts are metaphors and metacommunication about the clients' core trauma experiences. Keep in mind that "multiple functions for self-injury may exist concurrently within individuals" (Klonsky, 2007, p. 235), so it is important to explore all of the possible motivators and address all of the secondary gains the behavior evokes for clients.

Case scenarios

Bob

Bob is 58 years old and small in stature, but he has worked hard to maintain a muscular build. The youngest of four children, he was physically abused by his alcoholic father and older brother for much of his childhood. His mother was a nonprotective bystander, never challenging the abuse. She often left Bob home alone with his maternal grandfather, an alcoholic who sexually molested Bob from the ages of 6 to 10 years. Bob survived the relentless abuse and perpetual betrayal of caretakers by dissociating. At age 18, he escaped his abusive family by enlisting in the army, where he did three tours of active duty in Vietnam. Although Bob found a surrogate family system in the army, he was profoundly retraumatized when several of his closest friends were killed in his presence by enemy fire. Like many veterans, Bob returned home with untreated post-traumatic stress disorder (PTSD) and spent the next 12 years coping and enhancing his dissociative states by self-medicating with drugs and alcohol.

Given Bob's family-of-origin dynamics and attachment issues, it made sense that in his early 30s he would marry an emotionally unavailable and distant woman. His wife was overly critical of Bob, verbally shaming him in front of their peers and leaving him with the sense that "whatever I did, it was never good enough." Whenever Bob attempted to defend himself or confront her about her excessive criticism, she would withhold physical affection, sometimes for several days. Although she agreed to have two children, his wife refused to be a stay-at-home mom, and by the time their kids were 2 and 4 years old, she was frequently out of town, forging a career in a high-powered job.

Determined to be a safe and available parent, Bob gave up using all substances and did the best he could to raise his children, often feeling like a "single parent taking care of kids who had been abandoned by their mother." Bob's unresolved trauma also influenced his decision to become an emergency medical technician (EMT). Although he professed to like the flexible hours, working as an EMT actually kept him in a perpetual fight–flight response, evoking the hypervigilance and adrenaline rush that were normalized in childhood and solidified in Vietnam.

Although Bob remained sober, he didn't work a program of recovery. Without the coping strategy of substance abuse, whenever his "emotional demons" would resurface, he would either dissociate or numb the feeling by making small cut marks with a razor blade on the inside of his palm. Bob never received counseling for his childhood traumas and PTSD. After years of Bob being a stellar employee, Bob's supervisor began to notice that he was quick to anger, becoming belligerent with colleagues. He seemed distracted and incapable of making quick medical assessments and vital decisions regarding triage and treatment.

He was encouraged to speak with a therapist, but he resisted the idea. His wife complained that he was sexually distant and then grew outraged and shamed him further when she discovered a large collection of pornographic videos hidden in their bedroom. His adult children no longer lived at home but maintained a close relationship with their father. They, too, sensed that he was struggling, and at their insistence, he agreed to begin therapy.

As Bob forged a trusting therapeutic alliance with me, it became clear that he had expanded his repertoire of dysfunctional coping strategies to address the unresolved trauma from his past. In addition to cutting, he had become addicted to pornography. He was drawn to videos that always included sadistic–masochistic homosexual scenarios and frequently masturbated to the point of physical discomfort. This evoked confusion, shame, and feelings of helplessness, as he did not consider himself gay despite his compulsion to watch the films. He felt deeply troubled by his growing preoccupation with pornography and lamented the fact that it was taking him away from sex with his wife.

He felt he was leading a double life. He was exhausted by the secrecy and angry at his inability to stop the behavior. His anger permeated the workplace and was often the catalyst for belligerent interactions with colleagues. His preoccupation with his sexual addiction, coupled with his fear of getting caught, affected his concentration and decision-making processes. His shame kept him distanced from his wife and friends.

(continued)

(continued)

Karen

Karen is 16 years old, tall, thin, athletic, and extremely attractive. She has one 19-year-old brother. They have a strained relationship, and she avoids interacting with him whenever possible. This protective stance is the consequence of her brother repeatedly cornering her in their home and threatening to do sexually explicit things to her. Karen experienced his taunting, abusive behavior as an attempt to "show how much power and control he could have in our relationship."

Karen's mother was oblivious to this sibling dynamic and often chastised Karen for ignoring her brother and being insensitive to his requests for connection. The ineffectiveness of Karen's mother was compounded by the fact that she battled her own undiagnosed, untreated depression and anxiety, having lost her mother to alcoholism when she was 13 years old. As a result of her upbringing, it made sense that Karen's mother self-medicated with alcohol and prescription drugs and was either emotionally unavailable to Karen or inappropriately enmeshed in her life, listening in on Karen's phone calls, opening her mail, and rifling through her drawers.

Karen's father was raised by rigid, religiously dogmatic, and alcoholic parents and was physically abused by both of them throughout his childhood. He suppressed whatever pain he endured as the child of alcoholic parents, as he quickly learned that complaining about either parent would lead to ridicule and violence at home, as well as being shamed with multiple forced confessions at church. As an adult, Karen's father developed an explosive temper that was frequently displaced onto Karen's brother, and throughout childhood, Karen witnessed much of this violence. Her mother never intervened, and Karen learned to "make herself as small as possible until the storm blew over."

Karen also mastered the art of zoning out as a way to mentally escape the family violence and her mother's drunken behavior. In contrast to the abusive treatment her brother received, Karen's father idealized her, unreasonably expecting her to excel in academics and sports. The intense, paternal attention she received put tremendous pressure on Karen and exacerbated feelings of jealousy and resentment from her mother and brother. In the name of familial loyalty, both children were expected to enable their mother's addiction by making excuses for her when she was drunk and "screwed up." They were also forced to put her to bed whenever she passed out and to eat the dinners she had burned in her drunken state. It was understood that neither child could complain about the family dynamics. Because Karen's father held a high-powered and very public position, the children were expected to make it all look good to the outside world.

It makes sense that Karen, as the child of an alcoholic growing up in a violent home, had to adopt many coping strategies to endure her situation. By the time she was 12 years old, she would escape the pain of her home life by sneaking out of her bedroom window in the middle of the night. Older friends would wait in their cars and bring her to local parking lots where she would get drunk and sexually act out. Karen would often black out or dissociate during these episodes, not remembering who she had been with or what she had done. Despite these peer interactions, Karen still felt different from her friends and attempted to impress them and fit in by shoplifting. When she didn't get caught, she upped the ante, stealing in more blatant ways.

When this didn't yield the parental attention she unconsciously craved, she began to significantly restrict her caloric intake. By age 14 she had full-blown anorexia and was hospitalized on three different occasions when she became medically compromised. In a family session during one of her hospital stays, Karen disclosed that she had been molested by an older cousin. Unfortunately, the therapist minimized the impact of this traumatic event, giving family members permission to deny its significance as well. This disavowal of a deeply disturbing event added another layer of trauma to Karen's life.

When she was unable to self-medicate through her eating disordered and sexually dissociative behaviors, Karen would burn her skin with cigarettes and cut the inside of her thigh, discovering that she could achieve a numb state that made everything temporarily better.

(continued)

(continued)

Despite myriad dysfunctional acting-out behaviors, Karen remained a straight-A student in school. She starred in many school productions, played on several sports teams, and was considered a model student by her teachers. No one knew the depth of her pain or recognized the dissonance between her public and her private personas. Friends and relatives labeled her brother as "the deeply troubled one" and saw her as "the perfect one." This message was reinforced at home, and Karen did her best to counterbalance her dysfunctional family with her overachieving drive and enviable academic accomplishments. As the pressure increased to "stay perfect," so did the need to engage in self-destructive behaviors. She was finally referred for therapy when a teacher caught her cutting herself in the high school bathroom after she missed a goal during a field hockey game. At the school's insistence, attending therapy sessions became a prerequisite for staying on her sports teams.

Karen was skeptical about the benefits of therapy and presented with sarcasm, belligerence, and, at other times, silence. For many months, she remained protective about her family dynamics, working hard to minimize, rationalize, and justify her parents' neglectful and abusive behaviors and her mother's addiction issues. Her need to remain loyal to her family precluded her ability to openly share her pain. Slowly, Karen began to forge a trusting therapeutic relationship, and as her bravado dissipated, the true depth of her anger, fear, and pain began to emerge.

Debbie

Debbie is 38 years old, overweight, plain in appearance, and overtly depressed. In an effort to please others, she is excessively acquiescent and will avoid rocking the boat at all costs. She has four siblings who are between 15 and 22 years older than she is, and despite her large family, she grew up feeling like an only child because of the age differences. Debbie always experienced her parents as old, both chronologically and because of their disconnection from popular culture. Growing up, she believed they were never interested in her school activities or her peers. They never attended her recitals, parent–teacher conferences, or swim meets. She believed they were "tired of parenting, as they had already done it four times." Her parents would often use fatigue, prior community commitments, or troubled health as excuses for their lack of participation.

Given her neglect, it made sense that Debbie became convinced that she was an accident and an unwanted child. The more she experienced her parents as disinterested, the harder she tried to win them over. She pursued the same hobbies her mother liked in the hopes that it would be a common bond. She never talked back to her father or challenged his rulings, believing that he would love her more if she were cooperative and compliant.

Her earliest recollection of engaging in self-destructive behaviors was around the age of 7. An older sister had been interested in painting, and there were many art supplies stored in one of the bedrooms. Debbie stumbled upon them and "rather than using a paint brush and paint to express myself, I was drawn toward the XACT-O knife and used it to cut myself." Although her mother punished her and her father yelled, it garnered the parental attention she had been seeking. "Cutting became a way of life and the only way I could get them to notice me." She also developed a compulsion to pick her lips.

Debbie does not have a single memory of her parents displaying physical affection or saying, "I love you." In fact, the memories that linger are the parental looks of exasperation when Debbie fished for a verbal compliment or the stiffening of her mother's body when Debbie would attempt to get a hug. Her siblings labeled her "overly sensitive" and "emotionally needy," and her father cautioned her that she would never find a husband if she remained "so high maintenance and demanding."

(continued)

(continued)

Personalizing her family's rebuffs, Debbie saw herself as ugly and defective and accepted the notion that her desire for affection and emotional intimacy was unreasonable. She learned to stop wanting or needing anything and spent much of her adolescence isolated in her bedroom, where she would read, draw, and fantasize about living with another family. By later adolescence she would bang her head with her fists whenever she felt frustrated or felt guilty for being angry at her parents or wishing she were with a different family.

Throughout high school and college, Debbie was desperate for a boyfriend but never dated because she was terrified of sex. In her senior year, she met the man who would become her husband. A shy, understanding, and hardworking man, he grew up in a violent home with a father who had a serious gambling addiction. Given their respective neglectful upbringings and their sadness about their childhoods, neither one of them wanted to bring more children into the world.

Although they have been married and devoted to one another for 15 years, Debbie continues to secretly cut herself and pick at her lips. She also uses food to make herself feel better whenever she starts to feel depressed. Over the past few years, Debbie has gained 65 pounds. The more she gains, the more she dislikes herself, which perpetuates her self-destructive behaviors. Her husband remains supportive, but his own family-of-origin experiences evoke anxieties about never having enough money, and his inherent fear of losing everything creates a compulsive need to work long hours of overtime. As a result, Debbie feels alone much of the time. She is reticent about expanding her social life, as she doesn't know how to go about making new friends.

Last year, Debbie discovered that shopping online and buying things from home shopping networks were powerful ways to pass the time and feel better. In response to the marital discord created by her purchases, Debbie often acquiesces and returns what she buys. However, returning the items leaves her feeling resentful and helpless, which often leads to additional shopping or self-destructive acts.

For many years Debbie wanted to see a therapist to address her destructive behaviors and depressed mood but was afraid to ask her husband for the money. When her bingeing, head banging, compulsive shopping, and suicidal ideation grew unmanageable, she finally summoned the courage to tell her husband. He was supportive about treatment but urged Debbie to do it in as few sessions as possible. Debbie continues to feel guilty about staying in therapy and describes it as an ongoing internal conflict and struggle. Debbie believes her husband would also benefit greatly from therapy, but she is afraid to broach the subject with him.

Keeping in mind these poignant case scenarios, take another look at the visual depiction of the cycle on page 68. When you are in session with your clients, it helps to draw the cycle on a large piece of paper and then walk your clients through each stage. To best demonstrate this, in the following chapters we will deconstruct each part of the cycle, giving you a deeper understanding of the dynamics that are operating and then apply Bob's, Karen's, and Debbie's experiences so the template becomes more personalized for each of them.

7

THE TRIGGERING EVENT AND
THE LOOP OF NEGATIVITY

The loop of negativity: triggering events

There is always a triggering event that precedes the act of injuring; it does not occur in a vacuum (Turner, 2002). Self-destructive behavior happens only when our clients deem it necessary. The first step is to help clients put the behavior into a context, that is, a triggering event that is experienced either internally or externally. The trigger may be perceived objectively as painful or threatening (e.g., being yelled at by an intimidating person), or it can be a benign event interpreted subjectively as threatening (e.g., the smell of a particular brand of cigar that the perpetrator smoked). Our clients react based on their perceptions of what is happening and the meaning they attach to it.

Given trauma survivors' levels of hypervigilance, hair-trigger startle responses, the perpetual state of flight or fight, and their vulnerability toward affect dysregulation (Hollander, 2008), it is not surprising when they experience extreme overarousal to seemingly benign stressors. Often the stimulus is, objectively speaking, fairly innocuous. What matters most is the subjective sense of being threatened and triggered.

The triggering event often evokes feelings of being neglected or mistreated. A personal interaction might conjure feelings of rejection, abandonment, loss, or separation: a significant other appearing disapproving of or disappointed in them. Other triggers may be elicited from the five senses: a smell, taste, texture, auditory cue, or visual image. These experiences may be consciously or unconsciously associated with a prior threatening event, an unsafe person, or traumatic episode (Walsh, 2008).

When abuse occurs in childhood, horrific acts are often paired with benign sensory stimuli, such as music playing in the background, cooking smells in the kitchen, or leaves falling outside of a bedroom window. Once the brain associates these images with the pain and betrayal of the abuse experience, subsequent exposure to similar sensory experiences will elicit the same emotional responses. This is further solidified by the fact that trauma is experienced and stored in the limbic system, which is where our five senses are located.

Because we are biologically hardwired to respond to a perceived threat with either flight, fight, or freeze reactions, it is understandable that a triggering event sets in motion a cascade of physiological responses that will, in turn, affect our thoughts, feelings, and behaviors. It is necessary for clients to put the self-destructive behavior into a contextual framework. When we introduce clients to the concept of a "triggering event," we increase their awareness of surroundings, relationship dynamics, sensory and somatic experiences, and thought processes as they pertain to prior trauma and the impulse to harm or injure themselves. Once internal and external triggers are identified, clients can create action plans that help them avoid, address, or extricate themselves from those triggers.

Bob's triggering events

- Watching war movies on TV or having a dream about Vietnam
- Feeling rejected by my wife when she chooses work functions and obligations over spending time with me
- Experiencing my wife withhold physical affection
- Interacting with drunk friends after work and smelling alcohol on their breath
- Hearing news reports about pedophiles molesting boys
- Being unable to resuscitate a patient in the ER
- Being ridiculed by my aggressive female boss at work
- Getting a visual flashback about my childhood sexual abuse

Karen's triggering events

- Watching my mother slowly get drunk and then pass out on the sofa
- Listening to my father and brother fight
- Trying on jeans and then feeling fat and ugly when I look in the mirror
- Feeling afraid of doing badly on a school test or paper and then worrying that my dad will be angry with me
- Having my brother corner me in the house while making gross sexual remarks
- Losing any track meet, field hockey game, or basketball game
- Going to family gatherings and seeing the cousin who abused me
- Being forced to cover up for my mother when she drinks

Debbie's triggering events

- Feeling rejected or unwanted by anyone close to me
- Receiving a look of disinterest or disapproval
- Feeling inadequate or awkward in social situations
- Feeling guilty whenever I spend money
- Getting visits from my elderly parents
- Getting bills in the mail
- Having to return items I've purchased online

The loop of negativity: negative thoughts

If the triggering event is not addressed, clients move to the next stage of the cycle: the activation of negative thoughts and negative feelings. Depending on the treatment paradigm, pessimistic thoughts will yield negative affect, or negative feelings create an internal monologue of defeating thoughts. Clients frequently experience the two simultaneously and are overwhelmed by negativity and criticism (Hollander, 2008). Glassman, Weierich, Hooley, Deliberto, and Nock (2007) substantiated the role of negative cognitions in self-destructive behaviors when they concluded, "Psychosocial interventions aimed at decreasing adolescent self-criticism may be effective in treating or preventing non-suicidal self-injury" (p. 2488). Cognitions and affect fuel each other in an endless negative loop. This part of the cycle is therefore depicted with arrows pointing to and from thoughts and feelings.

The cognitions are dangerous and overwhelming in their negativity because they are so distorted. This predilection toward inaccurate and "frozen in time" thinking—superimposing past experience on the present—also makes sense. It is one of the inevitable consequences of childhood trauma. Van der Kolk, McFarlane, and Weisaeth (2006) discussed the ways in which intrusive thoughts stemming from traumatic events can be cognitively processed. Some people can use these thoughts to learn from the experience, plan for the future, work toward a state of acceptance, and adjust their future expectations. In this case, the event is "integrated in memory and stored as an unfortunate event belonging to the past."

However, for many trauma survivors, the brain processes the intrusive thoughts and trauma-based experiences differently, and "the sensations and emotions belonging to the event start leading a life of their own" (van der Kolk et al., 2006, p. 8). This continues to manifest in adulthood. Trauma survivors are prone to dichotomous mind-sets: stark contrasts of black and white that manifest as all or nothing, always or never. When they are triggered, the distortion is "This will *always* happen to me" or "It will *never* get better." These thoughts are developmentally consistent with childhood concrete thinking and the disempowered hopelessness of a traumatized child.

Trauma survivors also automatically engage in self-blame, often exaggerating their missteps and taking ownership of problems, while simultaneously downplaying their positive contributions and intrinsic worth. Holding themselves unfairly responsible for negative outcomes is a way to reclaim a pseudo-sense of control. Clients think, "If I caused this problem, that means I can come up with a way to fix it."

In actuality, this replicates the family-of-origin dynamic of unfairly blaming victims, while perpetrators take no responsibility for their role in the abuse or neglect. Survivors learn to internalize perpetrator messages of negativity, criticism, and blame (Conterio & Lader, 1998). The research by Glassman et al. (2007) corroborates the relationship between emotional abuse and internalized critical self-talk, with self-destructive behaviors as the inevitable punitive response to these cognitive distortions. Historical layers of self-hatred and inaccurate self-blame exacerbate this phase of the cycle. Unfortunately, personalizing events fuels our clients' negative and distorted sense of self and sets them up to fail. They cannot fix a problem they did not create in the first place. Adding insult to injury, clients create internal guilt, proclaiming they should be able to fix or change another person or an external event.

Another cognitive distortion survivors have is the irrational belief that if they feel something strongly, it must be true. If survivors feel damaged, responsible, unworthy, and so on, then those feelings must be accurate reflections of their character. When a triggering event elicits a negative cognition such as "I am unlovable," clients assume the thought must be accurate. They do not question or reevaluate its merit. These thoughts create additional negative cognitions, and clients remain stuck in an endless loop of negativity.

Bob's negative thoughts

- I am trapped in my job.
- Things will never get better in my life.
- I'm sick and weird.
- I should have done more to save the patient in the ER.
- Drunk people aren't safe to be around.
- I'm not good enough for my wife.
- I don't deserve to be loved.
- There are no safe places in the world.

Karen's negative thoughts

- My family sucks, and I'm stuck with them.
- I am fat and ugly, and no one will want to be with me.
- I should do something to get my mother to stop drinking.

- I will always be different and never fit in with my friends.
- I'll never be able to make my father happy enough.
- Don't trust what people say. Most of them don't care about you.
- No one will ever protect me.
- The things that happened in the past are unimportant, and I shouldn't be upset about them.

Debbie's negative thoughts

- I am not lovable.
- My needs are too intense and unreasonable.
- Never ask for what you want—you'll never get it.
- If my husband knew the real me, he wouldn't want me.
- I don't deserve to be happy.
- I don't have the right to be angry or unhappy. So many people had it worse than I did.
- Even though I'm married, I'm really alone.
- My body is gross.

The loop of negativity: negative feelings

Negative cognitions and the triggering event itself always elicit negative feelings. Upsetting interactions or self-defeating thoughts would create painful feelings for anyone. But the stakes are much higher for traumatized clients who lack the essential tools to work through, resolve, and move beyond painful experiences. For many clients, triggers that are reminiscent of prior abuse or neglect scenarios will instantly evoke anger, depression, despair, or terror. Distorted thoughts inherently create feelings of inadequacy, worthlessness, helplessness, and disempowerment. Some events trigger feelings of isolation, loss, and alienation (Alderman, 1997). Triggering interactions with others can lead to feelings of embarrassment, invalidation, rejection, and betrayal. Klonsky (2007) supported the notion that harmful behavior is preceded by acute emotional distress, including feelings of guilt, self-hatred, loneliness, anger, and anxiety.

Clients physically hurt themselves to bring about a sense of relief by temporarily reducing emotional upset. Mikolajczak,

Petrides, and Hurry (2009) described emotional regulation as one of the primary functions of self-harm, focusing on the fact that the behavior distracts clients away from intolerable feelings. In fact, their research showed that "eighty percent of the young people who deliberately harmed themselves reported doing so in an attempt to regulate unpleasant emotions" (p. 190). Van der Kolk et al. (2006) echoed the sentiment that many clients attempt affect regulation through self-mutilation, eating disorders, and substance abuse. Klonsky (2007) cited research from 11 different studies of self-reported reasons why clients hurt themselves. In all 11 studies, "reasons suggesting an affect regulation function were heavily endorsed" (p. 230).

Given our prior discussion of the role attachment plays in the internalization of necessary coping resources for comforting and self-soothing, it makes sense that clients who were not allowed to successfully attach to their primary caretakers are bereft of internal resources to modulate emotions or undo cognitive distortions. Self-injury, therefore, becomes a way to regulate intolerable affective states and the only way a trauma survivor knows how to self-soothe (Herman, 1992; Nixon, Cloutier, & Jansson, 2008; Strong, 1999). Mikolajczak et al. (2009) said, "Self-harm may be a desperate attempt to down-regulate the negative feelings that are exacerbated by ineffective emotional coping strategies" (p. 190).

Ironically, feeling negative or difficult emotions is a doable proposition for anyone. Our capacity to experience a wide range of emotions is part of what makes us human beings. And all feelings, no matter how intense they may seem, inevitably have a beginning, middle, and end. However, the concept of experience being time limited is often lost on trauma survivors.

Clients are often afraid to get close to strong feelings because they lack the internal resources that help them navigate or "ride through" the discomfort of powerful emotions. They don't trust in their ability to handle emotions without becoming overwhelmed, falling apart, acting out, or behaving inappropriately, so their automatic response to the bubbling up of feelings is to push them away and shut them back down. Van der Kolk et al. (2006) supported this notion, stating, "Traumatized people seem to try to compensate for their hyper-arousal by shutting down . . . on a psychobiological level by emotional numbing to both trauma-related and everyday experience" (p. 218).

Bob's negative feelings

- Helpless
- Frozen
- Damaged
- Ashamed
- Unsafe
- Weak
- Scared

Karen's negative feelings

- Trapped
- Alone
- Guilty
- Embarrassed
- Unsafe
- Angry
- Powerless

Debbie's negative feelings

- Lonely and alone
- Rejected
- Guilty
- Unsafe
- Ungrateful
- Numb
- Defenseless
- Neglected

The mounting discomfort and lack of self-compassion that grows from an uncontrollable continuous loop of negative thoughts and feelings inevitably brings clients to the next stage in the cycle: unbearable tension and anxiety.

8

UNBEARABLE ANXIETY AND THE FROZEN LOOP

Unbearable tension and anxiety

Clients often somatically experience this stage in the cycle. Overwhelming negative thoughts and feelings of despair manifest physically on the body. Clients may experience muscle tension, headache, upset stomach, jitteriness, shortness of breath, heaviness in the chest, and so on.

The pain inflicted on physical and sexual abuse survivors originates on the body. As stated earlier, many sexual abuse survivors mistakenly blame their bodies for participating in sexual acts, particularly if they experienced arousal or orgasm (Ferentz, 2001). This is further fueled by perpetrators looking to assuage their own guilt by telling their victims they wanted sex or they liked it. These clients are left with a deep sense of body betrayal and self-loathing. The rage that cannot safely be expressed toward perpetrators gets internalized and connected to the victim's body instead. Being physically violated leaves survivors with a sense of disempowerment, and this loss of control is somatically reexperienced when they are overwhelmed with anxiety.

Because childhood trauma memories often get imprinted and stored on the body, it makes sense that survivors are somatically vulnerable. Van der Kolk, McFarlane, and Weisaeth (2006) identified the dynamic of abuse-related somatization, and trauma specialists can attest to the large percentage of trauma survivors who present in their offices with physical complaints that have no organic cause.

When anxiety escalates, clients often feel as if they are "going crazy," thus exacerbating their already anxious states. Many clients begin to turn on themselves. Embarrassed, frustrated, and frightened by their growing anxiety, they chastise themselves in an attempt to stop the anxious feelings. Paradoxically, the more clients berate themselves for being anxious, the more anxious they become. As anxiety rises there is the additional fear that it will never end. Consider the possibility that this particular belief echoes the commonly held childhood notion that the traumatic experience will never end. As therapists we should be sensitive to the fact that developmentally, children have a distorted sense of time, and episodes of abuse really do feel interminable.

In addition, clients experience anticipatory anxiety as they solidify their plans to hurt themselves (Alderman, 1997). Using self-destructive behaviors to feel better is exhilarating and frightening. Clients who have injured before know they can rely on these behaviors to alleviate bad thoughts and feelings. It is comforting, even thrilling, to experience that immediate relief and gratification. They also know there are many disadvantages to hurting themselves: feelings of guilt, shame, and powerlessness. Perhaps they have promised themselves they will stop or they are fearful of disappointing others. As the internal debate rages, the level of anxiety escalates.

Bob's unbearable tension and anxiety

- Heart racing
- Psychomotor agitation
- "Pressure on my chest"
- Shortness of breath
- Heightened irritability

Karen's unbearable tension and anxiety

- Jitteriness
- Shallow, quick breathing
- Muscle tension and tightness
- "Feeling like I'm going to throw up"
- Trouble swallowing

Debbie's unbearable tension and anxiety

- Tingling sensation in fingers
- Thought racing
- "Feeling like I'm having a heart attack"
- Tightness in throat
- Stomachache

At this point, clients feel genuinely out of control and helpless. Intense anxiety can actually alter consciousness. When clients are unable to reequilibrate themselves, the tension becomes untenable and leads them into the next, inevitable phase of the cycle of self-destructive acts: the need to dissociate.

The frozen loop: dissociation and analgesia

Dissociation

Once clients reach this stage of the cycle, they are often too overwhelmed to recognize, much less utilize, healthy external resources. For trauma survivors, dissociation makes perfect sense, as it is both a knee-jerk response to extreme threat and stress and, historically, the only reliable way to cope, achieve, and sustain self-protection. Najavits (2001) explained how important it is to view this symptom with "compassion rather than self-blame." She stated, "Dissociation can be viewed as the mind's natural response when it feels severely overwhelmed, rather than as 'crazy'" (p. 111).

Our clients have mastery over dissociation, as they have used it throughout their lives. It requires no conscious effort to disconnect from the present moment. Historically, it is a way to mentally escape that which they cannot physically escape. It is designed to reduce tension and to provide clients with a protective detachment from negative thoughts, feelings, and experiences. It can be experienced as a state of depersonalization or derealization (Herman, 1992).

Many researchers have suggested that chronic dissociative defenses are the natural outgrowth of disorganized attachment in infancy and are likely to be recapitulated in the face of subsequent trauma. When clients with prior histories of abuse and neglect become triggered and overwhelmed in the present, they will quickly revert back to a dissociative state. This disconnected state short-circuits the relationship between one's cognitive process and what is being experienced on the body (Conterio & Lader, 1998). Briere and Gil (1998) further explained the relationship between abuse, dissociation, and self-destructive behaviors, connecting sexual trauma to dissociative defenses and other PTSD responses that then promote and enable anxiety-reducing behaviors, including self-destructive acts. Van der Kolk et al. (2006) corroborated the notion that where there are high degrees of dissociation, there is self-mutilation and substance abuse.

Ironically, the fact that the response has become so automatic for clients is what makes it problematic. Gratz and Chapman (2009) explained how dissociation can take on a life of its own, creating perpetual disconnection, discomfort, and distress. Before clients can contemplate alternative ways to respond to threat or stress, they are out of their bodies and "on the ceiling." A strategy that once saved them in childhood actually disables them in adulthood. Clients cannot accurately assess a situation or formulate an effective safety strategy if they are frozen and no longer in the prefrontal cortex or reasoning part of their brain. They are unable to defend or assert themselves or make healthy behavioral choices.

In this state, they are recapitulating the freeze response from childhood. When children are threatened, they cannot physically fight back or escape. Their safest responses are being completely still, pretending to be asleep, holding their breath, or dissociating to survive the ordeal. No wonder our clients continue to operate from a "victim mentality" despite the fact that actual abuse is no longer occurring. Powerful coping strategies such as dissociation keep these clients frozen in time, unable to differentiate between the past and the present.

Dissociation can play a dual role in regard to self-destructive behaviors. Even thinking about the prospect of hurting the body can evoke a "zoned-out" state. In the short term this feels like a good, protective option for our clients. But in the long term, that altered state of consciousness can be scary and disempowering. When those feelings set in, hurting the body can be a way for clients to short-circuit the dissociative state. "Because self-harm can involve physical pain, it can capture people's attention and bring them back to the present moment" (Gratz & Chapman, 2009, p. 83). Many clients report that the visual shock and visceral warmth of blood on the skin regrounds them and reconnects them back to a body that otherwise feels completely numb.

Analgesia

Clients feel a subjective sense of numbness when they are in a dissociative state. They may lose a sense of time, the environment, and their own bodies. The combination of dissociation and detachment creates an analgesic effect: clients no longer feel any pain on their bodies (Strong, 1999; White & Shultz, 2000). Many clients who hurt themselves report feelings of numbness or emptiness during the act (Conterio & Lader, 1998; Herman, 1994). Miller (1992) said, "Many women describe being physically numb or not present, either before they hurt themselves or during the act of self-harm" (p. 100). It's understandable that in a zoned-out pain-free state, clients easily hurt themselves in ways they could never do if they were "fully forward." Even when clients claim they can feel the injuring, they are not experiencing the full extent of pain inflicted by the act (Alderman, 1997).

How is it possible to tolerate carving into skin with a razor blade or piece of glass? Think about the discomfort you feel when you get a paper cut. Think about what happens when you accidentally touch a hot stove top. The natural, instinctive response is to immediately pull away from the heat source. It is completely counterintuitive to subject our bodies to pain. The powerful combination of a dissociative state (with its accompanying analgesia) and a prior trauma history (which normalizes hurting the body) makes self-destructive actions possible, allowing clients to override their protective impulse to pull away from something painful.

Bob's dissociation and analgesia

- My body feels numb.
- I have a headache that won't go away.
- It feels like I'm standing outside of myself, watching myself.
- Everything is in slow motion.
- I feel I'm looking at things through a glass shield.

Karen's dissociation and analgesia

- I feel like my life is a dream.
- I shut down when I have sex.
- A black curtain comes in front of my face and blocks everything out.
- I feel like everyone is moving very far away from me, getting smaller.
- People talk, and I can't hear what they are saying.
- I can't feel my body in my skin.
- Sometimes I don't feel like I'm alive.

Debbie's dissociation and analgesia

- I feel like I live behind a brick wall.
- I lose track of my environment and the time.
- I have migraine headaches.
- I have a tingly sensation in my hands.
- My mind goes blank.
- I lose my peripheral vision.

Once clients are caught in the frozen loops of negativity, dissociation, and analgesia, they are primed for the next phase in the cycle: doing their self-destructive behavior.

9

SELF-DESTRUCTIVE BEHAVIORS, POSITIVE OUTCOMES, NEGATIVE OUTCOMES, AND EMOTIONAL VULNERABILITY

Self-destructive behaviors

Given the dynamics of depersonalization ("What's happening is not happening to me") and derealization ("This is not really happening—it's a dream") that often accompany dissociation, the extent to which our clients injure may not be within their conscious control. Clients cut deeper or burn more severely than they actually intend to when pain is not fully experienced (Alderman, 1997; Strong, 1999; Turner, 2002). It can be helpful to gently point out to clients that, paradoxically, this exacerbates a *loss* of control over their bodies.

Unfortunately, clients injure themselves in a variety of creative ways. Cutting with sharp objects (knives, scissors, razor blades, pen caps, nail clippers, etc.) is the most common method. The majority of clients use multiple methods (Conterio & Lader, 1998). Additional forms of self-destructive behavior include burning oneself, banging one's head, hitting and bruising limbs, picking at skin and wounds, engaging in trichotillomania (pulling out eyelashes, eyebrows, beard hair, hair on the head, and pubic hair), deeply biting, severely scratching, inserting objects into the body, taking scalding showers, swallowing chemicals, and engaging in injurious masturbation. Other behaviors such as limiting caloric intake; bingeing; purging with laxatives, enemas, or self-induced vomiting; having unsafe and promiscuous sex; and abusing alcohol and drugs should be considered forms of self-destructive behaviors as well (Miller, 1994).

There is much agreement within the field that behaviors that are harmful and destructive are done in response to profound emotional distress and represent a desperate attempt to reequilibrate one's emotional state. At this point in the cycle, clients find themselves over-aroused and incapable of healthy self-soothing and turn to destructive behavior as a way to regain some semblance of control over their emotions and their bodies. One of the primary functions of harmful acts is affect regulation, a coping strategy designed to self-regulate dissociation, hyperarousal, and untenable thoughts (Gratz, 2007; Hollander, 2008; Klonsky, 2007; Mikolajczak, Petrides, & Hurry, 2009; Nixon, Cloutier, & Jansson, 2008; Swales, 2008; van der Kolk, McFarlane, & Weisaeth, 2006; Yates, 2004).

In addition to this and other important functions served by self-destructive acts, we should also explore the meaning and metacommunication of the behavior, keeping in mind that the location and method used by clients are often not arbitrary and can yield information about the trauma narrative. Remembering that the behavior is a form of communication is essential. Clients can feel that a self-destructive act is the only way they can articulate their feelings and needs, a last resort option for clients who are afraid that direct communication will make them too vulnerable (Gratz & Chapman, 2009).

Bob's self-destructive behaviors

- Forcing myself to watch explicit, upsetting pornography
- Engaging in excessive, painful masturbation
- Cutting the palm of my hand
- Abusing drugs and alcohol (in the past)

Karen's self-destructive behaviors

- Getting drunk
- Shoplifting
- Not eating (anorexia)
- Burning skin with cigarettes
- Cutting thighs

- Having unprotected, unsafe sex
- Sneaking out of the window at night and driving with drunk friends

Debbie's self-destructive behaviors

- Bingeing
- Picking my lip
- Banging my head
- Compulsively shopping and spending

Positive outcomes

Once clients have engaged in their self-destructive behavior, there are immediate positive outcomes. We must stay cognizant and respectful of the fact that the behavior is inherently reinforcing. One of the best payoffs is the body's release of endorphins as it is injured (Alderman, 1997; Klonsky, 2007; Mikolajcak et al., 2009; Nock & Prinstein, 2005; Sandman & Hetrick, 2005; Swales, 2008). These endogenous opiates are the body's natural painkillers. When the body has been physically traumatized, it is biologically hardwired to respond with these chemicals to help counteract the ensuing pain. This endorphin rush most insidiously reinforces the behavior. Clients genuinely feel better after they hurt themselves. This is exactly what they want to accomplish.

Research supports the notion that endogenous opiates maintain and reinforce self-injurious behavior (Sandman & Hetrick, 2005; White & Schultz, 2000). This has even led some to hypothesize about an addiction to behaviors such as cutting and burning (Gratz & Chapman, 2009). After the body has been injured, the release of opiates produces an intense degree of pleasure that trauma survivors want to keep reexperiencing. "The release of endorphins, like the injection of morphine, creates a gratifying sensation and provides positive reinforcement for the preceding behavior" (Richardson & Zaleski, 1983, p. 938).

The role that endorphins play in reinforcing and sustaining acts of self-mutilation has led researchers to experiment with the use of Naltrexone as an adjunctive treatment strategy (Crews, Bonaventura, & Rowe, 1993; White & Schultz, 2000). Naltrexone is an opioid antagonist and has the effect of blocking the euphoria normally experienced when endorphins are released. Interestingly, these studies report a decrease in what they term "self-harming behaviors" when the reward of an endorphin release is blocked. Other studies have shown that self-harm and self-injury, which are traditionally defined as acts of self-mutilation such as cutting, burning, and head banging, can not significantly decrease with the use of Naltrexone (Gratz & Chapman, 2009), so the jury is still out regarding its efficacy.

Self-injury (as defined in the previous paragraph) is not about committing suicide; it's about stopping the pain and feeling better (Alderman, 1997; Ferentz, 2002; Gerson, 2008; Hollander, 2008; Strong, 1999). Once it has occurred, there is a temporary alleviation of depressed feelings, anxiety, and tension (Nixon et al., 2008). Nock and Prinstein (2005) identified this "automatic positive reinforcement function" as one that counteracts anhedonia, emptiness, and detachment by eliciting certain sensations and feelings. Once a client engages in a harmful behavior, the negative thoughts and feelings are eliminated.

Klonsky (2007) cited in his meta-analysis of the research exploring the functionality these behaviors several studies that support the notion that "self-injurers reported feeling more tense, anxious, angry, sad, and uptight before the self-injury, and more relaxed, calm, happy and relieved afterwards" (p. 234).

Many clients report feeling regrounded and reconnected to their bodies. The shock of seeing blood or the sensitivity of nerve endings on the skin can help bring clients "forward" again. Attention is drawn back to the body. It is not uncommon for clients to say the blood reminds them they are alive (Herman, 1992; Hollander, 2008).

Part of the reason why reintegration occurs is because wounding the body can short-circuit an escalating dissociative state (Alderman, 1997; Swales, 2008). Initially, "leaving the body" feels reassuring and safe. Prolonged dissociation, however, paradoxically leaves many clients feeling unsafe, alone, and disempowered. As necessary as dissociation is, it is equally necessary to have a mechanism that regrounds. Sachsee, Von der Heyde, and Huether (2002) emphasized this by stating, "Self-mutilating behavior may be regarded as an unusual but effective coping strategy for the self-regulation of hyper-arousal and/or dissociative states and for regaining control over an otherwise uncontrollable stress response." (p. 672).

Many clients describe the same phenomenon of reconnecting to their bodies when they engage in eating disordered and addictive behaviors. Some clients report that the way to curtail a dissociative state is to binge to the point of physical pain or nausea. Others say they can feel certain parts of their bodies again when they purge. Clients who engage in sexual addictions do so, in part, to reconnect with their bodies through sexual arousal and orgasm. Clients who compulsively gamble and shop describe simultaneous physical sensations of pleasure and angst, but they are grateful and relieved that at least they are feeling something.

Our clients experience another positive outcome when they use self-destructive behaviors to distract from other untenable or unresolved issues. Many clients dedicate a significant amount of time to the behavior. Because it is their most reliable coping resource, they spend time fantasizing about and planning for ways to injure their bodies, buy the food they will binge on, or get the drugs or alcohol they will use to become numb. Some clients incorporate specific, time-consuming, preparatory rituals into the act. Time may be devoted to cleansing and caring for the wound after the body has been harmed, just as ritualistic time might be spent before or after a binge or purge. Time is also expended creating cover stories for the injuries, the smell of vomit in the bathroom or the money missing from the back account, so the secret can be maintained.

As time and energy are devoted to thoughts and actions related to self-destructive behaviors, less time can be devoted to other aspects of clients' lives. Self-destructive behavior provides an ongoing distraction and keeps uncomfortable material at bay. This resonates for clients who have spent a lifetime minimizing, rationalizing, or denying prior abusive experiences and relationships. Given the consuming nature of these acts, clients cannot work on dysfunctional relationships, seek out healthier ones, work on self-care, resolve trauma, move forward in their careers, or be emotionally available to others when they are preoccupied with a secretive, shame-based behavior.

Clients who have been physically or sexually traumatized understandably feel an inherent loss of control regarding their bodies. Boundaries have been ignored and invaded. Survivors have experienced physical pain and/or confusing feelings of sexual arousal. Essentially, a victim's body is at the mercy of the perpetrator. To stay safe, victims must comply, perform, and be readily available to meet the needs of their abusers. Conversely, self-destructive behaviors allow clients to reframe the experience as a way to recapture control over their bodies (Swales, 2008). In a convoluted way, hurting oneself can feel reparative to those people who never felt as if their body was their own. For the first time, clients have the autonomy to decide when, where, and how their bodies will be hurt (Cutter, Jaffe, & Segal, 2008; Turner, 2002).

In addition, victimized clients may be perpetuating a learned paradigm that says, "In order for the body to be comforted, it first has to be hurt." Oftentimes, after harming a loved one, if the perpetrator isn't a sociopath, he or she may be left with lingering feelings of guilt that need to be extinguished. In an effort to do so, they may console their victim with loving words or physical comfort, convincing themselves that their victim is no longer hurt. They also want to reduce the likelihood that their victim will tell, or they may attempt to confuse the victim into "liking" what was done to them by rewarding them with a treat, present, or extra attention. For neglected children who have no consistent resources for healthy attachment, although these gifts are confusing, they are necessary and welcome. From a neurological standpoint, the brain begins to pair "being loved" with "being hurt," and the unconscious message that gets normalized is "you have to endure getting hurt first before you can get your emotional needs met."

Clients may begin to unconsciously reenact this, particularly when they engage in acts of self-mutilation, unsafe sexual practices, and eating disordered behaviors. To get the attention, care, comfort, and social engagement they need and crave, they first abuse the body and cause it pain. Klonsky (2007) corroborated this idea, stating, "Self-injuring, then, may provide a soothing and gratifying opportunity to competently care for oneself by examining, cleaning, bandaging, or otherwise tending to the wound" (p. 236).

Bob's positive outcomes

- I have a temporary feeling of relief.
- My negative thoughts disappear.
- Feeling pain reassures me I'm alive.
- I feel "back in control" of my body.
- Trauma memories go back underground.
- Vietnam demons go away.

Karen's positive outcomes

- I forget about my family problems.
- I get my parents' attention for a while.
- Bad thoughts disappear.
- I feel "back in control" of my body.
- I feel "in control" of men when I act out.
- It distracts me from my mother's drinking.
- My father and brother stop fighting and focus on me.
- Peers think I'm tough and cool when I cut myself.
- I have a release for my anger.

Debbie's positive outcomes

- I reclaim a feeling of control.
- I get concern from my parents, siblings, and husband.
- Guilt from negative thoughts subsides.

- Anxiety about being alone goes away.
- I have a release for my anger.
- I "bang" bad thoughts out of my head.

Negative outcomes

As is the case with all destructive coping strategies, these behaviors inevitably yield negative outcomes as well. This is an important part of the cycle to process with our clients. Most clients experience a profound sense of powerlessness and helplessness once the initial payoffs subside. Mikolajcak et al. (2009) corroborated that self-harm "temporarily reduces psychological distress, but at the cost of physical injury and long-term impairment of psychological and physical welfare" (p. 182). Swales (2008) concurred that "the emotion-reducing effects rarely last for long (minutes to a few hours), and self-harm in the longer-term can be a source of stress in itself" (p. 3).

Some clients have only partial memory or no memory of actually injuring themselves. This makes sense given the role dissociation plays in the process. Often clients "awake" to discover their body is injured or bleeding. Many clients report "standing outside of themselves" while they binge, purge, engage in unwanted sex, or withdraw more money from the ATM to continue gambling. Clients who use punitive, harmful, or injurious behaviors to reclaim control paradoxically feel an unfathomable loss of control as they struggle to understand what happened to their bodies, finances, or sense of integrity. This loss of control is exacerbated when clients attempt to extinguish the behavior only to discover they have, unwittingly, done it again. Should they experience depersonalization or derealization during the act, they may be unable to stop the cutting, unprotected sex, or eating disordered behavior even if they want to do so. When clients are unable to modulate their self-destructive behavior and do more damage than they intended, they recapitulate a loss of control over the body and their lives and are left feeling revictimized.

Another negative outcome is a deepened sense of shame. Trauma survivors are already vulnerable to this emotion, having bought into perpetrators' messages of blame. Self-destructive behavior becomes another ugly secret. It perpetuates a sense of humiliation and victimization reminiscent of prior traumatic experiences. Most clients never talk openly about the ways in which they hurt themselves or compromise their safety. They believe they will be perceived as weird, disgusting, out of control, and damaged. They do not trust others to understand or accept the behavior, partly because they don't comprehend or accept it themselves.

Along with shame can be feelings of guilt, disappointment, worthlessness, and self-hatred. Clients often attempt to make pacts with themselves or with us about not acting out again. They are reluctant to reveal another episode to us, fearing that we will be disappointed or angry with them. When they do relapse, they may grapple with self-loathing, feelings of failure and inadequacy, disappointment, hopelessness, and the genuine concern that they will be rejected or "fired" by us or by loved ones.

When clients feel the need to act out, a standard safety contract sets them up for inevitable failure. Clients feel a deep sense of failure when they contract to abstain and then relapse. Engaging in their self-destructive behavior again means they've let everyone down, and there can be renewed anxiety about others disapproving of them (Swales, 2008). Initially they may be convinced the behavior is behind them, and when it reoccurs, it is overwhelmingly disappointing. Many clients experience feelings of self-hatred, using their weakness as proof of their worthlessness.

Because behaviors such as bingeing and purging are inherently antisocial acts, clients often feel a renewed sense of isolation after engaging in these activities. They are alone in the behavior and alone in its aftereffects. They become convinced that no one will be able to understand or help them. The act itself leaves them feeling like their own worst enemy. The compulsion to harm oneself takes clients away from family and friends and can create intense interpersonal conflicts. Clients feel compelled to stay away from others after self-destructive acts, afraid new wounds or the telltale signs of eating disordered or substance-abusing behaviors will be discovered.

Dealing with the issue alone or not dealing with the elephant in the living room at all becomes reminiscent of childhood abuse and neglect. This invalidating environment was described by Linehan (1993), who recognized the impact of growing up in a family system where a child's experiences and reactions go unacknowledged and unsupported by caretakers. Clients have to manage something scary, confusing, and shame-based on their own. Self-destructive behavior, like childhood trauma, becomes another cross to privately bear.

Bob's negative outcomes

- I feel more shame.
- I have confusion and fear about my sexuality.
- I feel like a sexual deviant.
- I have genital and hand pain.
- There is more secrecy.
- I feel increased isolation.
- I fight with my wife.
- My effectiveness at work is threatened.
- I have more anger that I can't control.
- I feel like I'm going crazy.
- I'm afraid it will jeopardize my relationship with my kids.
- I'm afraid I'll lose my sobriety.

Karen's negative outcomes

- I have anxiety that people will find out that I'm bad.
- I feel stupid and different.
- I'm afraid of getting pregnant.
- I feel weak when I don't eat.
- I feel "out of control" like my parents.
- I feel "troubled" like my brother.
- I'm embarrassed about the burns and scars and hate my body more.
- I feel it threatens my success at school.
- I get angrier when my mother doesn't respond.
- I have to keep more secrets.

Debbie's negative outcomes

- I have anxiety that my parents will be upset or angry.
- My siblings don't trust me with their children.
- I feel abnormal.
- People stare at my lips, and I feel self-conscious.
- I get angrier when my relatives "give up on me."
- People stare at me because of my weight.
- I fight with my husband.
- I'm embarrassed when I have to keep returning things I buy.
- I'm risking my financial credit.

Emotional vulnerability

The aforementioned negative outcomes create an additional layer of vulnerability in our clients. The aftereffects of harmful behaviors leave them with a new set of internalized negative cognitions and upsetting affect, solidifying preexisting depression or inaccurate thinking. If guilt and shame were a part of their adverse outcomes, those feelings will color their sense of themselves and increase their isolation and disconnect from the world. This heightened sense of being alone adds to their emotional vulnerability.

Whatever short-term positive reinforcement our clients felt when they acted out now disappears, and clients are left with the more lasting feelings of disempowerment and despair. That negativity is manifested on their bodies as well. A defeated and futile mind-set causes posture to collapse and muscles to tighten or constrict. The nonverbal messages they transmit get received by others, profoundly shaping and influencing the nature of subsequent interpersonal dynamics.

The likelihood of clients in this vulnerable state successfully and safely socially engaging with others gets reduced, and there is an increased chance of their being exploited, ignored, taken advantage of, and not taken seriously. This is a crucial part of the cycle, because walking around with cognitive, emotional, and somatic vulnerability actually sets our clients up for the next triggering event.

As they approach social interactions and their environment with a sense of hypervigilance, suspicion, defensiveness, fear, and anxiety, they are more likely to misinterpret, distort, and personalize benign encounters. They will quickly become triggered when they subjectively perceive situations to be threatening, and once triggered, they are off and running, looping back into the repetitive cycle of self-destructive acts.

Bob's emotional vulnerability

- I'm easily angered at work, which creates more fights with coworkers.
- My fear of getting caught makes me more defensive, even paranoid.
- Scars on my palm make me look weird to the outside world.
- I'm afraid to let anyone get too close to me.
- I'm always on the verge of yelling or crying.
- Memories live just below the surface, always threatening to come out and overwhelm me.

Karen's emotional vulnerability

- I get upset if anyone looks at me the wrong way.
- I think peers are talking about me and making fun of me.
- I can't trust anyone.
- I'm terrified of anyone getting too close to me, which keeps me isolated.
- I'm exhausted from pretending to be normal.
- I'm always waiting for the other shoe to drop.

Debbie's emotional vulnerability

- I'm terrified I will always be alone.
- I assume people will be repulsed by me.
- I can't get close to anyone.
- I'm afraid to tell people what I feel and need.
- I'm exhausted from being hypervigilant.

10

TREATMENT

Identifying intervention sites and working with the triggering event

Working with the cycle

The advantage to incorporating a paradigm that focuses on a cycle of self-destructive behaviors is that it gives us many potential places to intervene—any of which can be effective. We should encourage our clients to choose where they want to first focus their attention in terms of short-circuiting their chronic behaviors. This gives them a sense of genuine power and control in the treatment process. We are also inviting our clients to explore possible treatment options that will ultimately give them a greater sense of control over their bodies. Clients understand that intervening at any point can be useful when they are given multiple opportunities to integrate healthier coping strategies. This sets them up for success rather than the failure to which they have become accustomed.

In addition, we are reducing their anxiety about falling short or failing when we communicate that there is "no wrong place" to intervene. We should normalize the fact that the work is not linear, and they can build on their successes wherever they achieve them. Starting wherever they feel most comfortable allows them to pace the work properly and increases the likelihood of cooperation and progress. All that is required is a mindset that Schwartz (1997) helps clients find in their work: a sense of compassionate, nonjudgmental curiosity about the issue.

As we educate our clients about the cycle of self-destructive behaviors and all of the potential "intervention sites," we should be observing our client's verbal and nonverbal communication, as this can lead us to the parts of them that hold interest or curiosity about alternatives to their harmful behaviors. It also shows us where they still feel overwhelmed or ambivalent about introducing an intervention, and it gives us the opportunity to process their concerns without pressuring them to work on areas they are not yet ready to address.

Once the cycle is explained, it is important to personalize it by allowing clients to "plug in" their experiences at each identified part of the model. The cycle comes alive and resonates when clients can identify and describe their actual triggering events; negative, distorted cognitions; and upsetting affective states. Clients are encouraged to identify the specific ways in which they physically and mentally experience untenable anxiety and the "somatic harbingers" that signal the onset of dissociation. We need to support clients through their embarrassment or shame as they work toward disclosing the different ways in which they engage in injurious and destructive behaviors. We also need to acknowledge and honor the positive outcomes they experience immediately following their actions, as well as the inevitable negative outcomes that linger afterward.

Clients should also identify how this part of the cycle leaves them feeling vulnerable and how that vulnerability manifests cognitively and emotionally. We can then connect the dots between that vulnerable state and the next triggering event. Although the template has universal application, the process of personalizing the cycle (in therapy) allows us to honor the individuality of our clients and their unique experience with self-destructive behaviors.

As we now explore each intervention site and process some of the creative modalities that can be implemented, keep in mind that most of these techniques can be used interchangeably throughout the cycle. For example, strategies that employ visualizations can be used to address negative affect and cognitive distortions (Daitch, 2007). Art therapy techniques have multiple applications as well. Breath work is a powerful tool for affect regulation and the management of triggers and unbearable tension and anxiety (Emerson & Hopper, 2011). Feel free to experiment with these modalities once clients are comfortable with them, applying these techniques to whichever part of the cycle works best.

Although all competent therapists understand the importance of doing treatment, and especially trauma retrieval work, within the context of a trusting therapeutic alliance and a safe clinical environment, it bears repeating. Before moving ahead with any work that clients will experience as emotionally charged, make sure the fundamentals of treatment are in place. These include a client's capacity to feel stabilized and grounded, an acknowledgment of external resources for support, the development and installation of an internalized safe place, and healthy mechanisms for comfort and containment. Van der Kolk, McFarlane, and Weisaeth (2006) reiterated this sentiment when they said, "Early exploration and abreaction of traumatic experiences without first establishing a sense of stability are likely to lead to very negative therapeutic outcomes" (p. 319).

You will discover that working with the cycle of self-destructive behaviors allows for the installation of many of these resources and can be the appropriate precursor to more intensive trauma work. Again, we should approach treatment with the understanding that the behavior will not be immediately extinguished. The process takes time, and decisions about reducing or stopping the behavior must always be in the hands of our clients.

Working with the triggering event

Because the cycle begins with the notion that self-destructive behavior never occurs in a vacuum, and a triggering event is the catalyst for the onset of subsequent dysfunctional coping, it makes sense that working with triggers is an important focus of treatment. We may be so fixated on the self-destructive actions, however, that we overlook the antecedents to that behavior. Initially our clients can be reticent to discuss triggers, as they would rather just use avoidance as a way to ward off additional PTSD symptoms. Matsakis (1996) agreed that it is "important for trauma survivors to understand and manage their trigger situations" (p. 26), because merely avoiding anything that is potentially triggering creates additional problems for survivors.

Start by didactically introducing the concept of "triggering" to your clients. Napier (1994) offered a great definition of triggering as "when your mood shifts from a sense of well-being to an overwhelming feeling of discomfort or vulnerability" (p. 75). Clients may not understand the process of having a cognitive, emotional, and somatic response to stimuli that is reminiscent of a prior scenario that felt threatening or traumatic—even though they are often triggered. Clients may understand the notion of "flashback," but it's important that they grasp the idea that flashbacks can manifest through thoughts, feelings, and bodily sensations.

When clients do get triggered, they chalk it up to being "weird" or "crazy." Many triggered survivors get labeled "crazy" by friends and family members who see the reactions as *overreactions* and express impatience about the survivor's inability to "just get over it" and move on with life (Matsakis, 1996). I like to reassure my clients that getting triggered is an involuntary response and is not indicative of any shortcoming on their part. In fact, I don't believe the goal of treatment is the eradication of getting triggered. I don't think that is a reasonable or fair goal given the primitive survival mechanisms that are hardwired on our bodies. Instead, the goal is for clients to be able to recognize when they are in the throes of being triggered and to learn how to reground as quickly as possible, thus minimizing adverse effects such as feeling disempowered or freezing.

In essence, clients need to measure their progress by how quickly they *identify and rebound* from a trigger, not whether they got triggered in the first place. This point can be elucidated when we remind clients that the limbic system does not change with insight (van der Kolk et al., 2006). No matter how much their prefrontal cortex "intellectually understands" that in their current reality they are safe and not trapped, when sensory experience activates a fight–flight or freeze response, the prefrontal cortex goes offline, and their reactions are mediated by more primitive parts of the brain that cannot assign reasoning or analysis to the experience.

Another fundamental part of this psychoeducational intervention is helping clients to discern between internal and external triggers. Internally mediated triggers are rooted in a "feeling sense" such as nausea, dizziness, butterflies in the stomach, or body pain. Externally mediated triggers often connect to something in the environment that the client hears, sees, smells, tastes, touches, and so on.

Once the client understands triggering, a critical next step is introducing the concept of "context." As we process acts of bingeing, purging, cutting, abusing substances, and so on, we should encourage our clients to connect them to time, place, circumstance, interpersonal dynamics, and so forth. Initially this is done retroactively in session, as clients get caught up in the planning and execution of their behaviors and typically don't have an awareness of the internal and external influences that activate and propel them forward. The use of *journaling* can be extremely helpful in promoting a more mindful awareness of what drives their behaviors. Inviting clients to document the circumstances that surround their self-destructive acts enables us to begin to see patterns and recurring themes. I incorporate a simple acronym to help clients capture the essential information in their journal entries: REACTS. Writing the word vertically in their journal reminds them to assess for the following potential triggers:

Table 10.1

R:	*Relationship Dynamics*—Who were they with before they got the impulse to hurt themselves? What was the nature of the interaction or conversation?
E:	*Emotions*—What were they feeling as they moved toward planning or actually hurting themselves?
A:	*Awareness of the Five Senses*—What did they smell, hear, see, taste, or touch when the urge to hurt themselves got activated?
C:	*Context*—Where were they? What was going on in the environment that might have been experienced as upsetting or threatening? Include the date and time.
T:	*Thoughts*—What were they thinking before the self-destructive act?
S:	*Sensations on the Body*—What did they notice happening on their bodies before they acted out?

Clients can document this pertinent information in a journal on their own either before or after the harmful act, or they can write about it within the safety of a therapy session. In any case, the verbal processing allows us to notice the recurring themes and the vulnerabilities that might increase their self-destructive behavior. You can use the journaling exercise in the workbook entitled USING "REACTS" TO IDENTIFY TRIGGERS on page 98.

Thirty-three-year-old Edith struggled with sexual acting out and restricting her caloric intake. She was able to write a journal entry, using the REACTS format, when she experienced the urge to look for a date with a stranger on Craigslist and deny herself any food:

Table 10.2

R:	Interacting with my boss at work—he's very demanding. Whatever I do, it's not enough. I was giving him the information he requested, but he didn't validate anything I said.
E:	Invisible, humiliated, inferior, inadequate.
A:	Seeing his condescending face, hearing sarcasm in his voice, smelling cigars on his breath.
C:	Alone in his office, after work hours.
T:	"I'm stupid at my job." "No one cares about what I think or say." "I'm not good enough, and I'll never be promoted." "He might fire me, and I'll lose another job." "Don't eat dinner—you don't deserve it." "Figure out how to get on his good side." "Go on Craigslist—you'll feel better."
S:	Face is flushed, hands are in fists, leg muscles are tight, knot in stomach, heart is racing, feel sweaty.

Once we identify the triggers, we can begin strategizing an action plan to address them. In Edith's case, there were several important internal and external triggers, including smelling the cigar (her perpetrator smoked cigars), being alone with her boss, being made to feel invisible, and struggling with self-doubt and feelings of worthlessness. The anxiety and fear this created in her prompted a knee-jerk response for self-punishment (denying herself food, putting herself at physical risk) and a need for comfort and connection (finding someone on Craigslist).

It's helpful to offer clients several options in regard to triggers. You can explore ways to reduce exposure to toxic triggers, avoid them if need be, or at least formulate an "escape clause" so clients don't feel held hostage by people or circumstances that are triggering. The concept of reducing or avoiding triggers may feel counterintuitive to trauma survivors who are used to simply enduring experiences that feel awful.

When you think about some of your triggered clients, you realize it may never have occurred to them that they don't have to be verbally abused by an aggressive boss or that they're not obligated to spend time with an older parent who abused or neglected them in childhood. It also never occurred to them, for example, that they would be within their rights to tell a significant other that his or her perfume or cologne is distressing because it's the same scent their perpetrator wore. In these cases, giving clients permission to limit their time with triggering people, to bow out of spending time with them, or, if it's a safe proposition, to even confront them about their abusive actions can all have the effect of reempowering them and reducing the feelings of helplessness or revictimization that these encounters evoke. Clients can explore this treatment intervention by using the workbook exercise called COMING UP WITH NEW BOUNDARIES OR AN ESCAPE PLAN on page 144.

Because dramatically altering existing boundaries can feel threatening or overwhelming to clients, encouraging small baby steps they can build on is the best approach. Start by inviting clients either to reduce the amount of time they spend in potentially triggering situations or to install an escape clause. This can include prearranging to have a trusted friend or loved one call or text them during the difficult encounter so they have an excuse to step away or regroup or have a built-in reason to leave if they choose. They can also keep themselves grounded by holding on to their car keys or keeping their keys visible throughout the encounter. Symbolically, car keys are a great reminder of not being trapped or stuck. They also provide clients with a visual reminder that says, "You are powerful, you can drive, you can leave whenever you want!"

Forty-five-year-old Stacey was repeatedly sexually abused in childhood by her father. Her mother was a nonprotective bystander and denied the abuse ever occurred. As an adult and only child, Stacey was expected to continue visiting her parents every Sunday, spending all day in the living room where she had been violated. With a conditioned sense of compliance and a frozen-in-time victim mentality, Stacey never realized that she could say "no" or in any way limit these interactions. After each visit, Stacey would go home and in a dissociative state cut and burn herself. The reenactment was feeling "cut down to size" by her father's abuse and "burned" by her mother's denial. The triggers related to all of the sights, sounds, and smells of her childhood home. Intervening at this stage of the cycle meant working to reduce the triggers by her limiting the amount of time she spent with her parents, prearranging to have cell-phone interruptions so she could get a respite from the triggers, and insisting that their family gatherings happen in a neutral restaurant. Eventually, Stacey was able to skip some of the Sunday meetings. This was a huge accomplishment for her and helped her reclaim a sense of power and control. The epilogue is even more hopeful: after summoning the courage to confront her father about the abuse and again being met with denial, Stacey made the decision to terminate her family visits. When she did, her self-destructive behavior completely abated.

When clients must attend a gathering or function, encourage them to "scope out" the space ahead of time if possible. Remind them to sit facing the doorway and closest to the exit and to make sure that no one is seated behind them. All of these small things can enhance their sense of safety and reduce the likelihood of getting triggered.

In time, clients can experiment with more direct limit setting: shortening the length of an uncomfortable encounter or even refusing to participate in conversations or events that feel unsafe. As they work to reduce the triggers in their life and begin to feel less hijacked by them, the cycle of self-destructive behaviors can potentially be short-circuited in its earliest stages. When clients avoid triggers or rebound from them more quickly, they stay grounded and present and spare themselves the onslaught of negative thoughts and feelings that disempower them.

11

WORKING WITH THE CYCLE

The loop of negativity

Given the inherent mechanisms of the self-destructive cycle, when clients are unable to reground from triggering they will likely begin to experience thoughts that are negative and distorted. Burns (1999) suggested, "The negative thoughts which cause your emotional turmoil nearly always contain gross distortions" (p. 13). However, the fact that clients' cognitions are not rooted in present reality is irrelevant. They are experienced as real because they hijack cognitive schema and resonate with distorted self-effacing core beliefs that connect with earlier traumatic experiences. Therefore, these thoughts must be identified and addressed using cognitive therapy techniques designed to label and then reframe them. This becomes another "intervention site" within the cycle of self-destructive behaviors.

Begin by incorporating the cognitive strategies you routinely use with clients. Special attention should be paid to some of the more common distortions we find with traumatized clients. You can process those distorted beliefs as your client does the workbook exercises entitled IDENTIFYING YOUR NEGATIVE THOUGHTS on pages 103 and 104. Burns (1999) brilliantly conceptualized the types of distorted thoughts we are likely to encounter, and they deserve our attention as we weave cognitive strategies into the treatment process. Look for the cognitive manifestations that were identified in an earlier chapter, including minimization and magnification, emotional reasoning, dichotomous thinking, mind reading, and overgeneralizations.

As we introduce this part of the cycle to clients, we want them to begin identifying the most common self-effacing, critical, or judgmental thoughts that accompany their harmful acts. Invite your clients to write out these thoughts on brightly colored index cards. Together, you and the client can label the cognitive distortion that accompanies the thought. A common example is "I am bad," which is emblematic of emotional reasoning (Burns, 1999). The labeling process allows clients to step back and see their thoughts from a different, more accurate perspective. It creates a new opportunity for them to reevaluate the validity of their thinking. This is a critical intervention, as emotional states and behavioral choices often emanate from our thoughts. When clients can learn to reexamine their mind-set, they are often spared the subsequent destructive, negative experiences that follow.

Once our clients have identified the thought and labeled the distortion it represents, we can explore a healthier reframe that can be written, in a different color and in much larger letters, on the same index card under the original distorted thought. "I am bad" can be reframed as "Something bad happened to me." Whenever clients become consciously aware of their negative thoughts, they can quickly read the reframes on their card and literally retrain their brains to go to a more accurate, positive thought.

Carl had a long-standing history of abusing pot and repeatedly cheating on his girlfriends and several past wives. After a lifetime of blaming his behavior on others, he learned, through the course of group therapy, to take responsibility for his actions. However, in doing so, he was left with thoughts that humiliated and shamed him. As a result, not surprisingly, his substance abuse increased. Working on his distorted thoughts became a major focus of treatment, as they evoked the psychic pain that fueled his need to get high. He identified his five most common negative thoughts on an index card and then practiced counterbalancing them with more accurate reframes.

- *After all the hurt I've caused, I don't deserve my sobriety.*
- I have taken responsibility for the hurt and made amends. I have the right to be healthy and sober.

- *If I get high, it won't make any difference.*
- Getting high profoundly affects every aspect of my life.
- *Cheating in all of my relationships means I am worthless.*
- Cheating in all of my relationships was a sign of my unresolved issues with attachment and loss. I am a worthwhile human being.
- *I will always feel depressed, and my life will never get better.*
- There are times when I am not depressed, and that shows me my life is actually improving.
- *Getting stoned will take away my pain.*
- Getting stoned brings more pain into my life and leaves me feeling out of control.

Your clients can practice this technique by using the workbook exercise entitled COMING UP WITH NEW RE-FRAMES FOR NEGATIVE THOUGHTS on page 150.

Historically, thought-stopping strategies were often employed to work with clients and their untenable cognitions. Classic thought-stopping techniques included snapping a rubber band on the wrist and pressing a sharp bottle top into the palm of one's hand. Although these techniques were deemed effective, they are, ironically, additional ways to injure the body. Therefore, these strategies are not recommended for trauma survivors who already hurt themselves.

I created a simple thought-stopping technique that clients find effective because it spares them the pain of an internal power struggle and feels more doable to them. Simply encourage your clients to say "not now" when an overwhelming and uncomfortable thought kicks in, rather than tense up and fight it. At the same time, have them extend their arms in front of them, palms facing in to each other, and then move their arms all the way to the left or right of their body, out of their peripheral vision. This is a nonverbal message to the brain that the thought is being "put to the side" rather than staying front and center in the mind. "Not now" as opposed to "No!" or "Stop thinking that" is a gentler, nonadversarial way for our clients to temporarily dismiss their unwanted thoughts. This strategy is explained in the workbook as well, see page 154.

Another strategy that I incorporate into this part of the cycle is a simple visualization I've created called "the paint roller technique." Clients are invited to imagine a large paint roller and a pan of brightly colored paint. As the thoughts continue to present themselves, the paint roller is dipped in the pan and gently rolls across and over them. Clients are instructed to follow the movement of the roller, either back and forth from left to right or up and down. I also encourage them to pair their inhalations and exhalations with the movement of the paint roller. They can use as many "coats of paint" as needed until the thought is completely covered over by the colorful paint. Again, we are avoiding an internal power struggle by allowing the thoughts to "just be there" as they are painted over by the roller. Details of this technique are outlined in the workbook on page 154.

If your clients respond well to simple thought-stopping techniques, you can also invite them to visualize or look at a picture of a stop sign or literally carry a child's toy version of a stop sign in their pocket. This also reminds the brain to "step on the brakes" when a negative thought surfaces.

There are other equally effective strategies that focus on the reevaluation of a destructive thought. David Burns wrote about a cost-benefit analysis that encourages clients to identify what they gain by holding on to a negative thought and what it costs them, emotionally and behaviorally, to operate from the thought. The price they pay for buying into self-effacing thoughts is often clear: it demoralizes; exacerbates low self-worth, shame, and the vegetative symptoms of depression; puts a glass ceiling on personal growth; and often sets clients up for revictimization.

Processing the ways in which clients *benefit* from negative, distorted, or judgmental thoughts may seem less obvious, but attributing those thoughts to an "inner critic," as per the Internal Family Systems model, can be quite helpful. Using this paradigm, we can suggest that the inner critic is a protective part, albeit a hurtful and debilitating one. Despite the fact that inner cognitions are hypercritical, guilt inducing, controlling, demanding, or perfectionistic, they protect by trying to keep clients from falling short, disappointing others, or taking risks that would potentially lead to rejection, ridicule, or failure (Earley & Weiss, 2010). Helping our clients find other healthier ways to feel protected in the world becomes an important part of treatment. Deconstructing the advantages and disadvantages to distorted thinking can be an excellent exercise, especially for clients who are inherently more intellectualized. Clients can practice this cognitive technique in the workbook exercise called IDENTIFYING THE ADVANTAGES AND DISADVANTAGES TO YOUR NEGATIVE THOUGHTS on page 156 of the workbook. The following is an example taken from a client's journal:

Twenty-seven-year-old Daniel has a serious gambling addiction. It has led to the inevitable breakup of several meaningful relationships in his life. Digging deeper, he connects to a core cognitive distortion—"I am unworthy of love"—and uses this strategy to process his ambivalence about addressing his addiction:

Costs

I feel shame.
It keeps me alone in the world.
I feel different from other people. I sabotage my relationships.
It sets me up to hurt myself.
It deprives me of a support system.
It leaves me feeling depressed and hopeless.
I feel compelled to get the rush from gambling.

Benefits

It protects me from rejection.
Keeping my distance means I won't get hurt.
I don't have to be social.
If I don't get married, I won't get divorced.

Burns also used the "double-standard technique" to show clients the disparity between the way they talk to and think about themselves and the way they talk to others. This disconnect can be striking: clients are quite forgiving, accepting, patient, and nonjudgmental of others in ways they never apply to themselves. The value of focusing on this disparity is not to evoke shame or guilt but rather to show clients they are quite capable of thinking thoughts that are kind, supportive, and loving. Even when our clients struggle with the idea that they deserve the same equitable treatment they show others, you can appeal to the notion that their hurt inner child needs and deserves to be treated with kindness.

When clients were repeatedly abused or neglected in childhood, we know they introject the perpetrator propaganda that has guilt-producing messages of blame, shame, or disgust. This comprises the "tape" that plays in their head throughout their lifetime. I believe that there is nothing more powerful than the way we talk to ourselves about ourselves, that incessant tape that reminds us of who we are and how we do or don't deserve to be treated in the world.

Making a new tape for survivors is a critical intervention. On this tape the messages must be loving, kind, and uplifting; support self-worth; and enhance self-esteem. Engaging in any kind of self-destructive behavior does not resonate with this new tape. Oftentimes clients need our help in "scripting" a reparative tape: they don't speak the language of self-love and self-care. If they are unable to populate the tape with enough loving and supportive thoughts, ask them to conjure a person from their past who cared about them or believed in them. Sometimes that person is readily accessible in their mind: a deceased grandparent, their third-grade math teacher, a friend's parent from childhood, a clergy person. Babette Rothschild (2002) referred to this as a "remembered resource," and she emphasized the value of reconnecting our clients to the loving messages from a past safe and nurturing figure in their lives. This strategy is explained in the workbook exercise entitled MAKING A NEW POSITIVE TAPE on page 159.

If your clients cannot identify anyone who cared about them (which we should gently challenge because they probably wouldn't still be alive or nearly as high functioning if *no one* cared about them), ask them to think of a loving character from TV, a book, or a movie. Again, they can usually conjure positive messages that would come from that character, and those can be incorporated onto the tape. We can certainly add messages of support, and the stronger the therapeutic alliance, the more those messages will be believed by the client.

You can bring this to an even deeper level by creating a specific script and making an actual tape recording of the affirming messages. Instructions for this are found in the workbook exercise called make a tape recording from the script you have written above on page 160.

Clients may initially ask you to make the tape for them, as they find your voice soothing, comforting, and believable. This is a good first step. The eventual goal is to have clients make the recording with their own voice. This deepens the authenticity of their experience and addresses the concept that there is nothing more important and powerful than the way we talk to ourselves about ourselves. Messages such as "I deserve to be happy," "I deserve support for my pain," "There are things in my life that I can control," or "What I'm thinking right now is time limited and will pass" are all new thoughts that can be put on our clients' reparative tapes.

Working with the cycle: negative affect

If clients are unwilling or uninterested in addressing the parts of the cycle that focus on triggers or negative thoughts, we can home in on helping clients manage their emotional states. This is a critical place to intervene, because given trauma survivors' issues with attachment and affect dysregulation, they are perpetually vulnerable to feeling easily overwhelmed by their emotions. This is compounded by the fact that they are bereft of the internal resources that are necessary to self-soothe or reground. Klonsky's (2007) crystallization of research exploring the functionality of self-destructive behaviors reminds us that "most self-injurers identify the desire to alleviate negative affect as a reason for self-injuring" (p. 235).

When we focus on this part of the cycle, clients begin to feel a sense of confidence and reassurance about their capacity to manage difficult emotions such as despair, rage, hopelessness, and helplessness. Once clients feel more capable of handling these feelings, they become less anxious and less afraid of them. This dramatically reduces the need to keep feelings under wraps or dysfunctionally short-circuit them with distracting or numbing behaviors.

Consider the small child who is running and falls and is suddenly overcome with physical pain and emotional distress. If that child has a secure attachment to a loving, available caretaker, he will experience a parent quickly coming to his aid. In addition to providing physical comfort and words of consolation and reassurance, parents also often label the experience for the child, attaching feeling words that help him gain an understanding of what he is emotionally experiencing. In this scenario, Mom or Dad might say, "It's OK, Timmy. I know you feel sad; that really hurts! I'm here, and everything will be all right. Let's go put a Band-Aid on it, and we'll make it feel better." In this moment, Timmy can introject his parent's description of what has happened. He is feeling hurt and sad, and a trusting caretaker is validating his right to have these emotions. The parent is also offering him the reassurance that he will feel better soon.

What would happen, however, if Timmy's parent ignored his pain, saying, "that doesn't hurt!" or admonishes him to "Stop acting like a baby and get up off the ground." Aside from the obvious lack of comfort and shaming this would evoke, it would also deprive Timmy of an opportunity to label and understand his feelings. In many cases, abusive parents negate emotions by saying to their victims, "Nothing hurtful is happening," which leaves children with confusing messages about the validity of their feelings.

In terms of effective treatment paradigms, this is an area where the value of utilizing components of dialectical behavioral therapy (DBT) should be acknowledged. Hollander (2008) did an excellent job of identifying the strengths of Linehan's model, paying particular homage to the fact that DBT emphasizes "the importance of incorporating acceptance strategies and validation into the treatment" (p. 74). Teaching clients how to first acknowledge and validate their emotional states before moving in the direction of shifting them is an important part of the work and can be a reparative experience for clients who never felt emotionally corroborated in childhood. Given that many of our clients grew up with parents who did not take the time to comfort or explain emotions, we realize how important it is to teach our clients how to reclaim an "emotional vocabulary."

> Forty-five-year-old Amanda has a childhood story that poignantly illustrates this issue. She grew up in a family with an emotionally shut-down father and a mother with a serious addiction to prescription drugs. She has many memories of her mother passed out on the living room floor, half undressed, while her father sat on the sofa reading the newspaper as if nothing was wrong. After Amanda made repeated attempts to enlist a response from her father, her unheeded and invalidated terror and despair eventually gave way to her own emotional disconnect. Her learned adaptation was to permanently shut down her feelings and become numb like her father. She accomplished this by developing a drinking problem and bulimia. As she continued to grow up, she carried the faint realization that she no longer had words for her feelings or felt anything about anything.

Van der Kolk, McFarlane, and Weisaeth (2006) described this state (known as alexythymia) as an inability to put words to one's emotional states or a state of "speechless terror." One way to reintroduce this vocabulary is to give clients a list of feeling words they can refer to several times during the day. Ask them to take a moment when they have awareness of an emotional response to see if they can connect the visceral experience to a word such as *embarrassed, overwhelmed, comforted, uneasy, trusting,* and so on. They can keep a simple log of the feeling words they relate to or put a check mark next to the word on their list. The exercise called DAILY LOG OF FEELINGS on page 165 of the workbook can provide a framework for this strategy.

Schiraldi (2009) has a comprehensive list of feeling words that gives clients a rich, new vocabulary to master. Going beyond one-dimensional labels such as *angry*, he provides clients with many words that address the nuanced layers of feelings, such as *fuming*, *infuriated*, and *irked*. He also provides examples of the behavioral manifestation of each emotion, such as clenching fists, speaking sarcastically, or interrupting others. Over time, affective and behavioral patterns will emerge, along with an increased ability to identify emotional states. As simplistic as it sounds, it is a necessary first step. There is also an extensive list of feeling words and a writing prompt in the workbook called CONNECTING FEELINGS TO A VARIETY OF SITUATIONS on page 163.

Introducing modalities such as journaling, drawing, poetry writing, and collaging offers clients a variety of ways to identify, depict, and process their emotional states. For the clients who have performance anxiety regarding an inability to adequately draw what they feel, just encourage them to focus on colors, shapes, and lines that speak to their affect. The images can be abstract, and clients can even use scribbling to discharge and depict emotion. The workbook exercise USING LINE, SHAPE, AND COLOR TO EXPRESS EMOTIONS on page 168 of the workbook and the exercise USING IMAGES AND WORDS FROM MAGAZINES TO EXPRESS EMOTIONS on page 170 will give clients an opportunity to explore this creative technique.

We know that many trauma survivors walk around with unmetabolized shame, guilt, and blame—important emotions that wreck havoc on their thoughts, behaviors, and self-esteem. Safely processing these emotions, both verbally and through artistic expression, is critically important to their healing and gives clients an alternative way to show us their pain narratives. Cohen, Barnes, and Rankin (1995) offered effective art therapy techniques to help clients achieve safety, containment, comfort, and sensory relief.

Once clients are able to identify feelings, you can open the door to teaching affect regulation skills. Remember that clients do not possess healthy strategies and will need your guidance in learning how to manage what they feel. As we help clients access their emotional states, we should be mindful of the fact that the expression of feeling is activating. Their familial point of reference regarding the display of emotion is often represented by two antithetical extremes: a parent who was out of control with his or her feelings and a repressed parent who expressed nothing. Clients have legitimate concerns about not wanting to look like or act like the parent who could not regulate or control his or her emotions. Sixteen-year-old Lacey exemplifies this dilemma when she says:

> My dad goes out gambling, and when he comes back, if he's lost a lot of money, he starts screaming at us. He can stay in a really bad mood, yelling at us for days until he goes out and wins some of the money back. My mom doesn't fight back or yell at him. She just takes it and tells us not to do anything to upset him even more. If my younger brother asks her to make my father stop, it's like she doesn't hear him. She's just blank. Sometimes my brother starts to act like my father—a screaming crazy person—but I never want to turn into my father, so when I start to feel angry and stuff, I try to be like my mom—blank. When the feelings are too strong, I cut myself, and that helps me to go blank.

Schiraldi (2009) addressed this issue when he encouraged clients to "distinguish between feelings and actions. You don't have to do anything with feelings if you choose not to" (p. 95). However, given the fact that traumatized clients have often suppressed their feelings for so long, it is important for them to learn how to safely and appropriately express themselves. We need to reassure self-destructive clients that if they do get back in touch with their emotions, with help, the "dam won't break," leaving them flooded and overwhelmed.

We must therefore teach our clients the counterbalance to the externalization of feelings, which is the capacity to contain them. Traumatized clients need to understand the difference between containing feelings and repressing them. Typically they are adept at the latter because this was so often modeled by trusted family members who used their own dissociative responses to shut down to stay safe. Once clients find the courage to reconnect with and express feelings, we don't want them shoved back in the bottom drawer where they will be denied or forgotten again.

Conversely, clients need the reassurance that they will not be hijacked by their feelings. If they fear that the floodgates will break, they assume they are vulnerable to drowning in a relentless river of emotion. Strategies for containment provide the reassurance that this work can stay manageable. Napier (1994) offered a lovely description of containment as a way to create "a safe space inside in which to explore and deal with your feelings" (p. 111).

We can introduce a wide variety of techniques to help with affect regulation, particularly ones that integrate both left- and right-brain functioning. Think in terms of a two-step process when working with this part of the cycle: helping clients to safely express feelings and then sufficiently contain them so flooding doesn't occur.

One strategy I created to assist clients with affect regulation is to teach them to gather up their feelings and visualize giving them a shape and a color. Make sure that the image is supplied by your clients and not suggested by you, as they know best what will work for them. In addition, when we allow clients to internally create their own images, we are giving them the message that they have the ability to access healing resources within themselves. Clients can also heighten their imagery by drawing it. By definition, putting images down on paper is a form of containment: amorphous and overwhelming emotion is contained within the boundary of the page.

Maria, a 52-year-old woman, has been struggling with anger for most of her life. Working with the first stage of containment, her overwhelming rage becomes visualized as a huge orange and red sun. As she sits with that image, she is encouraged to magically and safely envision that all of the rage is being absorbed into the sun. In the next step, she is encouraged to put the sun into another container, to heighten the sense of safe storage. Maria imagines that the sun is put into a large asbestos box with a lid to keep it inside. Again, she is invited to sit with the imagery to assess for its efficacy. If Maria says the affect feels "somewhat," "sort of," or "almost" contained, she is invited to add additional layers. She puts a red and gray fireproof blanket made of scratchy wool over the box, then heavy black chains over the blanket, and finally glittery, soft, smooth, silver angel wings over the whole thing. At this point her body language clearly indicates a relaxed, comfortable state, and she reports that a sense of genuine containment has been accomplished.

The workbook visualization exercise called IMAGINING INTERNAL CONTAINERS TO STORE OVERWHELMING EMOTIONS on page 175 and DRAWING CONTAINERS FOR OVERWHELMING EMOTIONS on page 176 will guide your clients through this process.

Notice how the descriptions of the containers captured color, texture, size, and so on. The more clients can attach sensory information to the imagery, the more vividly they will see it and the more deeply it will be installed. Given that trauma survivors are often acquiescent as a way to stay safe, listening for vivid description is a great way for us to assess for the authenticity of their experiences.

It's important to watch for clients' nonverbal responses during this process. Ideally we want to see the activation of their parasympathetic system: slower breathing, a softening of musculature, and a release of body tension. This tells us that a sense of safety is being enhanced, and the imagery is resonating for them.

Once containment is established, clients are given the option to keep the emotionally charged material in its container until they choose to revisit it during the course of the week or, if need be, to keep it contained until they are back in the safety of our office. To ensure that material won't leak out of its containment, you can suggest that everything is put into the equivalent of a bank vault with a timer that doesn't allow it to be reopened until their next session. This heightens their sense of control, reassures them that they can go about their daily lives without the intrusion of debilitating affect, and ultimately teaches them that there are strategies other than self-destructive behaviors that can be utilized to manage affect.

Many trauma survivors are visually astute and have instinctively used imaging strategies to survive, so they are quite receptive to the concepts of visualization and guided imagery. Carolyn Daitch (2007) wrote an excellent book that is chock-full of effective visualizations to help with affect regulation. Her concept of "dialing down" overwhelming emotion or reactivity is a readily accessible resource and resonates with clients.

The basic premise is the pairing of the image of a dial with numbers from 1 to 10 and a needle that can move in either direction. Each number represents the level of intensity of an identified emotion. Clients begin by placing the needle on the number that represents the strength of what they feel. Typically the starting point for rage, disappointment, and so on is between 7 and 10. As clients breathe, their exhalation can control the dial, moving it down as the feeling lessens. This is a creative form of biofeedback: teaching clients about the mind–body connection and their ability to control affect by activating their parasympathetic system. It helps to encourage clients to simultaneously notice what happens to their bodies as the upsetting feeling begins to dissipate.

I have added one additional dimension to this strategy: inviting clients to give the targeted feeling a color and to visualize gradations of the color that coincide with the increasing or decreasing numbers on the dial. The workbook exercise called CREATING A COLOR WHEEL TO DECREASE OVERWHELMING EMOTION on page 178 offers a variation of this technique.

Forty-three-year-old Winona was grieving the profound loss of her infant in childbirth. Convinced that her body killed the baby, she was punishing herself by withholding food. Her grief was all consuming and triggered a deep state of depression. Winona ranked the intensity of her grief as a 10 and described it as "a dark midnight blue." As we worked with undoing cognitive distortions, she visually practiced dialing down the intensity of the feeling. She watched the numbers decrease to 1 as the color softened and turned into "a soothing baby blue." This gave her another way to measure the shift in her emotional state. It also gave her back some control, as she could decide "how blue" she wanted to be in the present moment.

This strategy is also effective because it pairs left- and right-brain processing. The numeric sequence appeals more to the left hemisphere, and the color palette appeals more to the right hemisphere. I also use this strategy to increase the intensity of *desirable* emotions such as positive self-worth, confidence, or safety. In this instance the starting number is usually quite low, and clients can be encouraged to use their exhalation and positive affirmations to move the needle upward. As they observe the color becoming brighter or bolder, it becomes paired with a stronger sense of their positive feeling.

When clients practice this connection between a vivid color (gold) with a positive feeling (empowerment) and an accompanying positive thought ("I am worthwhile"), they can eventually just go to the color gold and simultaneously feel the positive emotional, cognitive, and somatic reverberations that have become associated with the color. You can deepen this experience by encouraging your clients to find an object or swatch of cloth that matches the color they've been visualizing. This becomes another accessible resource for them when they are looking to quickly increase a positive state of mind.

Another approach that has become quite popular and is extremely effective is the use of emotional freedom technique (EFT). Created by Gary Craig, this deceptively simple "energy psychology" allows clients to tap on specific meridian points, helping to ease the flow of energy and alleviate feelings of distress. There seems to be additional benefit derived from the fact that this soothing self-touch is paired with a positive affirmation and an acknowledgment and acceptance of all emotions. Vorobioff (2011) wrote about the application of EFT to help alleviate the distressing components of anger, guilt, and loneliness.

When I teach clients tapping, I encourage them to do an alternating left and right touch, in an attempt to borrow from the precepts of EMDR (eye movement desensitization and reprocessing) and to activate the left and right hemispheres of the brain. A great advantage to this strategy is that clients can do it at anytime and experience relief relatively quickly. The workbook exercise entitled PRACTICING TAPPING FOR AFFECT REGULATION, on page 185 of the workbook, gives clients a step by step guide to the strategy. There are also some excellent demonstrations on YouTube that can assist clients in gaining confidence with the tapping scripts and meridian points. I have also found that the abundance of these videos invites a nonjudgmental curiosity and helps to normalize the use of EFT as a viable tool in affect regulation.

An additional modality that has been around for centuries and is getting newfound respect in the trauma world is yoga. When an esteemed and preeminent researcher and clinician like Bessel van der Kolk endorses the use of yoga to overcome trauma and reclaim the body, you know it is a modality worthy of serious consideration (Emerson & Hopper, 2011). There are numerous benefits to incorporating yoga into treatment. For trauma survivors, yogic breath work can be a safe and relatively easy way to reground and install an immediate anchor for safety. Weintraub (2003) wrote eloquently about how "Yoga philosophy and practice, including postures, breath work, and meditation can help you manage or even overcome depression" (p. 19). Modalities such as yoga, qigong, and tai chi offer our clients nonthreatening ways to reconnect with sensations on their bodies, increase a state of mindfulness, and evoke a healthy sense of power and control. These somatic experiences profoundly influence clients' affective states. Creating positive mind–body connections translates into feeling comforted, safe, energized, powerful, grounded, serene, and so on.

Thirty-year-old Stan had been profoundly physically abused in childhood by a trusted authority figure in his life. No one in his extended family recognized his trauma, and he became highly dissociative in order to survive his chronic ordeal. As a result, in adulthood, Stan felt completely disconnected from his body, so much so that he could run 26- or 50-mile marathons and triathlons on a broken ankle or with pneumonia. Despite the fact that he took pride in these accomplishments and his ability to block out all pain, on some level he realized he was doing lasting damage to his body. Through therapy he realized he had been abusively pushing his body to counterbalance internal feelings of guilt and shame about not being strong enough to fight off his female abuser. Stan found the courage to begin doing simple yoga poses and discovered a new way to feel strong, grounded, and present in his body. This immediately caused a positive shift in his depressed mood and feelings of helplessness and hopelessness. It also ended the cycle of subjecting his body to wrenching physical abuse.

When we consider a variety of treatment options to address the "negative feelings" part of the cycle, the role of medication should not be minimized or ignored. Van der Kolk et al. (2006) endorsed the use of medication in the treatment of PTSD as a way to reduce the frequency and severity of intrusive symptoms, dissociation, depressed mood and numbing, hyperarousal, and aggressive impulses toward self and others. Amy Weintraub (2003) concurred, saying, "The road to recovery from depression may be finding a balance of medication, talk therapy, and Yoga" (p. 7). Every major psychiatric organization and authoritative body recognizes the important role that medication can play in the treatment of clients with depression and anxiety disorders.

Engaging in the "medication conversation" with clients is often not a onetime proposition. Be prepared to spend a good amount of time processing clients' initial ambivalence or resistances, along with what I call "medication myths." Many clients have either heard about medication secondhand or on the Internet, or they may have had a brief and unsuccessful experience with medication in the past and assume the outcomes will be the same in the present. The workbook exercise called PROCESSING YOUR FEELINGS ABOUT MEDICATION on page 189 of the workbook will give you and your client good information to process in subsequent sessions.

Given the potentially disempowering dynamics and power differentials between trauma survivors and their therapists, it is important that our clients don't feel bullied or forced into taking medication. Just as we work to keep the decision to stop hurting themselves in their arena, we also want the decision to try medication to be of our clients' own volition. Having said that, it's important that clients make this decision from an educated place, truly understanding the pros and cons with informed objectivity. It is our ethical responsibility to broach the subject of antidepressants, anxiolytics, and mood stabilizers with our clients and to make sure they fully understand the benefits before ruling out this modality as a viable option.

Many clients view taking medication as a weakness. This may be a learned value from family and friends, and most of them do not have an accurate understanding of the medication and base their opinion on fear and misinformation. Rather than making assumptions, we need to get clear information from clients about why taking medication is perceived to be a sign of weakness. In the course of this conversation, we can actually reframe taking medication as a sign of strength. It is a *proactive* step to better one's life, reduce pain, and increase overall functioning.

Resistance to taking medication can also reflect clients' core survival beliefs that they have to do everything on their own without any assistance because nothing else can be counted on in life. If this thought is operational, it's an opportunity for us to remind clients of the difference between "then" and "now." Believing that they have to fend for themselves is accurate information about how it *used to be* in their lives, but it is not applicable to their current life circumstances. In this regard, agreeing to take medication for affect regulation can have the reparative effect of helping clients buy into the newfound idea that it's acceptable to get outside support, and they don't have to handle the vicissitudes of life alone.

One of the medication myths that surfaces in these conversations includes the fear that they will get addicted to an antidepressant. Set clients straight by teaching them that pharmacologically speaking, antidepressants are *not* addicting. For a substance to be addicting, three properties must be present: physical dependence, tolerance (requiring higher and higher doses to achieve the same effect), and withdrawal. Antidepressants *do not* cause physical dependence; that is, they are not craved. Although some clients may need more medication, this is not due to the development of tolerance. Some clients simply need higher doses to achieve relief of symptoms. And when clients are properly weaned, there is no significant withdrawal phenomenon from antidepressants in most clients.

Another myth is the notion that drugs will alter their thinking. The ironic truth is that anxiety, dissociation, trauma, and depression can profoundly alter our clients' judgment, memory, focus, concentration, and quality of thoughts. The right medication can reequilibrate all of that so clients are better able to make decisions from a place of sound judgment.

If your clients are ambivalent because they have had unsuccessful experiences with medication in the past, be sure to get a clear picture of what they used and how compliant they were. Oftentimes, clients' declarations about the ineffectiveness of medication are based on a 3-day trial at a sub-therapeutic dose with no physician follow-up. If side effects were the reason for discontinuation, let clients know there are newer drugs with lower side effect profiles, initial nuisance side effects often resolve, and they will never be forced to stay on medication that makes them feel uncomfortable.

I have consulted on many cases where clients were already on medication yet remained symptomatic. If you have clients in a similar situation, struggling with symptoms of depression or the debilitating effects of anxiety, their medication needs to be reevaluated by their prescribing physician. Getting a response from medication is not the same thing as getting to remission, an alleviation of all of the diagnostic symptoms. That should be our goal. Consider the strong possibility that your clients can dramatically improve if their physician considers changing the dose or the drug or using a second drug for augmentation. We can play the role of advocates in this process, empowering our clients to go back to their doctors or getting a signed release to discuss this directly with their physicians.

Although many clients are socially and culturally conditioned to "pull themselves up by their bootstraps" or "just grin and bear it," keep in mind that without a "pharmacological safety net," they may have great difficulty remembering, internalizing, processing, or integrating the work you are trying to introduce and focus on in session. Medication is not a panacea, but it often is the first step toward helping with affect regulation, restoring good eating and sleeping habits, and allowing our clients to reclaim that glimmer of hope that makes subsequent healing work even possible.

When your clients decide to try medication and their affective or anxiety disorder is straightforward, I suggest involving their primary care physician whenever possible. There are many advantages to this, including the fact that it is less stigmatizing and more cost-effective for clients to see their family physician or internist. Primary care physicians are well trained in the recognition and treatment of depression and anxiety disorders, and many have extensive experience in psychopharmacology. It is also a way to provide a streamlined, holistic approach to clients' mental health and medical care.

Many trauma survivors avoid seeing a doctor for a Pap smear, mammogram, colonoscopy, or prostate exam because those procedures are too somatically triggering for them. In addition, they often need to be connected to a physician to deal with addiction issues or complications from cutting or burning or if they've become medically compromised because of bingeing, purging, or restrictive eating. When a primary care doctor can see them for medication, you are also increasing the likelihood that their other medical needs will be addressed in time as well.

12

WORKING WITH THE CYCLE

Unbearable anxiety and the frozen loop

Unbearable tension and anxiety

If clients are unable to short-circuit the "loop of negativity," we can offer them ways to intervene as they reach a state of heightened tension and anxiety. I find it helpful to first introduce some psychoeducation to explain the physiology of anxiety: how and where it manifests on the body. As you work on this part of the cycle in session, encourage clients to home in on and identify the ways in which their bodies manifest an anxious state. Anxiety is typically experienced through heart palpations or heaviness on the chest, sweaty palms, dry mouth, a feeling of dizziness, a constricted or collapsed body posture, nausea or stomach upset, thought racing, and other symptoms of psychomotor agitation. When clients can identify the "physical harbingers" of anxiety, it is the first step toward being able to intervene. The treatment for anxiety often starts with our clients' abilities to accurately label what's happening as feeling anxiety or panic rather than thinking they are "going crazy" or having a heart attack.

Once clients understand their sensations as anxiety based, we can incorporate strategies that are already a part of our relaxation repertoire when treating these symptoms. Many clients benefit from modalities that incorporate breath work because anxiety is connected to a fight–flight response and is experienced somatically. Controlled, conscious breathing is a great way to reequilibrate an overly activated sympathetic system. Simple, rhythmic breathing seems to work best as it is easiest to master and can quickly reconnect clients back to their bodies.

Make sure your client fully exhales, as trauma survivors often have histories of holding their breath to "listen" better when in a hypervigilant state or as an inevitable part of a freeze response. Emerson and Hopper (2011) concurred that the rapid, shallow, and breath-holding breathing patterns of anxious, hyperaroused, or frightened trauma survivors "leaves [their] bodies in a state of tension and dysregulation and may add to an overall sense of unease in the body" (p. 108).

There are some wonderful breathing exercises that can be borrowed from modalities such as "sun breath" in the yoga tradition, mindfulness, Buddhist meditation, and Ericksonian hypnosis. Here are a few "scripts" that can be readily incorporated into a therapy session and then used by clients, outside of session, when they reach this stage in the cycle. In all cases, it helps for clients to have both feet firmly on the ground and to be sitting in an upright but comfortable position so the diaphragm can be fully utilized.

Fran, age 14, was frequently plagued by anticipatory anxiety in response to being teased by peers. Because she couldn't always control her external environment, we worked on reducing her anxious state by helping her achieve a greater sense of internal safety—which was in her control. In session we practiced inhaling through the nose while slowly counting to 3. Fran then held her breath for 3 counts and slowly exhaled through her nose for 5 counts. The additional count on the exhalation allowed her to fully release the breath. In the next breathing set, she was encouraged to pair her inhalation with a soothing word—she chose *calm*. Then on her slow exhalation, she chose the word *safe*. Fran began to notice how her body slowed down in response to the breathing and how this helped counterbalance the hyperarousal she felt from her anxiety.

Another simple strategy is to have clients place their arms, palms up and hands open, in their lap. As they inhale, their fingers slowly close into fists and then slowly reopen on the exhale. Matching the rhythm of breathing to the opening and closing of their hands helps clients to slow down their breathing and focus on their bodies in a way that activates the parasympathetic system and evokes a state of calmness.

Clients can also learn to incorporate hand-in-hand meditation, a Buddhist form of breath work designed to enhance mindfulness and reduce anxiety. Starting with both hands, palms up, in their lap, clients are invited to put one hand on top of the other and to simply notice the sensation of one hand in the other hand. These sensations include any differences in weight in the right hand and left hand, differences in the warmth or coolness of each hand, and an awareness of the air traveling between the hands and the fingers and on top of the palms. This heightened awareness of an accessible body sensation can then be transferred to the breath, noticing the difference between breathing in and breathing out. Clients can then toggle back and forth between an awareness of their hands and their breathing. In addition to its inherently calming effect, this meditation gives clients a healthier way to feel a sense of control and mastery over their bodies.

An Ericksonian approach invites clients to observe the differences between inhaling and exhaling across the body. Noticing sensations across the stomach, chest, top of the shoulders, or inside the nose can heighten a sense of awareness, focus, and calm. Encourage your clients to attend to the shifts that breathing creates on their bodies: expanding and releasing, rising and falling, tensing and letting go. The workbook exercise called PRACTICING MEDITATIVE BREATHING on page 193 allows clients to experiment with different breathing techniques and then document the impact they had on their level of anxiety.

The advantage to using the breath is that it is always available to clients. However, some clients already feel self-conscious about their breathing, as anxiety can quicken it and cause breathing to feel uncomfortable. In these instances, using art, visualization, and guided imagery can be quite helpful. Cohen, Barnes, and Rankin (1995) offered a creative option by walking clients through a simple art exercise that allows them to "draw" the breath. Using line, shape, and color to visually depict the depth, rate, and speed of inhalations and exhalations can be a safe way for clients to be more attuned to their breathing. They can also begin to play with the idea of taking more control over their breathing by deliberately drawing more slowly, using soothing colors, and making the lines on the page more elongated and fluid. This becomes a creative form of biofeedback and teaches clients about the power of the mind–body connection. The workbook exercise called USING LINE, SHAPE, AND COLOR TO DOCUMENT BREATH on page 194 walks clients through this process.

If your clients still resist the idea of slowing down their breathing, incorporate another art therapy technique that mirrors where they are somatically yet helps them to discharge the energy and hyperarousal that anxiety evokes. Invite your clients to illustrate their heightened state by choosing the appropriate colors and scribbling or making staccato marks on paper with magic markers or colored pencils. Using this media rather than paints or pastels will help to keep the imagery inherently contained. As their experience is validated, it will paradoxically begin to calm them down. You can then attempt to have them shift the imagery so the breath becomes slower and deeper. This exercise is called DISCHARGING TENSION WITH ART on page 195 of the workbook.

Much of the early groundbreaking work that was done in the treatment of anxiety and panic was by Dr. Claire Weekes. She understood the necessity of helping clients "float" with their somatic and cognitive symptoms rather than "fight" against them (Weekes, 1990). The idea of relaxing into anxiety or panic seems counterintuitive to clients who want to immediately disconnect from the feelings. However, fighting the sensations by tensing the body or cognitively bullying oneself actually exacerbates an anxious state and prolongs the experience.

As part of a treatment strategy, you can teach clients to go with the anxiety by pairing it with a visual image of floating. As always, we want clients to conjure imagery that works for them, but some effective suggestions include a balloon, feather, or cloud floating in the sky or a slow-moving leaf or an empty canoe floating on a river. As mentioned when we discussed containment, the more vividly they can describe the imagery, the more deeply it becomes installed. When some clients reach this stage of the cycle of self-destructive acts, their escalating anxiety can be short-circuited through this combination of mindful breathing and imagery that literally slows down their physiology. The workbook guided imagery exercise entitled FLOATING WITH ANXIETY/PANIC is on page 197.

We can also introduce other ideas including the use of relaxation CDs: sounds of nature, soothing music, or a calming voice that can bring clients to a more relaxed state. Encourage your clients to preview these CDs by listening to them in the store before purchasing them. This will ensure that there is nothing inadvertently triggering about the music or the tone of voice on the CD.

Some clients find it beneficial to read positive affirmations when their tension mounts, as they feel soothed and calmed by reassuring messages of hope or faith. In addition to words that are spiritually based, reassurances about the fact that anxiety is time limited and will always pass can also prevent the mounting escalation of such uncomfortable thoughts and feelings. Give clients specific mantras to use that will quickly ground them and counteract cognitive distortions when they begin to feel their anxiety building. Helpful reframes include the following: "Right now I am 'doing anxiety or panic,'" "I know that in a few minutes my body will calm down," and "I can use my inner resources to help myself through this time-limited, uncomfortable feeling."

Clients can also use the same image of dialing down their anxiety as was described in the section on affect regulation to deescalate their mounting visceral tension. The workbook exercise called REDUCING TENSION AND ANXIETY on page 199 will walk clients through this process. Schiraldi (2009) also offered some strategies for progressive muscle relaxation exercises that activate the parasympathetic system and deescalate anxiety.

As is the case with other parts of the cycle, the most important thing is to make sure clients choose strategies that feel safe, comfortable, and easy to do. Clients who begrudgingly agree to incorporate techniques at different intervention sites will not experience much success and are at increased risk to revert back to their self-destructive behaviors when they feel triggered or overwhelmed. Strategies that are halfheartedly attempted and fail reinforce the distorted idea that nothing will help and can cause clients to lose faith in the process. We must therefore continue to monitor both verbal and nonverbal responses to our suggestions and give clients the message that they possess veto power to overrule any strategy they feel hesitant about doing.

The frozen loop: dissociation and analgesia

This is one of the most important parts of the cycle, as some degree of dissociation seems necessary for clients to actually pick up the razor blade and cut more deeply than they intended, force excessive amounts of food into their bodies, "stand outside of themselves" and start drinking again, keep rolling the dice when they are broke, and so on. When we can help clients to really short-circuit this sensation, following through with destructive acts becomes a much more difficult proposition.

We must always remember that we do not have the power to take away someone's dissociative abilities, and we should reassure our clients of this reality as well. Even if we possessed that skill, it's not the goal of treatment; to do so would disempower our clients even more. At this stage of the cycle, the goal is to help our clients understand and identify their dissociative states and then to choose to either "go to the ceiling" or "stay forward and grounded in the present." This concept of proactive decision making helps us avoid a potential power struggle and reiterates the idea that clients do have choice and control over their behaviors.

Napier (1994) offered a compassionate spin on the treatment of dissociation when she encouraged clients to "use dissociation, voluntarily, as a resource." She described this process as "therapeutic dissociation," suggesting that clients can hold a dual awareness of being grounded in the present as adults while simultaneously bearing witness to, and sharing experiences of, parts that hold and feel rekindled past hurts.

Just as we discussed the harbingers of anxiety, our clients have physical cues that indicate the onset of a dissociative state as well. Because it happens in such a knee-jerk way—perceived threat is instantly met with dissociation—clients need guidance in reconnecting, in a conscious way, to their dissociative experiences.

Clients can sometimes get "spacey" or "zone out" right in the middle of a therapy session. This is especially true when we are discussing self-destructive behaviors. We should take advantage of this gestalt opportunity and process the experience as it unfolds in our office. For example, ask your clients, "Do you know what just happened?" "Are you aware of where you went?" "Can you describe what you were feeling on your body when you started to zone out?" Look for experiences that include clients losing peripheral vision or feeling tunnel vision, reporting that they can see your mouth moving but can't hear what you are saying, feeling like a black curtain or black cloud is hovering over them or in front of their eyes, having a tingling sensation in their extremities, having a specific kind of headache, losing body sensation or feeling numbness, feeling disoriented or disconnected from the environment, and so on.

Once clients can articulate these sensations, you've increased awareness and created the opportunity to introduce the concept of choice. I invite clients to incorporate the following cognitive strategy into their coping repertoire: "I feel myself starting to dissociate because I'm aware of those physical harbingers. Is it in my best interest to check out, or would it be most empowering for me to stay grounded in the present?" The operant phrase relates to what is most empowering for clients. This can be a confusing paradigm shift for them, as they have historically associated power and safety with zoning out to escape an untenable experience.

We have to reframe their ideas about dissociation. The mechanism that was lifesaving in the past is the very same strategy that puts them back into a freeze or feigned death response and renders them helpless in the present. When our clients are in a dissociative state, they are essentially in the more primitive parts of their brain. This means the prefrontal cortex is off-line, and clients are unable to use their capacities to analyze, reason, use good judgment, and so on. They are therefore not in the best position to self-protect or advocate for themselves. It may take time for our clients to accept that this "life jacket" is actually detrimental to their wellbeing. Van der Kolk, McFarlane, and Weisaeth (2006) agreed, saying, "Dissociation can be an effective way to continue functioning while the trauma is going on, but if it continues to be utilized after the acute trauma has passed it comes to interfere with everyday functioning" (p. 192).

Once our clients assess that staying forward is the optimal way to serve their best interests, they will need guidance in learning how to avoid full-blown dissociation. The introduction of grounding strategies becomes an important intervention in this part of their work. There are a variety of simple techniques that can help clients reconnect to the present. As we process these options and allow clients to test them out in the therapy session, we can assess for their efficacy and work through any initial resistance or roadblocks. Sometimes *identifying* their dissociative state, *relabeling* it as disempowering, and *giving themselves permission* to stay forward is all that is required for clients to short-circuit the process. At other times, once clients identify their dissociative state, they will need the additional support of visual cues, physical movement, or somatic sensations that serve as reminders of being grounded.

Whenever 60-year-old Colette explored her childhood neglect, she felt herself zoning out in session. Our first step was making sure she had both feet on the floor. Her dissociation usually caused her to contract and constrict her body, moving intuitively into a fetal position to feel safer. We counteracted this by getting her into a standing position, encouraging her to bend her knees and bounce a bit so she could feel herself rooted to the floor. Incorporating yoga positions such as "mountain pose" or "warrior pose" also enhanced her sense of being physically grounded. Sometimes, she would take off her shoes to feel her feet on the floor or roll her feet over a foot massager. At other times it helped for her to do jumping jacks, stomp, rub her hands together vigorously, clap, or snap her fingers. She also learned to put one hand on her belly and one on her heart, anchoring herself to the movement of breath and the rhythm of her heartbeat.

We can also introduce somatic sensations such as tapping along the outside periphery of the body, putting cold water on the face, sucking on an ice cube, or holding a cup of warm coffee, tea, or hot chocolate to activate their senses of touch and smell. Clients can grab on to a piece of jewelry such as a wedding ring or bracelet from a loved one and pair it with cognitions of safety. As we discussed earlier, car keys are terrific for regrounding, as they represent being an empowered adult who is not trapped. As simplistic as this may sound, these strategies can bring clients back into their bodies and their current environment. When clients are zoning out, they are often able to do only the easiest strategies.

When dissociation gets activated in our office during session, in addition to the aforementioned strategies, we can incorporate a movement therapy technique of mirroring back simple "hand and sound calls." Start with very easy patterns such as clapping twice and slapping the thighs once. Clients are asked to watch, listen, and repeat the movement sequence. This forces them to attend to the present moment, gets the prefrontal cortex back "online," and derails their ability to zone out. You can make the calls a bit more complicated by combining clapping, snapping, placing arms across the chest, tapping the toes, and so on.

When clients begin to dissociate, there is also an increased vulnerability for flashbacks. Flashbacks can manifest in a variety of ways, and it's important to educate clients about that possibility. Clients typically associate them with visual imagery, but they can also be experienced viscerally through body pain, nausea, dizziness, and so forth. In addition, there are "cognitive flashbacks," which are thoughts rooted in the past that get misinterpreted as information about the present, such as "I am helpless" or "It will never get better." Flashbacks can also be experienced emotionally, often through affect such as terror, despair, and rage.

Because flashbacks instantly make clients travel back in time and relive deeply upsetting facets of their prior trauma, it makes sense that they would perform self-destructive behaviors to quickly numb, distract, and short-circuit these overwhelming sensations. "In PTSD the past is relived with an immediate sensory and emotional intensity that makes victims feel as if the event were recurring all over again" (van der Kolk et al., 2006, p. 8). Therefore, helping clients to better manage their dissociative and abreactive states is an essential part of the treatment process. This can be accomplished by teaching clients a few flashback-halting protocols that should be practiced in your office.

Babette Rothschild (2002) did an excellent job of creating simple flashback-halting protocols. She helps clients identify their experience but is mindful of the importance of containing the experience and not opening the door any wider. She encourages clients to simply give a title to their trauma memory ("the time that Grandpa hurt me") rather than evoke any details about the experience. Her emphasis is on helping clients distinguish the past from the present, and her strategies are extremely effective. The workbook exercise called FLASHBACK-HALTING PROTOCOL on page 207 gives clients the opportunity to create scripts for regrounding.

In addition, Milton Erickson's work with hypnosis can be used as a flashback-halting protocol, helping clients reconnect with their present environment. Clients are encouraged to say out loud, in sequence, a number of things they see, hear, and feel as they begin to lose a sense of being present. This, again, forces them to notice their current surroundings, a critical component of regrounding and mindfulness. The exercise called FLASHBACK-HALTING PROTOCOL #2 on page 211 of the workbook will guide your clients through this technique. You can also incorporate the Ericksonian strategy of depersonalizing a visual flashback by encouraging clients to put their imagery on a movie screen while standing or sitting all the way back from it. They can then control it with an imaginary remote control that allows them to mute the sound, fast forward it, freeze-frame something important, and so on.

Inspired by the wonderful contributions of these brilliant clinicians, I would like to offer another simple flashback-halting protocol. I encourage my clients to write out the miniscript on a brightly colored index card and carry it with them. They can fill in the blanks as they relate to each unique experience of abreaction. This protocol allows clients to label the manifestation of their flashback and reminds them that if they feel younger than their actual age, they are, by definition, in flashback mode. The script also encourages clients to reframe the experience as something that can be useful rather than something to fear, which begins to take some of the power away from it. In addition, the script introduces the concept of "dual awareness," reminding clients that despite the intensity of their experience, in actuality they are grounded in the present, which, unlike the past, is safe and empowering.

Flashback-halting protocol

As I experience this *image, thought, feeling, or body sensation*, I realize that I feel _____ years old. This tells me that I am having a *visual, cognitive, emotional, or somatic* flashback. I am being given information back about how I used to *think or feel* in the past. In the present, I can use this information to grow and heal. In the present I can access support. I am not alone.

Seventy-one-year-old Anthony had been held hostage by flashbacks for most of his life. Never understanding their root cause and always feeling powerless when he abreacted, he stumbled on the strategy of "spending 10 hours a day playing video games, as a way to distract my mind and keep the demons at bay." Incorporating this simple flashback-halting protocol gave him a newfound sense of control and reduced the need to self-medicate through his computer addiction. By filling in the blanks for each statement, he came to realize that feelings of being trapped and afraid, the visualization of his childhood basement, and the body sensation of intense stomach pain were emotional, visual, and somatic flashbacks about being hurt at 8 years of age. His willingness to then work with childhood pictures of himself, to reconnect with and comfort his hurt inner child, became a breakthrough in his treatment.

Practicing the use of this script during session helps to strengthen it as a viable resource for clients when they are not in your office. If any of the other flashback-halting techniques resonate with your clients, encourage them to write them out on the brightly colored index cards as well.

13

WORKING WITH THE CYCLE

Self-destructive behaviors and CARESS

We should always be looking for ways to give clients alternative "life jackets," offering strategies that provide the same, albeit healthier, positive outcomes that their self-destructive behaviors yield. Given the fact that standard safety contracts can often exacerbate the problem, asking our clients to simply refrain from their self-destructive behaviors will usually backfire. Hospitalization, although occasionally necessary for clients who cannot maintain stabilization and become a true danger to themselves, should be considered a last resort. Gratz and Chapman (2009) concurred, saying, "There is no evidence that hospitalization is better than outpatient treatment." They further stated, "Hospitalization for self-harm really isn't necessary; it's like using a wrecking ball to hammer a nail" (p. 122).

A better way to intervene at this part of the cycle is to introduce the concept of CARESS: *C*ommunicate *A*lternatively, *R*elease *E*ndorphins, and *S*elf-*S*oothe. As we have already discussed, CARESS is an alternative to standard safety contracts that eliminates the power struggle between our clients and us. CARESS is specifically designed to help clients achieve, in healthier ways, the same positive gains they get from self-destructive behaviors. Most clients are tuned in to the fact that self-destructive behaviors ameliorate tension and anxiety and quell the resurfacing of painful memories and affect.

They may be less aware, however, of the fact that punitive, harmful acts are a form of metacommunication and the destructive behaviors are representative of their pain narratives. When we target this part of the cycle, it is important to introduce a psychoeducational piece that focuses on the dynamics of metacommunication and reframes the behavior as both a reenactment and a restorying of prior traumatic experiences. CARESS allows our clients to share their pain more productively, while simultaneously giving them creative ways to short-circuit uncomfortable affective states and move toward an experience of feeling soothed.

As an important aside, although I have never encountered this personally in my work, it is worth acknowledging that you may come across a client who feels triggered by the word *caress*. By definition, it means an embracing, soft touch—something we want clients to feel comfortable doing for themselves. It is meant to be a reparative alternative to self-punishment. If, however, the word connotes something unsafe, particularly for sexual abuse survivors, you can modify the contract to stand for CARES and still maintain all three essential components.

As we have already discussed, when clients become triggered, the prefrontal cortex goes off-line, making it impossible to operate from a place of rational or analytical thinking. Therefore, when the urge to cut, purge, or drink kicks in, it is unreasonable to expect clients will have the cognitive capacity to turn to healthier coping strategies. With this in mind, it is helpful to encourage clients to create a CARESS box in your office that will be kept in a safe place at home. (If you are working in a residential treatment center, every client should have his or her own CARESS box. It should be readily accessible and accepted by staff as a viable first-response when a patient begins to act out.) The box is used as a streamlined container, holding all the tools that will be needed to effectively implement CARESS when the self-destructive impulse strikes. We increase the likelihood that they will follow through with the protocol if everything is in one place and clients don't have to frantically search for their resources.

To enhance their emotional investment in the process, encourage clients to paint, collage, or draw words and images on the box that represent feeling safe, comforted, and soothed. Allow this process to unfold over several sessions if necessary, continuing to assess for the activation of the parasympathetic system to confirm that their choice of words and images is evoking a calming response.

Of course, when our clients reach this stage of the self-destructive cycle, they are either intensely hypoaroused (freeze and dissociation) or shifting into hyperarousal (fight–flight) as they contemplate the destructive act. We now understand that in either of those states, clients are at a grave disadvantage, and their capacity to think clearly about acts of self-care has been sorely compromised. This same dynamic holds true during a therapy session: clients can't process or integrate what we teach them if they are not grounded and present. To this end, the "C" in CARESS can also stand for "centering" clients before they can move ahead with the protocol.

There are many strategies that can assist clients in reconnecting with the present moment, and they should be practiced in session to help clients achieve some beginning mastery. This, in turn, will enable them to take greater advantage of the benefits of the CARESS model. Some of these ideas have already been identified as interventions that can be used when addressing the dissociative/analgesic part of the cycle. You can incorporate them here as well.

As we previously discussed, encourage clients to experiment with the following strategies to evoke a more centered state before moving into CARESS: simple breathing exercises while focusing on the sensations of inhaling and exhaling on the body; stating out loud what they see, hear, and feel in their current environment; using simple regrounding phrases to say as a mantra; using tapping, yoga poses, and other simple movements to reconnect with the body; and identifying their present location and age. It will not always be possible for clients to start from a more centered place, but don't let them become discouraged. In many cases going to the CARESS box is the conditioned cognition and action step that begins the centering process for them.

Once you have worked on the concept of centering and clients have personalized the box, you can begin to process the three stages of the CARESS protocol. You must reiterate that you are not asking your clients to refrain from their self-destructive behaviors.

Rather, when they get the urge to act out, *before* they do, they will *first* employ the strategies from CARESS. In this way we are trying to retrain their brains to associate the impulse to harm with an automatic CARESS response rather than their conditioned self-destructive one. CARESS is presented as an alternative option to the coping strategies they've been using; the decision to utilize it is always up to them.

As you set the stage for the protocol, focus on the importance of using a timer. This can be an alarm on a clock, cell phone, oven, or egg timer. Each facet of CARESS is deliberately limited to 10 to 15 minutes so clients never become flooded or overwhelmed by the strategy. Because they will often be doing CARESS by themselves, the timer becomes an external resource for boundaries and regrounding and reassures us that they will not become lost in the work.

Clients should set the timer at the start of each CARESS phase. When it goes off, they can either move on to the next phase of the work or reset the timer for one more cycle. At the end of the second cycle, however, clients are encouraged to move on to the next step. Clients are less likely to need to do their self-destructive behavior when they can successfully incorporate all three phases.

It is helpful to explain the function of each phase of the protocol as you walk your clients through the three parts of CARESS. In this way, clients understand the rationale behind each step and are more likely to try all three components. The actual contract is as follows.

CARESS

I agree that when I get the impulse to engage in a self-destructive act, *before* I do, I will choose to incorporate one behavior from each category below. (Set a timer so you have an external boundary to reground you after 10–15 minutes.)

CA: Communicate Alternatively (10–15 minutes)

Hurting the body is a way to communicate feelings, thoughts, needs, and unresolved trauma memories. Here are other, less destructive modalities to communicate:

- Draw or paint the body part and the injury you'd like to inflict; add words to images.
- Draw the emotions that accompany the urge to do something self-destructive.
- Make a collage of words or images that capture thoughts and feelings.
- Write a poem about your feelings.
- Depict the body part with clay and sculpt the injury.
- Write a graphic description of doing your self-destructive behavior.
- Write about what was happening when you felt the urge to do something destructive.

RE: Release Endorphins (10–15 minutes)

Clients feel better after engaging in a self-destructive act because the brain releases endorphins (naturally occurring opiates) in response to pain or body trauma. Here are other ways to experience the release of endorphins:

- Run up and down the stairs or around the periphery of your house, or march in place.
- Do 100 jumping jacks.
- Use a piece of exercise equipment.
- Do a part of an at-home exercise tape, or put on the radio and dance.
- Listen to a funny comedian on a CD or video.
- Watch a funny movie or TV show.
- Watch a YouTube video of a baby laughing or silly pet tricks.
- Read something that tickles you.
- Hold or stroke and hug a stuffed animal or live pet.
- Hug a pillow, rag doll, or tree.

SS: Self-Soothe (10–15 minutes)

Clients need to learn new strategies that promote self-care and decrease anxiety from future triggering events. Here are some additional ways to be comforted:

- Wrap in a quilt and rock in a rocking chair.
- Take a warm shower or bubble bath.
- Light scented candles or oil.
- Read positive affirmations.
- Massage your hands with soothing lotion.
- Listen to a relaxation tape, or play soothing music.
- Slowly blow bubbles to slow down breathing.
- Call a 24-hour hotline to hear a comforting voice.

Let's explore the contract in more detail, so you fully understand how to process it with your clients.

CA: Communicate Alternatively

This phase gives clients another way to show the pain narrative so it can be witnessed, processed, and transcended. The use of right-brain-based creative modalities will make sense to clients once they understand that trauma memories are not stored in the part of the brain that handles language (Broca's area). In addition, their perpetrator's injunctions against telling have made it impossible for them to simply talk about their experiences. Therefore, they need alternative ways to communicate their narratives, accessing them with the help of modalities that bring information forward from the more primitive parts of the brain.

Clients are empowered to choose which communication strategies feel safest and most comfortable for them, because the CARESS model is rooted in the reparative notion of helping clients retain a sense of control. The options are designed to integrate both the right and the left hemispheres of the brain, as this will enable clients to best process and work through the material. As clients select the strategies, it helps to write down their choices on a brightly colored index card or Post-it note. This can also be placed in the CARESS box as a kind of cheat sheet, which further reduces our reliance on clients needing to think clearly when triggering has occurred. The workbook exercise called USING CARESS on page 225 will help your clients plan out their strategies and identify the items they will need to keep in their CARESS box.

One strategy for CA incorporates art therapy techniques to sublimate harmful urges. Clients can draw or collage the body part they want to injure, along with a visual depiction of the actual injuries. They can also mold the body part out of clay and then use their fingernail to show the injuries. This effectively helps them to visually sublimate the depiction of pain and affect that is often etched onto the skin by cutting, burning, or bruising the body.

You can even encourage clients to draw, paint, or collage the words and feelings they vomit when purging or the emotions that accompany the desire to drink, use drugs, starve themselves, gamble compulsively, or sexually act out. This becomes a way for clients to nonverbally articulate and decode the deeper emotional underpinning of these behaviors. You may feel understandably nervous about encouraging art that depicts self-destructive behaviors or intense feelings, fearing this will cause an exacerbation of the behavior. But I have found that helping clients show their pain and communicate their needs and feelings dramatically reduces their desire to actually act on the behavior. Keep in mind that one of our clients' primary goals is to tell their stories and have them witnessed, and art therapy techniques allow them to safely do that.

Although clients are encouraged to use these artistic techniques when they are incorporating CARESS outside of your office, these are strategies that can also be woven into therapy sessions. Clients do, in fact, get the urge to hurt themselves in our offices, particularly when the content of the session is emotionally charged or threatening. Pay close attention to the subtle ways in which these behaviors can take place: pressing innocuous but sharp objects such as pens, pencils, paper clips, or fingernails into the palm of their hand; biting their nails; or pulling their hair. When this occurs, use the gestalt moment as an opportunity to teach clients about the sublimation process as an alternative way to communicate.

Offer them paper, markers, crayons, colored pencils, and so on and direct them to draw what they are thinking, feeling, or wanting to do on their bodies. If clients are unwilling to draw, Koosh balls with elastic strings that can be tugged or a variety of foam or squishy squeeze toys can also be used as alternatives to hurting themselves. The idea is to get the behavior off the body. If you are trained in sand narrative work and have a sand tray in your office, this can be another profoundly helpful way to help clients communicate and process the metacommunication of their actions. Along with the classic items we use in sand tray work to help clients explore their feelings and interpersonal relationship dynamics, be sure to have objects that can represent self-destructive behaviors such as empty, single-serve alcohol bottles; a plastic martini glass; a toy toilet; assorted plastic food; Band-Aids and other first aid items; a fake razor blade and knife; a fake cigarette; money; a pair of dice; and so on.

For clients who have performance anxiety about using art, you can encourage them to journal, write a poem or song lyric, send themselves an e-mail, simply talk into a tape recorder or mini Dictaphone, or leave themselves a message on their voice mail. Regardless of the modality, we want clients to freely express their thoughts and emotions about what they feel compelled to do or to provide information about the nature of the self-destructive behavior. When clients are able to safely communicate by creating a tangible product that can be witnessed and processed—rather than get high, purge, starve, gamble, or leave a cut, bruise, or burn on their bodies—the cycle of helplessness and repeated victimization is short-circuited, and true healing can begin.

RE: Release Endorphins

The rationale behind this phase of treatment is to offer clients additional ways to short-circuit overwhelmingly negative thoughts and feelings through the release of naturally occurring opiates. Remind clients that the reinforcing component of self-destructive behaviors is the release of endorphins through self-mutilation, binge-ing, or purging or the temporary euphoria elicited by substance abuse, gambling, compulsive shopping, or self-imposed starvation. Although our brains release endorphins in response to intense pain, we can also experience this pleasurable sensation through hugging, laughter, and an intense burst of physical activity.

After the timer has gone off and clients have had the opportunity to give a new kind of voice to their pain, moving to this phase of CARESS is a healthier way to short-circuit their upset state. It is again necessary to negotiate with your clients regarding which options they want to try. In this phase of treatment, clients often like a combination of the three strategies, incorporating a few minutes of physical exertion, laughter, and hugging.

When clients want to release endorphins through movement, make sure they are physically fit enough to engage in the activity. This is particularly applicable to obese, medically compromised, or very underweight clients. You should also rule out the possibility that this is an attempt to do "exercise bulimia," a form of purging that juxtaposes excessive exercise with an insufficient amount of caloric intake. If exercise is a safe option, clients can spend 10 to 15 minutes doing activities including doing jumping jacks, running around the periphery of their home, going up and down the stairs, using a treadmill, putting on music and dancing, following an exercise routine from a DVD, kickboxing or shadowboxing, or playing a high-impact motion-control video game system such as Wii or a controller-free motion gaming device such as Kinect.

When possible, the idea is to sustain a high level of exertion so clients feel the endorphin release. Extensive research has gone into studying the positive effects of exercise on mood. In addition to providing a sense of empowerment, heightened control over the body, and a feeling of competence, exercise gives us an endorphin kick, which serves as a healthy distraction and has a positive impact on thoughts and feelings. The release of endorphins enables long distance runners to endure the grueling physicality and discomfort of the race. This same concept resonates for trauma survivors.

The second option involves laughter, a surefire way to short-circuit untenable affect and thoughts. Although a mere smile can have a positive impact, we want to encourage clients to go for belly laughs. This can be accomplished in a number of creative ways. Clients can cue up a funny scene from their favorite movie or listen to or watch the standup routine of their favorite comedian. I have found that incorporating YouTube videos is a great way to elicit laughter and create a healthy distraction. In addition to viewing the treasure trove of TV and movie clips from the past, clients can search for either "silly pet tricks" or "babies laughing." These videos invariably make anyone laugh.

Once again, it is important to process these options with clients ahead of time. If there are unresolved issues related to abortion, miscarriage, infertility, the death of a child, or the loss or death of a pet, then these would not be appropriate suggestions. If, however, you assess that there is nothing emotionally loaded or potentially triggering about the topics, watching a child dissolve into a fit of laughter will evoke the same response in even the most stubborn clients, given the way our mirror neurons work.

The third option, hugging, can either stand on its own or be incorporated into the other strategies. It is important to emphasize that we don't want clients to hug another person. CARESS has to be workable when they are by themselves because they typically are alone when the impulse to do something self-destructive takes over. Having clients wrap themselves in a blanket; hug a pillow, stuffed animal, or doll; or hold a pet usually works. Some clients even like to hug trees! The idea is to release that surge of warmth that we feel when we wholeheartedly hug something. This is also a good place to introduce the EMDR (eye movement desensitization and reprocessing) butterfly hug: placing the arms across the chest and alternating gentle taps on the upper forearms with the palms of the hands. I also like to introduce the concept of "hugging the inner child" by inviting clients to hold a soft pillow close to their bodies while visualizing that they are hugging their younger, innocent self.

SS: Self-Soothe

Once clients have communicated and successfully short-circuited their negative thoughts and feelings, the timer is reset, and we want the end point of their work to be something self-soothing. In truth, they don't know how to do this in healthy ways, or they wouldn't be grappling with self-destructive behaviors. In this regard, clients will need your input and suggestions about how to self-soothe appropriately. Again the emphasis is on activities that can be done solo: clients shouldn't have to wait for the physical availability of someone else to feel better. This might initially feel counterintuitive, as many survivors can be codependent.

Some of the activities that you can suggest might include having clients take a warm shower or bubble bath, listen to soothing music, give themselves a hand massage with their favorite lotion, read a book of positive affirmations or about something spiritual or grounded in the 12-step movement, call a hotline to talk to an empathic person, meditate, sing a lullaby to themselves, hold and drink a warm cup of tea or cocoa, "nest" in pillows and blankets, massage their temples and wrists with a relaxing scent such as lavender, take a short walk through a garden, lie on the grass and watch the clouds in the sky, listen to a guided imagery or relaxation tape, watch an inspiring video, or look through a book of beautiful photography.

It is quite possible that clients will not easily buy into these options as viable, but this is due to the fact that they are foreign and new, not because they are invalid and won't be effective in time. Invite your clients to choose strategies that they have some curiosity about, and encourage them to hold on to the idea that in a short while and with practice and repetition, these behaviors will resonate and feel more comfortable.

Once clients have agreed on several possible behaviors under each of the three categories, make sure they are all written down on an index card. The last step is for clients to gather all of the resources they will need, depending on what they have chosen to do. This might include paper, markers, hand lotion, the URL for the video, a soft blanket, a CD of soothing music, the phone number for the 24-hour hotline, and so on. All of the items should be placed in their CARESS box for easy access.

When clients find the courage to try CARESS, it is important to process what worked and what needs to be renegotiated. Some clients will take to it instantly, doing all three things and reporting a great reduction in self-destructive behaviors. Others will be initially resistant, doing only part of CARESS or just thinking about it without putting any of it into practice. Our job is to be patient, supportive, and encouraging. We should reinforce the smallest baby steps our clients take toward new behavior, never shaming them when they don't follow through. Consistently remind them that when they begin to apply it, it will work. Besides, even thinking about or envisioning new behaviors can have a positive impact on our bodies and brains, so reward clients for taking that meaningful first step.

I want to reiterate that there is something deliberately missing from the CARESS model: calling us when they get the impulse to hurt themselves. Many caring and well-meaning clinicians encourage their clients to reach out to them when they want to hurt themselves or are on the verge of relapsing. Although I appreciate the generosity of this gesture, I believe it is a major mistake. It gives clients the subtle message that they *need* us in order to be OK, which inadvertently creates codependency. It also sets up a dangerous and unrealistic expectation about our availability and our boundaries. Clients should not expect us to be on call 24/7, and we shouldn't be. We want our clients to believe that they have what it takes to heal. CARESS reinforces the notion that everything they need to reconcile their issues exists inside of them.

14

WORKING WITH THE CYCLE

Positive outcomes, negative outcomes, and emotional vulnerability

Positive outcomes

I am a strong believer that we don't continue to engage in a behavior unless we get something from it. This does not imply, in any way, that our clients are masochistic. It does imply, however, that what we do holds conscious or unconscious meaning, expectation, and assumptions. Our clients may perpetuate behaviors to gain mastery, power, or control over something or someone. Other behaviors are chronically repeated because the outcome, or secondary gain, is pleasurable and gratifying. Frequently, behaviors are held on to because clients hope or expect the next time they engage in it an unsatisfying result will finally change for the better. In any case, it is important to address this part of the cycle with clients who chronically engage in self-destructive behaviors.

Some clients can easily articulate what their behaviors do for them, and they understand how powerfully reinforcing the positive outcomes are—even if they are short-lived. Other clients actually feel as if the behaviors hold them hostage. They feel compelled to engage in them, almost against their will, and focus more on the residual shame, guilt, and helplessness they evoke rather than the short-term gains. For these clients, when the positive motivation for engaging in their behaviors isn't clear, they are more likely to see their actions as proof of their "craziness."

The treatment of self-destructive behaviors typically focuses on why they are problematic. From a well-intended place, we might encourage our clients to home in on everything that is dysfunctional or wrong with their behaviors, hoping this will motivate them to stop. From clients' perspectives, this can be experienced as disrespectful and pathologizing and may paradoxically cause them to dig in their heels, clinging even more tightly to their behaviors. When this is operational, many clients become primed to drop out of treatment, legitimately claiming that we don't get it.

When we give clients permission to explore and express the ways in which their self-destructive behavior works for them, we depathologize the issue and deepen the therapeutic relationship by indirectly communicating that we do get it: the behavior serves an important function and feels *necessary* to them. This does not mean we are encouraging the behavior or ignoring the fact that it may be creating serious issues for our clients. However, we are acknowledging that for a *part* of them, the behavior is useful, and in all likelihood there is ambivalence and conflict raging inside about whether to relinquish it (Ferentz, 2011). Richard Schwartz's conceptualization of internal "polarization" (1997) is an excellent point of reference to work from, as is his brilliant notion of "firefighting parts," oftentimes the parts responsible for clients' acting out in self-destructive ways.

This inner conflict needs to be creatively fleshed out in therapy. There are a number of strategies that can be effectively implemented. The first step is to encourage clients to conceptualize the part of them that feels the need to do the behavior. Invite clients to conjure a vivid description of that part: how old it is, what it looks like, how it feels on their body, how they feel when they access this part of themselves. The workbook exercise called IDENTIFYING THE SELF-DESTRUCTIVE PART OF YOU on page 228 offers clients a safe, nonjudgmental way to explore this.

Once the self-destructive part has been identified, clients can be encouraged to let this part speak through writing or drawing. I often have clients use their nondominant hand, as this will evoke less intellectualization and censoring of authentic affect, thought, and memory. Two-handed writing can also be employed by vertically dividing a piece of paper in half, having clients pose questions on one side of the page using their dominant hand, then letting the self-destructive part respond on the other side of the page with their nondominant hand. This can be a great, nonthreatening way to invite a conversation between parts that historically have been adversarial and disconnected from one another. The workbook prompt called USING YOUR NON-DOMINANT HAND TO LET THE SELF-DESTRUCTIVE PART EXPRESS THE POSITIVE OUTCOMES on page 239 will explain this technique.

Forty-year-old Harriet (H) illustrated the power of two-handed writing in this conversation with a self-destructive part (SD) of her that cuts and drinks. You can hear the initial conflict and resentment between the parts and then notice the shift to a more empathic and cooperative stance once they begin really listening to each other.

Table 14.1

H:	Why do you insist on cutting me and drinking?
SD:	You NEED me! If I don't pick up the razor blade or get the alcohol in us then we're screwed. You don't get it!
H:	I think that YOU don't get it. Whenever you cut me or get me drunk, people think I'm weird, and then I have to pick up the pieces—make it look good to the outside world.
SD:	You think YOU have to hold it all together? I'm the one who keeps it together. Why don't you just back off?
H:	Listen, I'm not stupid. If I back off then you take over. Don't you realize how hard my job is? I've got to keep you in check and try to prevent you from acting out.
SD:	Maybe if you'd just let me numb you with cutting or booze then your job would get easier. Did you ever think of that? Just let me do my thing! Stop criticizing me for trying to keep us SAFE!!!!
H:	When I let you do your thing, I get hurt.
SD:	If you don't let me do my thing, you'll be hurt even more!!
H:	So now what do we do???
SD:	You tell me!! You're the high and mighty expert around here.
H:	Well, sometimes I don't want to be the expert!!

SD: Yeah, well sometimes I don't want to have to be the bad guy around here!

H: What do you mean? I thought you loved your job creating excitement, making a mess.

SD: YOU'VE got the good job! You're the one with the answers, the one who makes the decisions, the one who everyone likes at work.

H: I'm tired. It's hard to keep it all together.

SD: I'm more tired! I'm the one with the razor blade. I know I scare the crap out of you. I'm way more alone in here than you are.

H: This is weird. We BOTH feel alone and hated.

SD: It's really hard to be the one who does self-destructive stuff. Have you ever considered that?

H: Not till now. It's really hard to be me, too. I can't back down from you. I'm afraid of you.

SD: I'm trying to protect you so you don't have to remember stuff from the past or feel the feelings that will overwhelm you.

H: Maybe there's other ways to feel protected. I guess I can appreciate what you're trying to do, but the truth is, I feel even more overwhelmed when my body gets hurt again, and that does bring back memories from the past.

SD: OK, but how else can we feel protected?

H: I'm not sure what the answer is yet—I'm just asking you to be open to letting me try something else.

SD: OK.

Another effective tool taken from the Gestalt paradigm is the "empty chair" technique. Clients can imagine the part that does the self-destructive or addictive behavior sitting in an empty chair and then engage in conversation with this part. Allow the empty chair to explain why the behavior feels necessary and what is at stake if the behavior is extinguished. As an aside, processing what will be *lost* if the behavior stops is just as essential as understanding what is gained by doing it (Ferentz, 2011).

Take as much time as is necessary to fully explore these initial questions. It is so important to help clients validate and honor the existence of this part. The long-term goal is to help shift them from their initial reactions of shame, self-loathing, and a desire to disown this part to empathy, compassion, and acceptance. This is often accomplished when we help clients reframe this part's actions as self-protective, encouraging them to explore the ways in which seemingly destructive acts serve a protective purpose. With our guidance, clients can see that their behaviors might protect by isolating them, so intimacy is avoided. This, in turn, decreases the risk of being hurt or rejected. Sometimes protection is achieved through the numbing or distracting effects of their self-destructive behaviors. This keeps out the painful thoughts, feelings, and memories from the past.

Allowing clients to explain the value of their self-destructive behaviors will differentiate the therapy you are providing from all of their prior therapy experiences, and this can bring hope into the room. It also enables clients to gain more insight about the less conscious dynamics that drive and sustain the behaviors. Once they are empowered by these insights, they feel less "crazy." The identification of positive outcomes is also a crucial intervention because it allows you and your clients to be curious about and explore other possible ways for them to accomplish the same ends. Once clients understand the reinforcing power of endorphins, they become more willing to entertain other ways to get that same endorphin release. This brings you back to the value of CARESS and gives clients the opportunity to begin experimenting with hugging, laughter, and physical activity as alternative strategies.

It's also useful to address the fact that hurting the body has the payoff of short-circuiting an uncomfortable dissociative state and can help clients feel reintegrated and reconnected to their bodies. Incorporating some of the regrounding strategies that were discussed earlier in regard to counteracting dissociation can be helpful in this part of the cycle as well. Sensorimotor experiments that allow clients to notice, create, and intensify physical gestures that feel empowering and freeing are a great way to help clients safely reconnect to their bodies, without first eliciting pain. Additional pay-offs can be explored with the workbook prompt entitled LETTING THE SELF-DESTRUCTIVE PART EXPRESS WHAT WILL BE "LOST" IF THE BEHAVIOR STOPS on page 240 and USING THE DOMINANT AND NON-DOMINANT HAND TO ENGAGE IN A "CONVERSATION" ABOUT THE BEHAVIOR on page 241.

Yoga poses and simple movement therapy techniques provide clients with healthier alternative ways to be present in their bodies, rather than relying on physical pain, the sight of blood, sexual arousal, the rush of gambling, or the high of illicit substances to feel alive.

Negative outcomes

Clearly this is a necessary part of the cycle to address, as these inevitable consequences perpetuate the self-loathing and vulnerability that profoundly contribute to the chronicity of the behavior. Many clients come in to treatment wedded to their behavior, buying into the idea that this is the only viable "life jacket" available to them. As a result, they may be initially reticent about owning up to the inevitable negative outcomes that these behaviors evoke. Reassure your clients that a conversation about these outcomes is not synonymous with their agreeing to give up the behaviors before they are ready to do so. This may make them more willing to look at this part of the equation.

When clients can find the courage to put aside their bravado and defenses and acknowledge the downside to their behaviors, they tap into intense issues. We must create a safe enough therapeutic environment for clients to be able to identify the universal feelings of shame, guilt, and disappointment in themselves; anger at their "lack of discipline"; anxiety about their helplessness; fear about disapproval from others; discouragement about the loss of control; and inadequacy and failure. Exploring these issues is a balancing act: We have to continue to hold out hope even as our clients face the painful reality about the toll their behavior has been taking.

Cognitive reframing is essential at this intervention site. Identifying negative outcomes is not meant to be shaming or discouraging. Rather it is an opportunity to see the behavior from a more authentic and integrated vantage point, and for many clients it is the first chance to even consider the possibility that what they are doing is creating more harm than good. It shines a spotlight on the inherently revictimizing component of self-destructive behavior and begins to challenge long-held beliefs that it is a necessary way to reclaim power and control. In their most honest moments, clients begin to acknowledge that everything about the behavior is, in actuality, incredibly disempowering.

When the timing feels right, a powerful intervention can occur at this place in the cycle when we ask clients to consider the possibility that by engaging in behaviors that promote abuse and neglect of the body, their metacommunication is "My perpetrator was RIGHT. I am worthless, and my body doesn't deserve to be nurtured or protected." Ideally, it will be anathema for clients to accept the notion that their perpetrator was right and that their present-day choices both corroborate and perpetuate how they were treated in the past. This can be a breakthrough in treatment.

Even if your clients don't react strongly to this idea, help them access the part of them that does understand how the behavior is so problematic. You can also encourage them to access a remembered resource from the past who would understand the dissonance of agreeing with the perpetrator's actions. When the issue is depersonalized, many clients can be more honest about the downside to their behaviors. It can help to have them write a letter to themselves, from their remembered resource, processing the adverse effects of their self-destructive acts. Writing it through the eyes of a supportive person tends to remove the shame. This writing prompt, A SUPPORTIVE LETTER TO YOURSELF FROM A "LOVED ONE" is in the workbook on page 245.

Fifteen-year-old Valerie was able to write herself a moving letter from her beloved, deceased grandmother. The letter shows remarkable insight and is devoid of the shame or blame Valerie usually exudes when she talks about her sexual promiscuity in the first person.

Dear Valerie,

I feel so sad when I think about you having sex with boys you barely know. I understand that this is a way for you to feel loved, and I wish I was still in your life so I could safely give you the love and attention you really need and deserve. These boys don't really care about you and probably forget about you right after you sleep with them. The problem is that *you* don't forget, and it leaves you feeling ashamed, dirty, and even more alone. No matter how many boys you sleep with, it won't help you feel better about yourself, and the short-term satisfaction that you get when someone agrees to be with you turns pretty quickly to bad feelings—so really, it's not worth it. I love you.

Love, Granny

When your client is ready, a second writing and drawing prompt in the workbook called IDENTIFYING THE WISEST PART OF YOU on page 248 and A LETTER FROM THE WISEST PART OF YOU on page 252 creates opportunities to reconnect with their own wisdom, which can be a huge step forward in strengthening self-compassion and moving them towards true healing.

Because trauma survivors are vulnerable to intrinsically and automatically putting themselves down, another meaningful intervention is to reframe a relapse or setback as an opportunity to learn and grow. When clients feel safe enough to tell us about their relapses, we can use them as teaching moments. It becomes an opportunity to revisit triggers and to retrospectively encourage clients to "rewind the tape," brainstorming with us about the tipping points and what they can do differently the next time they are confronted with a similar situation. This can be strengthened with the workbook exercise entitled RE-THINKING THE MESSAGES YOU GET FROM OTHERS ABOUT RELAPSES on page 254 and RE-THINKING YOUR OWN MESSAGES ABOUT RELAPSES on page 256. You can also help your clients by identifying even the smallest successes in breaking the cycle: they thought about doing CARESS, they acted out for a shorter period of time, they regrounded more quickly, they didn't hurt themselves as severely as they have in the past.

Last, take the time to reassure your clients that you are not disappointed in them. You don't intend to fire them, and you haven't given up on their capacity to grow and change. Given the dynamics of traumatic transference, these clients assume your actions will mimic the same disapproving, distancing, or angry responses they got from their primary caretakers. It is a reparative experience for them to see you hanging in there with patience, empathy, and compassion.

Emotional vulnerability

As you continue to work from their personalized cycle, take the time to process your clients' areas of vulnerability. A great way to help them connect with this is to go back to the body. Encourage them to notice what happens somatically as they sit with the negative outcomes. Does the body become rigid, tense, constricted, collapsed? Clients can more readily access their vulnerable states by noticing what their body is saying through gaze, posture, muscle tone, and breathing. Sometimes the body holds vulnerability in very specific places. Pat Ogden described the patterns that get implicitly imprinted on our bodies and how these patterns give us crucial information about our histories, affective states, and childhood memories. Even more important, the way we use our bodies elicits predictable responses in our interpersonal relationships. Therefore, when our clients somatically manifest vulnerability, the response from others is often an exploitive one, which perpetuates their victimization and helplessness.

At this intervention site, clients greatly benefit from psychoeducational and sensorimotor approaches to assertiveness training. We can help clients reduce their vulnerability in the world by teaching them how to make and sustain eye contact, along with having a conscious awareness of their posture, stance, and tone of voice. Role-playing more assertive verbal and nonverbal responses to potentially triggering scenarios and interpersonal exchanges will help clients slowly gain mastery over their learned passivity.

Clients often need our help in distinguishing between "assertive" and "aggressive." When clients assert themselves, they are able to ask for what they need while remaining sensitive to other people's feelings. When they are aggressive, they ask for what they want without taking into consideration the needs and feelings of others. This was modeled, repeatedly, by their perpetrators. Being assertive is often a new concept for our clients. Growing up with trauma and dysfunction, they are shown only two ways to be in the world: passive (victim) or aggressive (perpetrator). Once they figure out that they don't want to be victims anymore, they tend to initially swing to the other extreme. Working on this issue in therapy allows them to find their way back to the middle, where they can finesse being assertive without feeling like a perpetrator.

Another effective strategy to counteract feelings of emotional or physical vulnerability is a guided imagery technique that invites clients to internally visualize a protective shield of colorful light that surrounds and protects them. They can also tune in to the warmth or coolness of this light or color. They are empowered, assertive, and safe when they are cocooned in this light. Go back to the body and help clients tap into the somatic sensations associated with this newfound sense of safety. Invite them to pair the somatic experience with a cognition that strengthens the notion of being safe and empowered. With practice, this becomes installed as an inner resource that can quickly be called on when clients spontaneously find themselves in vulnerable situations or when they know, in advance, that they will be confronted by something or someone triggering. Clients can practice this exercise, called PROTECTION OF LIGHT AND COLOR, in the workbook on page 259.

Throughout his childhood, 16-year-old Edward had endured a lot of teasing and inappropriately physically aggressive behaviors from his older brother. They grew up sharing a bedroom, so the taunts and painful "wrestling matches" felt relentless, and Edward confessed that he never felt his parents adequately protected him.

Because his brother was too intimidating to confront, Edward had been communicating and trying to process his rage through self-mutilating behaviors. When his brother went off to college, the self-destructive behaviors dramatically decreased. However, his brother was coming home for spring break, and concerned that he would start cutting again, Edward wanted a way to feel safer and less vulnerable in his presence. One of the resources he embraced was visualizing a bronze shield of warm light that gave him a sense of strength and power. He imagined his brother standing near him and intensified the imagery, memorizing the empowered changes he felt in his legs and on his chest and arms. We deepened the experience by pairing the sensations with cognitions that promoted self-protection and self-advocacy. As a result, he exuded a more powerful persona and reported that his brother left him alone when he came home.

Vulnerability can also be reduced when therapy focuses on strategies designed to improve limit setting. This often takes the form of teaching clients how to say "no" in a way that is convincing and believable. The more in sync a verbal "no" is with clients' body language, the less taken advantage of they will feel. In addition, we need to help clients redefine the boundaries in many of their personal and professional relationships. This will initially feel counterintuitive, and they will need your permission to hold those newly formed boundaries. They will also need assistance in working through their fears and anticipatory anxiety about how others will receive these new boundaries. This can be explored with the workbook exercise called IDENTIFYING AND RE-THINKING BOUNDARIES IN SIGNIFICANT RELATIONSHIPS on page 261.

Finally, clients benefit when we encourage them to seek out and strengthen their external network of support. Normalizing for clients their need and right to attach and socially engage with others helps to repair earlier losses and gives clients the experience of not being so alone in the world. At its core, emotional vulnerability is rooted in not feeling tethered to anything, and self-destructive acts perpetuate this sense of isolation. As we support our clients in their endeavors to reconnect, we help them heal primitive attachment issues and offer them newfound resources for comfort and affect regulation. In time, this renders self-destructive behaviors unnecessary, and this becomes the first step toward being able to let them go. The workbook drawing or collaging prompt entitled CREATING AN IMAGE FOR CONNECTION AND ATTACHMENT on page 264 will help strengthen this idea.

In the last section of the book, we'll shift the focus from helping our clients to helping ourselves.

PART III

HELPING OTHERS
WHILE TAKING CARE
OF OURSELVES

15

FOCUSING ON US

In the world of trauma treatment, the clinicians who are drawn to the field are often trauma survivors themselves. This can be quite advantageous if the therapist has resolved his or her own issues. Along with a sound clinical knowledge base, the reconciliation of traumatic experiences can bring a unique level of empathy and understanding to the work. This enables us to join with clients on a deeper level. Yet Rothschild (2006) posed an important question when she asked, "Is it possible that empathy is a double-edged sword, wielding both help and harm? Does the same tool that facilitates our understanding of our clients also threaten our well-being at times? The short answer is yes" (p. 10).

We increase the likelihood of burning out when our empathic responses don't have accompanying good boundaries or create inappropriate expectations about our roles. Alderman (1997) reinforced this idea when she cautioned, "Too much empathy and you may lose your objectivity and become over invested in your client's progress" (p. 193).

When therapists have transcended their own pain narratives, they can serve as inspiring role models for clients, offering a genuine sense of hope and reinforcing the notion that one can be a successful, happy, grounded, and highly functioning adult, despite a difficult past. If, however, we have not adequately resolved the impact of prior dysfunctional experiences, working with this presenting problem can be particularly difficult and triggering. "As a trauma survivor (you) have an additional response that makes understanding and managing your reactions both more difficult and more complicated" (Matsakis, 1996, p. 114).

By definition, we are required to maintain an outward focus in our work. In all of our professional training, the emphasis is placed on our clients: what they need and how they think and feel. Our assessments flow from listening and observing, to reading between the lines, to interpreting subtle verbal and nonverbal cues including tone of voice, word choice, and body language. All of this demands a heightened awareness of our clients and their processes. The stakes are even higher when we are treating self-destructive behaviors, as the emergent need to assess for client safety can put us in a constant state of hypervigilance during a session.

Although this outward focus is necessary and goes a long way toward enhancing our efficacy and strengthening the therapeutic alliance, it often detracts from our ability to monitor our own internal processes and experiences. It is extremely challenging to hold a twofold awareness during sessions: juxtaposing an outward focus on clients with a simultaneous inward focus on ourselves. Ironically, helping professionals don't think to ask themselves, "What do *I* feel right now?" or "What is the impact of this emotionally charged material on *me*?"

Charles Figley (1995) wrote extensively on compassion fatigue and eloquently described "the transformation in the therapist's inner experience resulting in empathic engagement with clients' trauma material" (p. 151). In short, he said the toll this work takes on us is "the cost of caring." Therefore, when we work with trauma survivors and ignore our own inner process, we are at increased risk for vicarious traumatization and secondary PTSD.

Bearing witness to clients' self-destructive behaviors adds to our vulnerability. The very nature of the behavior is unsettling at best and can evoke anxiety, genuine concern, self-doubt, and even fear in us. Alderman (1997) described the pain we are vulnerable to feeling when bearing witness to our clients' pain. When we mistakenly take ownership of fixing the behavior, putting all of our energy into trying to get clients to stop their harmful actions, the emphasis on the "other" is even more intensified. Figley (1995) suggested that even when the therapist is not a trauma survivor, "the presence of a survivor client in our office is an inescapable reminder of our own personal vulnerability to traumatic loss" (p. 154).

To work productively with this issue, it is imperative that we acknowledge and monitor our inward responses. "Unlike with other professions, being a competent therapist requires simultaneous exploration of one's inner world and private thoughts" (Wicks, 2008, p. 82). Achieving this dual awareness by focusing on our client and simultaneously noticing our own cognitive and emotional processes may feel counterintuitive to therapists who are trauma survivors. However, we will have greater success treating this issue when we understand and accept the notion that we are only as effective professionally as the extent to which we take care of ourselves personally. In essence, we must learn to take our own emotional temperature and pulse before we can be truly helpful to our clients. We cannot successfully ground them if we are not grounded. Robert Wicks (2008) reinforced this idea when he stated, "When vicarious PTSD disrupts the clinician's frame of reference, the results may change his or her world view, sense of professional and personal identity, and spiritual, psychological, or philosophical outlook" (p. 36).

As we take on the challenging work of helping clients reconcile their pain narratives, we must also make a commitment to take care of ourselves. Let's explore some of the more common concerns that can arise in this work, along with some concrete ways to enhance our sense of safety and containment while maintaining appropriate boundaries. Sometimes our ability to engage in self-care gets hijacked by potential clinical pitfalls that can emerge in this work. As we process ways to help ourselves, we will simultaneously identify the pitfalls to be mindful of and avoid.

All of these scenarios and self-care strategies are equally applicable to clinicians who do and don't have prior histories of trauma, abuse, and neglect. Although you will find that many of the strategies are also applicable to our clients' need for enhanced self-care, be sure to hold a "dual awareness" and consider the ways in which you can personally benefit from some of the self-help exercises.

The therapist vignettes that elucidate and normalize these pitfalls are compilations of various experiences I have had consulting with and treating talented and caring clinicians who specialize in working with trauma and self-destructive behaviors.

16

CREATING A SENSE OF INTERNAL AND EXTERNAL SAFETY

Clinicians who work with trauma survivors understand the imperative of establishing internal and external safety before beginning to address emotionally charged material. It's common knowledge that clients will become flooded, abreact, be unable to access or integrate new insights, and potentially terminate therapy prematurely if we don't create an enhanced sense of safety for them throughout the therapy process. Ironically, it may not occur to us as mental health professionals that we, too, need to feel a genuine sense of internal and external safety before moving forward with such challenging and fatiguing cases. This is one of the first applications of the dual awareness concept: taking care of our own sense of safety while simultaneously attending to our clients' ongoing comfort level.

When we look at the notion of external safety, we are talking, in part, about the aesthetics and logistics of our practice settings. We should pay attention to the layout of our office space: where we sit in relation to our clients, the phone, the windows, and the door. For clinicians who are trauma survivors, it can be triggering to be with a client's pain. This triggered state can be exacerbated when we feel physically trapped or disempowered in our own office. External safety is further enhanced or compromised by office decor. Everything from the color of our walls to the decorations, artwork, and office smells can subtly affect our physiology throughout the day. Given the amount of time we spend in our office space and the "toxic" energy that permeates it, making it as visually pleasing and comfortable as possible becomes an essential consideration.

You probably have the ability to be in control of the office decor if you are in private practice. There are many clinicians, however, who rent space from other professionals or work in larger agency, hospital, or school settings. There is certainly less control in those cases. Yet it is worth considering the positive impact of placing a scented candle or potted plant on a desk or a calming picture in a small frame or using appropriately soothing music within the confines of your office space. "The idea is to have a 'power object' or activity that can help you to remain rooted in now, in yourself, and in your office rather than slipping into you or your client's past or distress" (Rothschild, 2006, p. 179).

The concept of internal safety is powerful because we have a much greater sense of control over it, regardless of the office setting. It begins with an increased awareness of our physiological responses and is enhanced by a willingness on our part to make whatever internal cognitive and somatic adjustments we need to make to strengthen the experience of feeling grounded in our bodies and in the present moment. "We are most vulnerable to compassion fatigue and vicarious traumatization when we are unaware of the state of our own body and mind" (Rothschild, 2006, p. 103).

Therefore, toggling back and forth between an awareness of our clients' process and our own responses helps us to track and monitor the extent to which we are operating from and sustaining a sense of safety. Noticing if our own breathing is quick and shallow, slow and deep, or being held, and focusing on the constriction or relaxation of our musculature and the extent to which we feel dissociative or "forward" create a road map for self-awareness. Rothschild (2006) cited several studies substantiating the idea that the lowest rates of professional burnout and debilitating levels of stress were found in professionals who had the highest degrees of body awareness.

In truth, as clinicians we are capable of great insight. This can certainly translate into ongoing awareness. Self-awareness, however, is only half the battle. The other half of the equation is acting on what we know by implementing behaviors that truly promote safety and self-care. When we tap into sensations that tell us we aren't feeling completely safe, we need to *do* something about it! Otherwise the same symptomatology that unsafe clients experience—flooding, abreactions, loss of focus and concentration, the inability to process new insights—will adversely affect our practice. In essence, the clarity of our thinking is profoundly influenced by the extent to which we feel comfortable and safe in our practice settings (Rothschild, 2006).

Potential pitfalls

- We focus exclusively on our clients' safety while we ignore our need for personal safety.
- We disregard or forget to monitor personal physiological responses during a session and as a result do not stay grounded and present.
- We minimize the importance of counterbalancing a sterile practice setting with objects that are visually pleasing and soothing.
- We forget the sequence of a session, including taking the time to get personally grounded before moving forward with triggering or toxic client material.
- We inadvertently undermine our own credibility by not practicing what we preach.

THERAPIST VIGNETTE

Steve, a seasoned therapist, contacted me to consult on a case involving a 35-year-old female client who had dissociative identity disorder. He was concerned that every time he opened the waiting room door, his client looked spacey, and he was spending much of the session trying to reground her. The client also reported that when leaving his office, she always felt a strong compulsion to hurt herself and would often do so in the parking lot. In addition,

(continued)

(continued)

Steve was worried that her lack of progress was rooted in his own feelings of constant fatigue and mild depression during the workday. This was somewhat surprising to me, as I knew Steve to be a first-rate clinician who was deeply empathic toward his clients.

Colleagues typically come to my office for consultation, but circumstances dictated that I meet with Steve at his office. This turned out to be a blessing in disguise. As I reenacted his client's experience of parking in a somewhat darkened lot, walking through a maze of office buildings until I reached the elevator for his suite, and then walking down a long, slightly mildew-smelling hallway, I was able to quickly theorize about what was happening for this client. Entering his rather drab waiting room, I was ushered into his office: a nondescript small space with no windows.

When I rewound the tape for Steve, walking him through the sensory experiences that were associated with reaching his office, he slowly began to understand the impact it was having on his client. Apologizing profusely, he explained that he was only renting the space from another colleague. None of the office furnishings were his, which I believed was taking a toll on his affective state as well. We began to brainstorm about simple ways he could bring a greater sense of warmth and security to his office, including adding a few plants and posters and placing a vial of scented oil and a CD player with soothing music in the waiting room. The bigger challenge was the triggering trek from the parking lot to his office. I urged Steve to consider finding an alternative space if he were to continue treating traumatized clients. He had become so inured to his surroundings that he lost sight of the extent to which it was compromising his clients' and his own sense of safety and comfort.

Within a few months, Steve successfully relocated, finding a space with windows where clients could park three steps away from the entrance to the office. Not only did Steve report that his traumatized clients seemed more grounded in the waiting room, he noticed that he felt far more energized and effective in his work as well.

Putting it into practice

1 The creative strategies we use with our clients to enhance a sense of safety are equally applicable when we are attending to our own needs. One of the best resources for safety is a collage that brings together an assortment of words and images that activate our parasympathetic systems and evoke a state of calm. Take a trip to your nearest bookstore and invest in a few of the pricier travel, mountain, and beach magazines with appealing glossy images. Cut and paste the words and images on either colored paper or cardboard. If the collage feels too unwieldy to keep in your office, take a picture of it with a digital camera and either print out a small color picture for your desk or download the image to your cell phone or computer's screen saver where you can have easy visual access. Just as we invite our clients to build on their self-soothing resources, we can deepen the sense of safety that the collage evokes by pairing it with grounding cognitions that keep us focused on the present and the sensation of being calm.

2 Take the time to access or create an inner image that you associate with safety. Using all of your senses in this guided imagery, focus on what you see, hear, smell, taste, and touch in your safe place. Deepen the internal experience by adding conscious breathing to the image as you notice the effect this has on your body. You can also bring on board positive thoughts that you use for grounding and empowerment. Once you have the imagery, consciously place it somewhere in your peripheral vision—above, below, or to the left or right of your sight line. Now, imagine a stressful or triggering situation with one of your clients. Notice the subtle or overt changes in your body and your breathing as you visualize this encounter. Holding that experience, "look" to where you placed your image of safety, along with the thoughts and feelings that go with it, and "pair" it with the more upsetting scenario. Practice bringing the calmer, gentler thoughts

and feelings into your body as you continue to sit with the triggering client interaction. Using a classical conditioning approach, you can train yourself to quickly move from stressful events to the visual, somatic, and cognitive resources that represent safety. In this way you can avoid getting stuck in a stressful encounter, decreasing the likelihood of activating fight, flight, or freeze responses.

17

ASSESSING YOUR AGENDA

As I have stated repeatedly throughout this book, we can't fix our clients or make them stop the behavior before they are ready to do so, despite our best intentions. Alderman (1997) articulated this eloquently when she said, "You cannot make your clients stop injuring themselves—nor can you make them want to stop injuring themselves. All you can do is provide an atmosphere in which change is possible" (p. 195). This can be hard to accept, but we will experience professional burnout unless we let go of this agenda.

Confusion about our clinical agendas often has its roots in our own unresolved family-of-origin issues. For example, "I couldn't get my father to stop drinking or cure my mother's depression, but I *will* get my clients to stop engaging in self-destructive behaviors." It isn't a coincidence that unresolved issues from childhood find their way into our work, although this is often an unconscious process. Think of the workplace as an opportunity to unconsciously reset the stage with the same script and familiar players that existed in our families of origin. It is deceptively easy to replicate our emotionally loaded past experiences within the context of work.

For many adults, looking back on the childhood experience of not being able to fix or change a troubled parent feels like a failure. Never mind that a child does not possess the power or control to change another person. Adults somehow think they should have known how to do it. Gravitating toward a helping profession and interacting with troubled clients create a second opportunity to fix or change what couldn't be fixed or changed in childhood. In other words, the agenda to rescue people or solve the problem is not completely altruistic when it connects to our own unfinished business. The ante is upped when our sense of self-worth and self-esteem becomes contingent on getting others to change their behavior. We will continue to struggle with a sense of failure when we operate from this mind-set. We cannot take ownership of and responsibility for stopping a behavior that we do not have the power to terminate.

Wicks (2008) called on us to practice from a place of "scrupulous honesty," understanding our agendas, our defensive coping strategies, and the games we may play with others in the name of protecting our own vulnerabilities. The more we understand our own agendas and motivations, the more our clients' behaviors and defenses will make sense to us.

Our work with clients will also be ineffective if we develop a treatment agenda from a conscious or unconscious place of anxiety, anger, or fear or the desire to rescue and reparent. This keeps the agenda stuck on a narrow path, a dance between the provocative behavior, the clients' resistance to change, and our need to change them. In this case, our clinical efficacy may be compromised.

Looking at this through the lens of the Internal Family Systems model, when we operate from parts of ourselves that are frightened, overwhelmed, angry, or anxious, we lose our objectivity and our ability to stay grounded, compassionate, and nonjudgmental. Goulding and Schwartz (2002) wisely encouraged therapists to pay close attention to their own parts, acknowledging any potential interference and, if necessary, "getting those parts to step back and trust the Self," or, if need be, to process with the client when the work is being adversely affected by the intrusion of the therapist's parts.

Maintaining an ongoing conscious awareness of the clinical process, and an honest assessment of our intentions, is at the heart of good psychotherapy and best serves our clients' needs. Taking the time to identify, clarify, revisit, and renegotiate the agenda is a pivotal part of the work. Keep in mind that "self-awareness is an ongoing, dynamic undertaking that requires daily attention" (Wicks, 2008, p. 131).

Potential pitfalls

- Our treatment agendas and goals are rooted in our unrequited issues and unmet needs and do not reflect what our clients want and need to accomplish.
- We interact with our clients from an anxious, angry, or fearful part rather than from our most grounded adult self.
- Our treatment strategies are based on a desire to fix or change our clients' behaviors.
- Our sense of self-worth becomes contingent on the extent to which our clients cooperate and change during the course of treatment.
- We feel responsible for the outcome of treatment.
- Our agenda becomes rigid and fixed early in treatment and is not revisited and renegotiated throughout the course of treatment.

THERAPIST VIGNETTE

Sandy was a dedicated clinician who entered the field to make a difference in the world and to help others in ways that she had never been helped when she was growing up. Sandy grew up with a violent alcoholic father who never agreed to treatment and died estranged from her. Sandy's mother stayed with her husband, never confronting him on his addiction and never allowing her children to bring it up at home.

At a young age, Sandy was savvy enough to realize that the family dynamics were dysfunctional, and she even intuited that her father's drinking was "not normal and probably the source of a lot of conflict in our home." Growing up, Sandy had many fantasies about her family confronting her father. She fervently wished

(continued)

(continued)

that her mother would find the courage to leave her father, and she experienced much despair when her mother would shame her for not wanting to collude with the family's lies.

After graduate school, Sandy specialized in working with trauma survivors, and her supervisor called her "a natural." She related to her clients' issues because they were often a reflection of her own personal experiences. As a beginning clinician, Sandy felt a "rush of freedom" when she talked openly about the dysfunctional dynamics in other people's families. She tried to transfer her exhilaration to her clients, encouraging them to speak the truth about the pain they endured.

Oftentimes, however, Sandy felt perplexed by clients who didn't seem to want to speak the truth. She would try to persuade clients to confront the secret keeping and colluding in their families. She frequently pushed clients to hold interventions with alcoholic family members, even if they didn't express a desire or an emotional readiness to deal with the subsequent fallout. She felt a surge of self-doubt and questioned *her* abilities as a clinician when she was unable to persuade a client to follow this course of action.

After a session when Sandy actually got overtly angry at a client for not confronting her alcoholic sister, Sandy began to realize that the agenda she was pushing in the therapy room was rooted in *her* unrequited need for confrontation and intervention growing up in her family. To her credit, she temporarily stopped taking on clients with a family history of addiction and began her own psychotherapy, determined to resolve her issues rather than project them onto her unwitting clients. Although she was initially concerned that she chose the mental health field for all the wrong reasons, as she continued to reconcile her painful past, she slowly discovered that with an enhanced awareness about not letting her own agenda dictate the direction of treatment, she could actually bring more to the table than the average clinician and could, in fact, make a difference in the lives of her clients.

Putting it into practice

1   Find a place to sit quietly and comfortably, and begin think-
    ing about the clients in your caseload who engage in self-
    destructive behaviors. See if you can focus on the content
    of these sessions. On a piece of paper answer the following
    questions:

    a   What are the specific treatment goals we are addressing
        in therapy?
    b   Whose goals are they: the clients' or my own?
    c   Have the goals been explicitly articulated and agreed on?
    d   Do we check back to make sure we are still on track? Do
        the goals need to be updated?
    e   Are we too focused on the behavior and ignoring the
        metacommunication and/or trauma narrative that lives
        underneath?

    Give yourself permission to frequently revisit these questions
    during the course of treatment.

2   Ask your client to respond to the same five questions and
    compare your answers to theirs. Look for similarities and dis-
    crepancies in your perspectives. Renegotiate or clarify the
    goals so they are more in sync. Periodically revisit the ques-
    tions to hold you and the client accountable for staying on
    the same page in treatment.

18

BEING CLEAR ABOUT YOUR CONTROL ISSUES

Self-destructive behaviors create many opportunities for potential power struggles, especially when standard safety contracts are an integral part of treatment. We must be clear about what we can and can't control. Wicks (2008) emphasized this in his work as well, noting the loss of energy and the wasted energy that results from a refusal to let go of the things that are not within our control to change. Operating from a place of humility, we have to let go of what we can't control.

Instead, we can put energy where we can be most influential and impactful: educating and supporting our clients, helping them to become curious about and compassionate toward their behaviors, and serving as good role models for self-care and self-protection. The notion of helping clients to approach their behaviors from a more compassionate point of view is one of the cornerstones of the Internal Family Systems model and a profoundly helpful concept to hold on to throughout the treatment process (Goulding & Schwartz, 2002).

If you are a trauma survivor, relinquishing control can be quite triggering and frightening. We may be operating from a childhood credo that says, "You can be safe only if you are in control." Although this is a cognitive distortion, it's a thought that survivors come by honestly. In childhood, perpetrator behavior was synonymous with being "out of control" whether the verbal or physical rage came from a parent's drunken stupor or acts of sexual abuse were activated in a dissociative state.

Therefore when someone is out of control, it means something bad can happen. Clearly we need to reconcile this issue, as our desire for excessive control will compromise the therapeutic alliance by retraumatizing clients who already feel helpless and disempowered in their relationships with authority figures.

The dynamic of control is a powerful and loaded issue in treatment. Clients with trauma histories had to relinquish a tremendous amount of control in their lives. Their self-destructive behavior is a misguided attempt to reclaim some semblance of control. Therapists who personally struggle with the issue may inadvertently create power struggles with these kinds of clients. This can manifest as subtly or overtly pressuring clients to be compliant and obedient. The therapeutic alliance is severely compromised once this dynamic takes hold.

In essence, the perpetrator–victim dynamic is now being recapitulated in the therapist–client relationship. Once clients believe they have to be accommodating to be safe and respected or to sustain their relationship with us, they are back in victim mode. They will either increase their acquiescence to please us or aggressively push back to show us who's boss. In the end, we are left with either clients who think, feel, and behave in ways that keep them disempowered and helpless or clients who up the ante and act out more. In both cases, these dynamics can paradoxically lead to an increase in self-destructive behaviors.

Potential pitfalls

- We can engage in power struggles with our clients by imposing standard safety contracts to alleviate our own sense of anxiety.
- We make the continuation of treatment contingent on our clients' willingness to stop their self-destructive behaviors.
- We do not allow our clients to establish the ongoing pace of therapy.
- We foster codependency by intimating that our clients can't get better without our help.

THERAPIST VIGNETTE

Several years ago, I was asked to provide clinical consultation to an eager young staff who worked in a residential treatment facility. Their client population—female adolescent trauma survivors—had extensive histories of self-mutilation. The concern was a sudden exacerbation of acting out and self-mutilating behaviors despite the fact that there were serious consequences and a loss of privileges whenever safety contracts were disobeyed.

It became clear to me that the well-meaning staff was inadvertently evoking power struggles with the teens. Their rigid insistence on standard safety contracts almost became an invitation for the girls to up the ante and increase their acting-out behaviors. The staff believed that adherence to strict rules, including the consequence of being separated from peer-group activities if cutting occurred, was in the adolescents' best interests.

Further processing of their policy revealed an undercurrent of anxiety coming from the mental health professionals, and this seemed to drive their clinical decision making. Their treatment philosophy was mired in a need to maintain control over the girls at all times. The girls clearly needed to feel that there were rules and boundaries, but the notion of "keeping them in check" had more to do with the staff feeling burned out, overwhelmed, and, at times, frightened by the teens' cutting behaviors.

It was particularly important to point out the paradox of responding to clients who were plagued by attachment issues with the consequence of separating them and *increasing* their sense of isolation when they acted out. Obviously, this was creating a vicious cycle: the need for attention and connection (inappropriately communicated through cutting) was met with further alienation and disconnection from others (being punished with isolation).

The idea of approaching their cutting from a different angle was not immediately embraced by the staff. The fear of not being able to control the teens surfaced in our discussions. But this very need to control was also a recapitulation of the perpetrator–victim dynamic that these girls endured in their families of origin and explained, in part, why they were having trouble trusting and joining with staff.

To the great credit of the clinical director, we began to explore a different treatment approach. We processed the idea of fostering cooperation rather than blind obedience, responding to cutting with CARESS (every girl got her own CARESS box), and actually looking for ways to enhance the teenagers' awareness of what they *could* appropriately control in their lives. We also provided staff with more retreats for self-care and more didactic trainings to help them understand the metacommunication of self-destructive behaviors. The impact on both staff and the adolescents was enormously positive.

Putting it into practice

1   Sitting comfortably in a quiet place, close your eyes and take a moment to visualize being in session with a client who chronically engages in self-destructive behaviors. Imagine yourself calmly and respectfully saying to the client, "I don't own your behavior, and I accept that I cannot control your choice to engage in it or not. That decision is entirely up to you." Notice the thoughts, emotions, and body sensations that come up for you when you sit with this visualization. If you become aware of fear, anxiety, anger, tension, or any other sensation, acknowledge it, without judgment, as you breathe. If it feels safe, give yourself permission to explore on a deeper level the root source of those responses. Feel free to write down your observations and insights. Be sure to breathe through the visualization. See if you can access the part of you that genuinely understands that the client's problem is not yours to fix and allow that loving and compassionate part to reassure you that it's all right to relinquish control.

2   Take a piece of paper and draw a line dividing the page horizontally and then vertically. Label the top left box "What I can control" and the top right box "What I can't control." In the top left box, make a list of all of the things you can

control in your work with self-destructive clients. Then move to the top right box and make a list of all the things you cannot control. Now move to the bottom left box and make a list of all of the concrete ways you can act on what you can control. This might include educating your clients about the dynamics of self-destructive acts, providing clients with concrete and emotional resources for support, offering clients healthier strategies for containment and affect regulation, and working with clients in a nonjudgmental way. Last, move to the bottom right box and make a list of how you can concretely let go of what you can't control. This might include "turning it over" in a spiritual way, engaging in positive self-talk to quell anxiety and calm yourself during sessions, seeking consultation so you are accountable for your actions, reminding yourself to breathe and stay physically grounded during sessions, listening more and problem solving less, and encouraging clients to be more proactive while you take a backseat.

19

HOLDING APPROPRIATE
BOUNDARIES

One of the greatest temptations we are faced with when working with clients with self-destructive behaviors is our desire to make ourselves a part of the safety contract (i.e., "Call me when you get the impulse to hurt yourself."). In fact, this behavior is fully encouraged by the mental health community. Many formulaic safety contracts used by mental health agencies and private practitioners include "calling the therapist" as a part of the safety plan. However, I believe it is imperative that we *don't* put ourselves into a safety contract. Clients should never perceive us to be their lifelines, as that would be an unrealistic, unfair, and unhealthy view of our role. It's also a potential recipe for disaster. If we buy into this socially sanctioned idea and find ways to be available to our clients 24/7, we are inadvertently modeling poor boundaries and setting ourselves up for professional burnout. If our clients are not clear about the limits of our availability, we are setting them up to feel grave disappointment, rejection, and outrage when they call and we are not available.

Our clients need to believe and trust that they have the fortitude, resources, and creativity to work on their issues—whether *we* are available or not. And we need to believe that about our clients as well. Keep in mind that they are survivors: they found ways to cope before we were ever in their lives. Granted, they need guidance in accessing healthier coping strategies, but we can often underestimate their resiliency and overestimate the extent to which they need us. To this end, it is essential that we teach clients containment and self-soothing as soon as possible in an effort to reduce their reliance on us, especially outside of sessions. When we work to install resources for the client, we are simultaneously decreasing their dependency on us.

Along the same lines, we shouldn't put more effort and energy into the treatment process and the attainment of treatment goals than our clients do (i.e., never do more for clients than they are willing to do for themselves). This breach of boundaries will inevitably breed resentment on our part, create codependency, impede client growth, and make progress our success—not theirs. Yet if we grew up with our own dysfunctional family, we may have spent an entire childhood putting more energy into the parent–child relationship than our parents did. Rothschild (2006) highlighted the notion that many psychotherapists had and have the role of caretaker in their families-of-origin and are used to putting others first. In this case, our template for meaningful relationships includes the cognitive distortion that says, "I have to be the one to work really hard to win over the other person so I am liked and appreciated and reassured that the client will stay connected to me." We need to be mindful of not inadvertently reenacting this with our clients.

In addition, we must be willing to set limits with clients, communicating what is and is not acceptable. This is not synonymous with telling clients what to do or how to live their lives. Instead, it is a "reality check" about appropriate versus inappropriate choices. Although we can't make clients attend AA or incorporate CARESS, we can weigh in and suggest that these options would be beneficial. We certainly have the right to refrain from doing a therapy session when clients show up intoxicated or high or to insist that they turn over their car keys when impaired.

Limit setting is often a life skill that was never modeled, reinforced, or honored in our clients' abusive families-of-origin. By definition, caretakers who parent in ways that are neglectful or traumatizing are unable to set appropriate limits with their own behaviors. This gets normalized for clients, and as they grow their inability to set limits translates into tolerance for abusive adult relationships and tolerance for self-destructive behaviors.

Therefore, despite the fact that it may be uncomfortable for us, setting limits with our clients gives them a gift that can translate into heightened safety and self-respect. It also helps them introject the concept of a lower threshold for unacceptable behavior in self and others.

Trauma survivors are known for their "testing" behaviors, and we have a responsibility to them and ourselves to never promote or endorse inappropriate boundaries in the client–therapist relationship. Clients can get mixed or confusing messages about the parameters of the therapeutic alliance when we don't maintain good boundaries. As stated earlier, this can lead to unrealistic expectations, inappropriate assumptions, and hurt feelings. However, having clear boundaries with self-destructive clients is particularly challenging, as we may feel an ethical obligation to be available to these clients more than our other clients. Rubin and Springer (2009) concurred that the needs of traumatized clients can seem overwhelming, and as a result, therapists can feel responsible for their clients' well-being and safety.

This increased sense of responsibility often leads to longer work hours with fewer breaks and less support. The thought of a client potentially relapsing, purging, cutting, or engaging in unsafe, unprotected sex can activate the "anxious caretaking part" of any well-meaning clinician. We may feel compelled to return their phone messages more quickly, text them, allow them to engage us in e-mail conversations outside of therapy, or repeatedly check in with a vulnerable client who isn't reaching out to us. Although this seems like the responsible thing to do, we have to wonder if this communicates to clients that they need us in order to be OK. It may also reinforce the notion that our mutual attachment and connection revolves around, and is informed by, the self-destructive behavior.

I do not mean to imply that clients who are in true crisis should be ignored, but a great way to reduce the likelihood of clients going into crisis is by installing and ramping up their internal and external resources for comfort and support as early as possible in treatment. Part of good boundary setting is giving the message, early on, that you have faith in their ability to internalize the lessons of therapy and subsequently call on them when needed.

There is another subtle but powerful and detrimental by-product that develops when we don't hold good boundaries with our clients. Many years ago, when I was a graduate student, I remember sitting in session with a newly recovering alcoholic young woman who was telling me about her abusive childhood. As she dispassionately described horrific physical abuse at the hands of her father, I began leaning toward her until I was, literally, on the edge of my seat. My face was full of expression: empathy, sadness, and anger over her maltreatment. As I got more and more emotionally invested and animated, a curious thing happened. She sat all the way back in her chair, folded her arms across her chest, grew silent and calm, and smiled at me. It was both eerie and revelatory. I was doing the emotional work for her—so she didn't have to experience it! It was a gross misstep on my part, a blurring of the boundaries and a message to her that I would own the emotional work in the room. Fortunately, I realized what was happening and forced myself to sit all the way back in my chair. This gesture subtly reconfigured the boundaries.

Without limit setting we may also jeopardize our own sense of safety. Ongoing attention must be paid to personal safety for clinicians who are trauma survivors, otherwise there is the likelihood of disabling flashbacks, the perpetuation of a victim mentality, and clinical missteps rooted in distorted assessments and poor judgment.

Potential pitfalls

- We put ourselves in the safety contract by insisting that our clients contact us when they get the urge to engage in a self-destructive behavior.
- We identify these clients as "special" or "different" and use those labels to justify or rationalize a lack of limit setting or boundaries.
- We show preferential treatment for these clients by being available after hours, allowing them to accrue debt, and continually going over the allotted session time.

- We become enmeshed in our clients' lives by overidentifying with their narratives or working after hours to help them.
- We do the emotional work for our clients by getting overly upset or angry or being moved to tears during session.

THERAPIST VIGNETTE

With the advent of e-mail and texting, I encountered a new kind of blurred-boundary violation when consulting on cases. Terry had many years of experience working with clients who engaged in eating disordered behaviors. Despite her expertise, she contacted me to discuss a specific case because she felt there was something about her work with this client that was creating an unfamiliar feeling of resentment and leading to burnout. As I listened to Terry describe, in glowing terms, all of the great strides her client had made in treatment, including the establishment of a trusting therapeutic alliance and a dramatic decrease in bingeing, I felt puzzled by the source of her resentment.

Then Terry produced a large stack of papers and said with a sigh, "This is the stuff that I resent." In all, there were more than 50 e-mails between Terry and her client. Some of the back-and-forth correspondence occurred late at night, and much of it was on weekends. What emerged were enmeshed boundaries. Interestingly, much of the content was emotionally charged or crisis oriented or revealed the kinds of insights we hope clients come to during the context of a therapy session.

When I asked Terry why she allowed her client to correspond through e-mail, she explained that it seemed to ground the client and helped her to feel more connected to therapy. As is often the case, Terry never intended for the e-mails to become a dominant form of reciprocal communication. Therapists will often say to their clients, "You can e-mail me if you feel compelled, but I won't e-mail you back." Clients instantly test this by pushing the boundaries and sending missives that are either crisis oriented,

(continued)

(continued)

laced with self-destructive thoughts or suicidal ideation, or filled with meaningful insights that intrinsically demand a response. Given that caring and concerned clinicians do respond, you have the makings of a runaway train.

It's difficult for us to extricate ourselves from an e-mail or texting relationship once the precedence is established. There are several obvious problems, not the least of which is the need to always be on call and immediately responsive. We can actually feel like we are being held hostage by e-mails. Ironically, clients start doing their "best work" behind the safety and anonymity of a computer screen or cell phone. But we lose the ability to factor into the equation critical nonverbal cues: facial expressions, body posture, tone of voice, and dissociative dynamics.

Also, consider the possibility that hitting the "send" button is a way for clients to disavow ownership of thoughts and feelings, turning them over, instead, to us. In addition, e-mails that are pseudotherapy sessions collude with the perpetuation of inappropriate, even invasive, boundaries. It was no wonder that Terry resented a client she actually cared deeply about.

Of course, retraining the client is easier said than done. Terry was particularly concerned about asking her client to give up a strategy that seemed to help her gain insight and self-expression. Because I felt strongly that Terry's client should not text her (we text with family and friends), I suggested that the client continue to type her thoughts on the computer, print them out, and bring them into the therapy session and not send them through cyberspace. In addition, I encouraged Terry to let the client read the e-mails out loud in session rather than just hand them over. This promoted ownership, allowed Terry to observe her client's emotional and nonverbal responses, and ultimately fostered much better boundaries between them.

Putting it into practice

1   Revisit your safety contract. Make sure you are not encouraging clients to call you when they get the impulse to engage in a self-destructive behavior. Turning to CARESS is a better option, as

it doesn't require the availability of another person to get them through a vulnerable period. It actually *strengthens* the idea that they have the inner resources to help themselves and to heal. Notice how it feels when you give yourself permission to extricate yourself from the contract. Your reactions may range from relief to guilt or a temporary increase in anxiety. Take time to validate and process these emotions. If your clients insist on interactive support, instruct them to incorporate other community resources including calling 24-hour hotlines, getting online Internet support from reliable organizations, or contacting a sponsor from a 12-step support group. These resources ensure an immediate response, helping clients to feel validated and heard.

2   Before starting a difficult session, take a moment and imagine that you are being shielded in a protective beam of colored light, just as we described when helping clients with their emotional vulnerability. Choose a color that feels soothing, and allow yourself to notice the temperature of that light. Intensify the color and the warmth or coolness of the light if you know the clients' material will be particularly challenging or triggering. In whatever way feels safe, imagine you are being cocooned in this soothing, protective light. Keep the image present in your mind throughout the session, knowing that you have the power to strengthen your protective shield as the session intensifies. This image can serve as a metaphor for an invisible boundary between yourself and your clients' toxic material. In addition, repeatedly remind yourself to sit back in your chair, put both feet on the floor, and exhale while the session unfolds. These simple gestures can enhance your sense of boundaries, reminding you that you don't own your clients' issues.

3   To imprint the above exercise using a sensorimotor psychotherapy technique, take a moment, close your eyes, and visualize sitting in session with an emotionally trying client who struggles with self-destructive behaviors. Focus on a circumstance where he or she is testing your boundaries, by either continually relapsing, demanding more of your time, or disclosing a particularly painful trauma experience that would cause you to "lean in" or want to work overtime to help her or him. Notice what you

experience on your body as you sit with that scenario. You may be able to even access the part of you that gets the most activated by the challenges of boundary setting. Incorporating the Internal Family Systems model, you can acknowledge and validate that part and then gently ask it to step to the side. Staying with your imagery, begin to lift one or both of your hands and arms into a defensive pose that says, "Stop." Notice the sensations it evokes on your body. Experiment with raising and lowering your arms, close to your body and further away from your body, until you find a pose that evokes a feeling of protection and boundaries. Because we often can't literally raise our arms in session, asking clients to back off or halt, you can install this as an internal resource by visualizing moving your arms without actually doing so. See if you can access the same physical sensations on your body. You can go back to this sensory visualization when you are in session and feel an internal struggle or ambivalence about setting a limit. Imagining your arms moving gives your body the message about boundary setting. This can either serve as a private reminder or compel you to verbally assert a needed boundary with the client.

4   When clients ask you to do something that tests the limits of healthy boundaries, ask yourself two simple questions: "Would I do this for *all* of my clients?" and "Would I be comfortable sharing what I'm doing with all of my colleagues?" If the answer is not a resounding "yes" to both questions, you may be on that slippery slope of playing favorites that often is the precursor to blurred boundaries. Therapists who are trauma survivors may unconsciously feel compelled to go the extra mile for their most vulnerable clients. These two questions are the litmus test for appropriate decision making within the client–therapist relationship. Apply them to issues including repeatedly going over the allotted time for a session, seeing clients after normal business hours, being asked by clients to see them outside of your office, making phone calls and pursuing resources for your clients, reducing or waiving your fees, or allowing clients to accumulate debt.

20

UNDERSTANDING YOUR TRIGGERS

It is imperative that we understand what triggers us when we work with this population. We can be triggered when clients express emotions such as rage, sadness, guilt, shame, depression, or despair. The triggering might be attributed to our own discomfort about the open expression of these emotions. If we've grown up in families that didn't model or allow for the healthy expression and reconciliation of these feelings, we may be anxious about not knowing how to help our clients manage them.

Perhaps we are worried that the affect will escalate to the point where the client will be unable to handle it. Or a particular emotion might hit too close to home, reflecting the same unresolved emotions in us. Sometimes the clients' inappropriate expression of a feeling mirrors the way someone in our own life exhibited that emotion. And at that moment, we are no longer grounded in the present time. Conversely, we can be triggered by "silent" clients, those who are highly dissociative or who have no emotional vocabulary and are never able to identify or express what they feel.

We can be triggered by the specific content of charged trauma narratives that resonate with our own experiences. At times we are fully aware of our own narratives and know when the client's story begins to echo our own. But there are also times when we can be caught off guard, and midway through the client's retelling of a traumatic event, we discover that pieces of it rekindle our own suppressed memories. Needless to say, this can be disquieting, even terrifying when it occurs. The accompanying involuntary experience of our own fight–flight or freeze responses can hijack our "professional self" during the session. When we are triggered, our adrenal glands are activated, we lose the ability to distinguish the past from the present, and our emotional, cognitive, and somatic responses can flood and overwhelm us (Matsakis, 1996).

For clinicians who are survivors, sometimes the trigger is the client's presentation of neediness, helplessness, or passivity. The more vulnerable the clients, the more we feel compelled to fix them or, conversely, distance ourselves from them. Our sense of them as impotent can even evoke a feeling of revulsion in us, particularly when it activates an internal feeling of unresolved self-blame about our own traumatic childhood experiences. Consider the situations where we were unable to protect a sibling or parent from abuse, never reported or confronted our abuser, or never felt a sense of vindication or justice about our trauma. In these cases, our own triggering might cause us to bully clients into taking a course of action that is either unsafe for them, contraindicated, or premature.

Clients who engage in self-destructive behaviors often present with false bravado when talking about their prior abuse. They use intellectualization (talking about their experiences with no affect), rationalization ("I deserved the abuse because I was a difficult kid"), and minimization ("It wasn't so bad; it could have been worse"). They employ these strategies to avoid dealing with the deeper pain that lurks underneath. Those defense mechanisms might reflect our own prior coping strategies, evoking intense discomfort in session. As a result we may be unreasonably hard on clients for using these defenses, or being inured to them, we might neglect to recognize their dysfunctionality. We are doing our clients a disservice in either case.

Countertransferential responses can also be activated when clients don't initially integrate what they are learning in session or stubbornly refuse to let go of their self-destructive behaviors. We can feel justifiably frustrated when clients attempt to "pace" the work by canceling appointments or "forgetting" what was processed in prior visits. When we become triggered and personalize these behaviors, this frustration can lead to deeper feelings of intense anger, rejection, and self-doubt. Just as we work with clients to identify and protect against their triggering events in the cycle of self-destructive behaviors, we must identify our own triggers and find ways to address them so our work is not compromised.

Rothschild (2006) reminds us that our countertransferential responses may manifest on our bodies, as much as they play out emotionally, cognitively, and in our behavioral choices.

Potential pitfalls

- We don't realize that we are responding emotionally to our clients' behaviors because we have been personally triggered.
- We don't have an awareness of the kinds of clients and presenting problems that are likely to trigger us.
- We get angry at a client's helplessness because it mirrors our own historical sense of disempowerment.
- We confuse a client's behaviors with someone from our family-of-origin who acted in a similar way.
- We take it personally when clients relapse, "forget" session material, refuse to follow through with a homework assignment, or cancel sessions.
- We discourage our clients from discussing specific behaviors or prior trauma or revealing a self-inflicted wound because we feel triggered or overwhelmed.

THERAPIST VIGNETTE

Robert was an experienced therapist who ran a psychoeducational group for male trauma survivors struggling with sexual addictions. Stuart, a close colleague, co-facilitated the group. Robert had received feedback from Stuart that he seemed to be very impatient with and not very empathic toward one of the younger men in the group. At Stuart's urging, Robert consulted with me to take a closer look at what was transpiring during group.

(continued)

(continued)

With great insight he admitted he felt frustrated by how slowly this group member worked and got agitated when the client processed the same material over and over in session. Robert felt concerned about the slowness of this member's recovery and said he worried about the client's vulnerability toward relapsing. "I try really hard to empower him, but he acts helpless a lot of the time, and if I'm totally honest about it, it actually pisses me off, although I feel embarrassed saying that!"

Robert quickly took to my reframe that the client's slowness might be a way of pacing the work, and his behavior could be useful information about his need for more containment or a greater sense of internal–external safety. But it was equally important for Robert to process his own frustration and anger without any judgment or self-reproach. When asked to consider the possible countertransferential dynamics, Robert recognized that the client's attempts at pacing triggered feelings of incompetence and inadequacy in him. "When the client seems to be stuck, I ask myself what *I'm* doing wrong. It's funny, but I don't ever think that Stu is doing anything wrong! I put that on me."

Given my responsibility to hold good boundaries, deeper exploration of Robert's countertransference went beyond the purview of consultation. But Robert felt comfortable enough to say, "This is my stuff coming up. When someone doesn't get better fast enough, I worry about relapse, especially in a young person. I feel responsible for fixing it—like I did with my younger brother growing up. And if they don't hurry up and get well, I feel like I own that." I encouraged Robert to pursue those important insights with a caring therapist. We also discussed the option of taking a break from co-facilitating the group, after the current one ended, in an effort to reduce the triggering until he felt his own issues were reconciled. Although the idea of not co-leading the group didn't feel like an option to Robert, he was willing to talk with a therapist, which seemed like a great step forward.

Putting it into practice

1   Find a safe, peaceful environment. Make yourself physically comfortable. Take a few moments and think about some of your more challenging clients and their emotionally charged therapy sessions. Now take the following "Countertransference Questionnaire," focusing on what you think, how you feel emotionally and somatically, and how you behaviorally respond when confronted with these various clinical scenarios. There is no formal scoring. You cannot fail. Simply use this information to nonjudgmentally increase your self-awareness so you can take the necessary precautions to reduce or manage personal triggering when it surfaces during a session.

A   When a Client Is Verbally Angry or Aggressive During Session
I think . . .
I feel . . .
On my body, I experience . . .
I behaviorally respond by . . .

B   When a Client Presents as Depressed or Hopeless
I think . . .
I feel . . .
On my body, I experience . . .
I behaviorally respond by . . .

C   When a Client Discloses Childhood Sexual Abuse
I think . . .
I feel . . .
On my body, I experience . . .
I behaviorally respond by . . .

D   When a Client Discloses Physical Abuse or Neglect
I think . . .
I feel . . .
On my body, I experience . . .
I behaviorally respond by . . .

E   When a Client Tests the Boundaries in Session
     I think . . .
     I feel . . .
     On my body, I experience . . .
     I behaviorally respond by . . .

F   When a Client Explores Material That Resonates for Me
     Personally
     I think . . .
     I feel . . .
     On my body, I experience . . .
     I behaviorally respond by . . .

G   When a Client Accuses Me of Not Understanding or Not
     Caring
     I think . . .
     I feel . . .
     On my body, I experience . . .
     I behaviorally respond by . . .

H   When a Client Cancels Repeatedly
     I think . . .
     I feel . . .
     On my body, I experience . . .
     I behaviorally respond by . . .

I   When a Client Discloses Self-Destructive Behavior
     I think . . .
     I feel . . .
     On my body, I experience . . .
     I behaviorally respond by . . .

J   When a Client Relapses
     I think . . .
     I feel . . .
     On my body, I experience . . .
     I behaviorally respond by . . .

21
ACKNOWLEDGING YOUR VULNERABILITIES

You may be particularly vulnerable when working with this population if you grew up with parents with a substance abuse problem, an eating disorder, a gambling or sexual addiction, or other forms of destructive behavior. This is especially powerful if your parent is not in recovery or died without recovering. Unresolved feelings of rage, resentment, grief, and helplessness that live within us can easily be rekindled if our clients relapse or are not ready to relinquish destructive behaviors. Because we are human, these countertransferential responses can find their way into session and are noticed by clients who are hypervigilant.

Working with traumatized clients who engage in self-destructive behaviors can be daunting even for therapists who grew up in loving and safe families. For clinicians who carry the extra weight of coming from their own dysfunctional backgrounds, there is an even greater predilection toward secondary or vicarious traumatization. For traumatized clients who already have a history of personalizing and owning the thoughts, feelings, and behavioral choices of others, it is likely that they will own our emotional responses too. This will shift their treatment agenda, heightening their external focus and compelling them to take care of us. In addition, these countertransferential responses can easily blur our clinical agenda, compromising our ability to do what is in the best interest of our clients.

It isn't always easy to be a clinician who practices from a place of humility. Clients come to us brimming with expectations and fantasies about who we are and what we do. In addition to thinking we are "the expert" with all of the answers, clients often believe we have it all together and lead perfect lives outside of the office. These assumptions are inadvertently reinforced because we sit on the opposite side of the patient's couch. Sometimes we can fuel the fantasy by refusing to engage in even the most superficial level of self-disclosure. When we reveal nothing about ourselves to clients, they fill in the blanks on their own, creating life scenarios for us that are devoid of stress, dysfunction, or discord.

Although it is not appropriate to divulge personal struggles to our clients or to take the emphasis off of them and let the spotlight rest on us, we have to at least be honest and humble within ourselves, recognizing our vulnerabilities and attending to them, so our efficacy and our personal sense of safety are never compromised.

We can all relate to the dynamics of feeling helpless, inadequate, or overwhelmed when the presenting problem is self-destructive behavior, even if it doesn't trigger us or personally resonate for us. We can depathologize these feelings by acknowledging that they are an integral part of the human condition. We can also model self-care by attending to them whenever they surface and by working from a grounded place—before and after sessions.

In the novel *The House of God* by Dr. Samuel Shem (1995), the repeated recommendation given to new medical residents when attending to a patient who is experiencing a medical crisis is "the first pulse to take is your own!" This is sage advice, as our efficacy is rooted in our own ability to be grounded and calm. Because we do challenging work that focuses on the ways clients hurt their bodies, we must have an awareness of our own bodies. We can use our own physiological responses as a somatic and emotional compass that will help us understand our deeper reactions to clients' behaviors. This, in turn, can remind us to increase self-protective strategies during sessions when needed.

Potential pitfalls

- We forget to exude humility in our work.
- We refuse to engage in even superficial self-disclosure and inadvertently communicate a superior air.

- We engage in too much self-disclosure, which keeps the spotlight on us, increases our vulnerability with clients, and offers them a distraction from their work.
- We don't maintain a dual awareness so we can notice and attend to our inner process as we simultaneously monitor our clients' processes.

THERAPIST VIGNETTE

Years ago, I was working with a client who was a trauma survivor and was grappling with eating disordered behaviors. She had forged a strong therapeutic alliance with me, often quoting my words, verbatim, months after I had articulated them in a session. During one visit, we were working on an issue that was serious and upsetting to her. As I tried to emphasize a point I was making, I gesticulated too dramatically with my hands, and the cup of tea I was holding went flying all over me. I jumped up, trying to stop the hot river that was flowing down my skirt and chair. I'm sure my face was red, and I looked as flustered as I felt. My client's reaction both surprised and confused me: rather than expressing concern or helping me with the mess, she started to laugh.

Once I got my own countertransference back under control, I asked her about her response. She quieted down and then said with great seriousness, sincerity, and relief, "In all the years I have been working with you, this is the first time that I actually believe you are human and fallible. I'm glad that you're capable of spilling tea all over yourself, because now I believe you can really understand my struggles. I always thought you cared—but I wasn't sure if you really understood my feelings of inadequacy."

This experience has always stayed with me. It reminds me that I have to recognize and attend to my own vulnerabilities, while appropriately communicating and normalizing humility through the client–therapist relationship.

Putting it into practice

1 When you are working with clients who engage in self-
   destructive behaviors, think about how you can address
   your own need for affect regulation and grounding. Begin
   by incorporating breath work, making sure you fully exhale
   throughout a session. When we bear witness to upsetting
   material, we often respond by unconsciously holding our
   breath. Sometimes this is a part of the freeze response, and
   sometimes we do it to listen more carefully. Try this experiment: Imagine that while you are reading this, someone
   suddenly comes up to you and says, "Listen! There's a scary
   noise in the next room." What happened to your breathing?
   Most people stop in their tracks, hold their breath, and listen. We do this as clinicians during sessions because we are
   so attuned to our clients. In our stillness, we listen to their
   words and their nonverbal communication as well.

2 You can also strengthen a sense of being grounded and
   reduce vulnerability through increasing your awareness of
   your body posture; pressing both feet into the floor; applying a subtle, comforting self-touch; and using internal positive self-talk to stay calm during difficult sessions. Although
   it may seem counterintuitive, make sure you lean back a bit
   when the client shares toxic material. Gently cross your arms
   and stroke your upper forearm with the other hand. In addition to your own self-soothing, this also activates our clients'
   mirror neurons, which will have the effect of evoking their
   parasympathetic system and de-escalating them as well.

22

PACING THE SESSIONS

Most of us who work with clients' trauma and pain narratives understand the need to properly pace the sessions. We toggle back and forth between the activation and the deactivation of our clients' sympathetic systems, keeping the work manageable by avoiding emotional and cognitive flooding. So too should we consciously pace the rhythm and type of sessions we schedule throughout our workday. Appropriate pacing enables us to regroup and reground in between clients and helps us maintain a sense of balance throughout the week.

Be cognizant of when you schedule challenging clients throughout the day and throughout the week, noticing when you schedule them in relation to other clients with similar issues. It's not recommended to do back-to-back sessions with this population, as mental and physical fatigue will take a toll on your concentration and the quality of your work. "Cumulative exposure to traumatic material and a lack of diverse job responsibilities increases the risk of vicarious traumatization" (Rubin & Springer, 2009, p. 247).

It's also more likely that you will get backed up if you see several clients in a row who are all grappling with self-destructive behaviors. This is understandable, as these clients present with affect dysregulation, ambivalent attachment issues, unclear boundaries, testing behaviors, and dissociative tendencies. They may require additional time for containment and regrounding. Although we work hard to end a session on time, it's not unusual to run a few minutes over. However, running

5 minutes over with each morning client quickly translates into being 20 minutes late for your afternoon ones. It also eliminates your opportunity to shake off a session or go to the bathroom, eat lunch, or catch your breath between clients. Cozolino (2004) emphasized strategies for pacing when he encouraged us to schedule breaks during a workday, avoid overbooking, and continually monitor our emotional and physical reactions to sessions. He also encouraged us to make adjustments to our workplace routines when needed.

For some of us, the idea of pacing our schedules is easier said than done. To have a balanced calendar, we might have to say "no" to new referrals. Because we have deep empathy for this population, we might feel guilty turning anyone away, especially when it seems like only a limited number of mental health professionals understand and work with clients with self-destructive behaviors. We also take great pride in being accommodating and may find it hard to reign in our availability, always opting to schedule appointment times based on what's most convenient for clients and not what works best for us. Wicks (2008) stressed that one of the many ways to strengthen your self-care protocol is to "know your physical and mental limitations and to learn how and when to say no" (p. 60).

Many clinicians believe that if they restrict their evening and weekend hours, they'll severely compromise their ability to maintain thriving practices. This has the subtle effect of one being held hostage by one's practice. It may breed resentment and, eventually, burnout. Ironically, the aforementioned anxiety is usually unfounded: clients who are grateful for your expertise are quite willing to see you whenever you have office hours.

There is an even bigger societal challenge that comes into play, as we are acculturated to associate long work hours with greater dedication to our jobs. The professionals who get the gold watch and the retirement dinner are the ones who put in 16-hour workdays. Yet it is safe to assume that their professional efficacy, the quality of their lives, and their interpersonal relationships are profoundly compromised. The better clinician is not the one who works longer hours; it is the one who works with balance and pacing and has a full life outside of the office.

Potential pitfalls

- We schedule too many complex clients back-to-back without the opportunity to regroup or reground if needed.
- We overbook clients.
- We never turn down new referrals for fear that it will limit our practice and eventually lead to a decrease in financial solvency.
- We buy into the mind-set that dedicated clinicians work overtime, and never go on vacation, or take sick days and mental health days.
- We don't limit prime evening or weekend work hours for fear that our clients will not be flexible with their time, resulting in a longer workweek for us.

THERAPIST VIGNETTE

Martin had been working for a community mental health agency for years and had recently decided to start a part-time private practice. He hoped to be financially successful enough to quit his agency job and work full-time on his own. Eager and talented, Martin never turned down a case. His practice grew quickly, and he developed a great reputation among his colleagues as someone who was always willing to see even the most challenging clients. Soon Martin was working the equivalent of two full-time jobs.

Martin claims that he was quite happy and would have continued at that pace. His wife, however, grew more and more frustrated by his long work hours. Martin said the "straw that broke the camel's back was when I started seeing more clients on weekends." Historically, this was family time, and Martin was showing up less often at his kids' sporting events and extended family gatherings.

(continued)

(continued)

As is often the case, Martin rationalized his workaholic pace by claiming it was the only way to build a successful practice and the only way he could accumulate the necessary expertise to work with such a tough population. In addition to working the long hours, Martin was scheduling tough cases back-to-back. He figured out that he could see 7 clients in 6 hours if he didn't take a break in-between. Given the fact that his caseload was so challenging, his clients took longer to reground at the end of a session. As a result, he began running over with many of them, and his workday grew longer. His wife pointed out that by day's end, 7 clients were now taking close to 8 hours of his time.

Martin did not acquiesce readily. His good intentions, coupled with anxiety about the viability of his practice and an underlying connection between self-worth and professional success, made him initially resistant to change. In the end, the unhappiness that it brought to his wife and children, along with a grudging admission of his growing exhaustion, forced Martin's hand and created an opportunity for him to reexamine the way he paced his private practice.

Putting it into practice

1   Accessing your most self-protective part and using your most objective eye, sit down with your appointment book and go through your day-to-day scheduling. Use data from several typical weeks in your practice. As you begin to revisit how you've scheduled your clients, take a moment and notice how your body reacts. Is there a sensation in your stomach, throat, or jaw or another place on your body? Do your palms get sweaty? Are you aware of your heart racing or heaviness in your chest? Observe, without judgment, whatever sensations emerge. Trust that your body is your best compass in terms of letting you know the true impact that your work schedule has on you.

2 Staying in this place of heightened awareness, continue to review your schedule and allow yourself to honestly answer the following questions on a separate piece of paper:

a Do you give yourself enough breaks throughout the day? Can you stop to go to the bathroom or to get a drink of water?

b Do you give yourself adequate time to reenergize or "shake off" in between clients?

c Do you schedule a sufficient amount of time for lunch every day?

d How many challenging clients do you schedule in a row?

e When do you have the most energy—at the start, middle, or end of the day? Have you booked your clients accordingly?

f Is your calendar balanced with activities that have nothing to do with work?

g What one small thing could you begin to do differently to enhance your pacing?

3 As you revisit these questions, make sure you answer them from your most compassionate and self-caring part. If you are a trauma survivor or a driven professional, you may have, as Jay Earley and Bonnie Weiss (2010) identified it, an unforgiving inner critic or an anxious, people-pleasing part that weighs in, refusing to afford you the level of self-care you really need. If you find it difficult to cut yourself any slack, take a moment to visualize someone in your life who loves you dearly and has only your best interests at heart. This can be someone currently in your life or a beloved figure from your past. Now go back to the questions and answer them again, responding in the way that your loved one would if he or she were looking at your appointment book.

23

DEBRIEFING AFTER
DIFFICULT SESSIONS

It is essential to physically release what our body retains so we don't hold on to our clients' energy or toxic narratives. Given the realities of confidentiality, we don't have many places to release what we've held on to all day. If we are not careful, each session can feel like a 50-pound weight has been placed on our shoulders. Imagine the cumulative effect when we are shouldering the weight of 6 or 8 clients. In fact, for therapists who are trauma survivors, much of the material that comes out in sessions can physiologically evoke a flight–fight response.

Because it isn't practical for us to bolt from a session or cover our hands over our ears when material is upsetting and triggering (although we'd often like to do just that), the only viable coping response is to freeze. Many therapists report feeling "spacey" during these kinds of sessions, and some actually dissociate. This can manifest as our losing our peripheral vision, feeling as if we are floating above the therapy room, seeing the client's mouth move but not hearing what he or she is saying, zoning out, going cognitively blank, often needing to stifle a yawn, losing sensation in our bodies, or needing clients to repeat themselves many times throughout a session.

Even when we externally go into a freeze response, internally our bodies are revving for a flight–fight response. Debriefing and releasing that pent-up energy is critically important. A physically suppressed or truncated fight–flight response is a major cause of subsequent somatic symptoms such as headaches, muscle tension, and stomach upset. It's not a coincidence that by Friday many clinicians have migraines, back and neck pain, and GI upset. Just as we recognize the therapeutic value of encouraging our clients to vent, share, and release their inner experiences, we must be mindful of our own need to do the same.

Charles Figley (2002) offered "the 3:1 ratio" rule as one important strategy for reducing compassion fatigue: "For every three hours of discussing a case that is traumatic, there should be one hour devoted to personal processing" (p. 215). Whether this is handled formally or informally, the goal is to bring attention to our own need for debriefing.

When we don't debrief, we bring the toxicity of the day home with us. This can unfairly impact interactions with our children and significant others, sapping us of the spontaneity, positivity, and vitality we want to bring to these relationships. Holding on to the emotionality of the workday is also fatiguing. It reduces the likelihood that we will have the energy to engage in hobbies that counterbalance work or important acts of self-care such as exercise. As we lose the vigor to do proactive and healthy self-care, we may become more vulnerable to unhealthy self-medicating behaviors such as drinking and overeating as a way to unwind after a difficult day.

Potential pitfalls

- We don't take the time after a difficult session to shake off the experience.
- We don't use supervision or peer consultation to process a tough session or get additional feedback about how to move forward with our clients.
- We don't notice the physical harbingers of our own dissociative responses, a clear indicator that we are being triggered or feel overwhelmed.
- We ignore the somatization of our stress and the subsequent increase in physical pain and discomfort it creates.

THERAPIST VIGNETTE

Vera was a social work grad student doing an internship in a psychiatric hospital. Many of the patients had been diagnosed with dissociative disorders and engaged in a wide range of self-destructive behaviors. Vera was eager to please and fascinated by the complexities of her caseload. She was encouraged to schedule back-to-back sessions to see as many clients as possible in the course of a week. Her enthusiasm for the work sustained her for long periods, and then she realized she was feeling dizzy and uncomfortable toward the end of the workday. This actually escalated into feelings of anxiety and a growing concern that she wasn't being effective with clients she saw in the latter part of the week.

Although Vera continued to ignore these red flags, she finally became concerned when she began experiencing feelings of derealization during some of her sessions. "It's almost like I am on the ceiling, looking down at myself doing therapy with my clients. I'm losing a sense of connection to them, and it's starting to scare me."

When we looked at what Vera was doing to debrief after her challenging sessions, it became clear that she was simply holding on to everything she witnessed, without decompressing or even processing what she had been exposed to every day. Vera admitted that she was reluctant to discuss her cases with her supervisor. Worried that she would be seen as too green and inexperienced, Vera wanted to impress her boss to maintain job security. She told herself she could handle it all and was completely unaware of the toll her work was taking on her mental and physical health.

Without consciously realizing it, Vera was actually in a freeze response during many of her interactions with her clients. Vera was overwhelmed by their complex trauma narratives and struggling with her own feelings of incompetence, and her outward professional facade belied her internal anxiety and the ongoing activation of her sympathetic system.

When she got home, unwinding often consisted of reading more clinical textbooks to stay on top of dissociative disorders.

Vera was able to see how all of this was weighing her down and came to understand that she needed to start shaking off these difficult client encounters by building breaks for self-care into her workday and reaching out to her supervisor for feedback, processing, and debriefing. In addition, Vera signed up for a spinning class at her local gym and quickly discovered the value of physically releasing what she was holding on to all week.

Putting it into practice

1 After a triggering or emotionally charged session, consider closing your office door and engaging in an activity to self-soothe. Use scented hand lotion or light a small candle for comfort and aromatherapy. Hold a mug of warm coffee or sweet-smelling tea in your hands, and listen to soothing music to help activate your parasympathetic system. Do some deep breathing as you look at pictures of loved ones on a cell phone or a screen saver to help you regroup and reground. Doodle on paper or color in part of a mandala (a circle with a symmetrical pattern in it) to feel a renewed sense of focus and boundaries. Have a book of positive affirmations handy, and read a few pages to cognitively reground.

2 After a session that leaves you dissociative or spacey, do a quick burst of physical activity (doing jumping jacks, shaking out your extremities, or swinging your arms and legs) to release what you have held on to during the session. Splash cold water on your hands or face, suck on an ice cube, open a window, or step outside for fresh air. You can also listen to music that wakes you up or read a paragraph from a magazine to get back into your left brain.

3 If you need to get rid of a client's particularly toxic narrative of abuse or a self-destructive act or the unsettling sight of a client's self-inflicted wound, either write down a brief description or scribble something with markers or colored pencils to represent the material. You can also make a symbolic representation of the material out of clay. Then allow

yourself to either contain it by placing it out of sight in a
drawer or envelope, tear up what you've written or drawn,
or squash the clay and get rid of it. This can be a powerful
reminder that you don't need to hold on to the client's material. It will also help to clear your mind and release body tension before your next client enters the room.

24

UNDERSTANDING THE CORRELATION BETWEEN FAMILY-OF-ORIGIN AND WORKPLACE DYNAMICS

It is not a coincidence that so many trauma survivors are attracted to mental health and helping professions. Survivors can bring special attributes to their professional work including the ability to read other people; great listening and problem-solving skills; deep empathy and compassion for the underdog; the capacity to stay grounded, focused, and intellectualized during crisis; an intense work ethic; and firsthand knowledge about the impact of trauma and the healing process.

All of these strengths can come into play for us as therapists after family-of-origin and subsequent traumatic issues have been identified and reconciled. Unfortunately, professionals who have not done their personal work can find themselves in toxic workplace scenarios, reenacting dysfunctional interpersonal dynamics with supervisors, colleagues, and clients.

It is so helpful to have awareness about the possible connection between our family-of-origin dynamics and current interpersonal and professional relationships. It also helps to understand the ways in which those dynamics are rekindled and replicated through interactions with clients and colleagues. Childhood experiences of feeling invalidated, invisible, powerless, misunderstood, unsupported, and unappreciated can all be replicated in the workplace and in relationships with self-destructive clients. As this unfolds, we may not realize how difficult it is to work on a tenacious issue such as destructive, harmful acts or a triggering issue such as childhood abuse or neglect, while we are simultaneously impacted by stress, mental and physical fatigue, and other somatic symptoms.

Remember that working with traumatized clients is not a linear process. Their ongoing ambivalence about attachment, receiving help from others, sharing their pain, and changing dysfunctional behavior—even when it is clearly healthier for them to embrace these things—is a pervasive part of the work. Adding insult to injury, many agency settings that deal with traumatized clients have their own toxicity or dysfunction built right in to their systems.

This can manifest as not providing adequate emotional support for clinicians, normalizing a workplace culture of being overworked and underpaid, operating from vague or constantly changing job descriptions, placing unreasonable demands on staff, minimizing or ignoring staff contributions, discouraging "out of the box" thinking, or adding layers of stress through mountains of seemingly unnecessary paperwork. This means that for clinicians who grew up in discordant, chaotic, or abusive families, the client–therapist relationship and the context of the workplace can evoke powerful triggering.

Clients' inevitable inconsistencies, broken vows to change, empty apologies for their insensitivities, accusations that "we care about them only because they pay us," and unpredictable, defensive, aggressive, or crisis-driven behaviors can be quite unnerving. The deceptive nature of clients who secretly engage in eating disordered behaviors, acts of self-mutilation such as cutting or burning, or substance abuse can quickly elicit childhood feelings of rage, helplessness, anxiety, and fear in us. The unsupportive, shaming, or condescending supervisor or colleague further exacerbates our vulnerable state.

The face of our own unrepentant, neglectful, abusive, uncaring parent can easily and unconsciously superimpose itself onto a client, supervisor, or colleague. All of the implicit memories we have about that person transpose themselves onto the client–therapist or collegial relationship. Issues including their narcissistic agenda to hurt us, the inevitability of the "other shoe dropping," our need to be hypervigilant, the intrinsic sense of things being hopeless, or our feeling unsafe in their presence can routinely infiltrate our thoughts, feelings, and body sensations while distorting our clinical judgment.

Taking it one step further, if we grew up with trauma, we were denied a carefree childhood and probably lived in a family that was joyless. It would make sense that once we found ourselves in the job world, we would unconsciously seek out and stay with a job that was joyless or oppressive. This is not because we are masochistic. Rather, an environment that is reminiscent of our past is familiar to us, and we are all most comfortable with what we know. Sadly, what *doesn't* resonate and feels dissonant is a workplace where we are treated with respect, allowed to use our voice, and encouraged to actually have fun.

Potential pitfalls

- We stay in a workplace that is toxic, unsupportive, or dysfunctional because it resonates with our family of origin.
- We don't realize that there are healthier places to work, and we don't need to settle for a dysfunctional work environment.
- We stay in a workplace with an unsupportive or clinically incompetent supervisor.
- We don't recognize that we have power in adulthood that we did not possess in childhood, which means we can extricate ourselves from a dysfunctional workplace and seek out healthier places to grow in our careers.

THERAPIST VIGNETTE

Carl's anger was palpable when he said during a therapy session, "I hate where I work. I feel totally unsupported, grossly underpaid, and buried alive in meaningless paperwork. And if that wasn't bad enough, my supervisor is a paper pusher who hasn't worked clinically with a client in probably 30 years." This was a familiar refrain in our work: Carl often bitterly complained about

(continued)

(continued)

his job working as an LCPC in a hospital setting. It was an equally repetitive refrain for me to ask Carl what he wanted to do about his untenable situation. And true to form, his answer was always, "You don't really get it—there is *nothing* I can do about it. It's just the way it is—it's that golden handcuffs thing. I have to grin and bear it until I am old enough to retire." Given that Carl was only in his early 30s, that seemed like an awfully long wait.

The juxtaposition of incessant complaining and a stubborn belief that nothing could be done about it was adversely impacting Carl, mentally and physically. He was completely and depressingly wedded to the idea that he was trapped and stuck. All of my attempts to empower him by offering an alternative perspective and an action plan to change jobs were met with instant disdain and disagreement. Carl put tremendous energy into continually trying to convince me that leaving his job was impossible. Realizing we were both caught on his cognitive distortion hamster wheel, therapy finally moved in a new direction when I asked Carl, "When else in your life have you felt like this?" At first he was thrown by the question. We had been so focused on his current job that asking him to shift gears and think about a prior experience of hopelessness and feeling trapped was a curveball.

The question, however, resonated somewhere deep inside because Carl grew very quiet and finally said, "That's how it felt in my house—trapped and stuck. No options and no choices. I even remember my sister saying, 'Just grin and bear it until you are old enough to move out.' Sounds like what I say about the hospital."

This was a breakthrough for Carl, and it opened the door to a deeper exploration of the parallels between work and his earlier childhood experiences. He saw the incompetence and ineffectiveness of his supervisor as mirroring similar qualities in his mother, who had been a nonprotective bystander in his childhood. Her emotional unavailability left him feeling totally unsupported, which was exactly how he felt at work. He also realized that the implacable notion of not being able to leave an untenable situation was modeled and normalized by her inability to leave a violent marriage.

Once Carl realized that he had a "frozen in time" attitude about work—assuming he couldn't leave and superimposing childhood feelings of helplessness onto his adult persona—he became willing to look at the possibility of changing jobs. There was a lot of anxiety and fear to work through in therapy. Carl needed to learn how to make decisions from his most empowered adult self and not a traumatized and trapped inner child. However, it was clear that his inner child needed much comforting and support as well.

The fact that Carl was willing to visualize and imagine a life beyond his current job was a major step in the right direction. As is often the case, Carl was able to take this powerful lesson and apply it to his clients' lives as well. He gained new insights about their "stuckness," and it ultimately enhanced his sense of compassion for them.

Putting it into practice

1   Divide a piece of paper in half vertically. On the left side write the heading "Family of Origin" and on the right side write "Workplace." Take a moment and think about your childhood and what it was like to be a part of your family. Starting with the family-of-origin side, choose one of the two options in each statement below that most accurately captures your experiences growing up. When you've completed the list of words, take a few deep, cleansing breaths. Now move to the right side of the page and focus on your current or most recent job and the workplace dynamics that exist there. Again, choose which of the two descriptive words that best captures your workplace environment. When finished, take another cleansing breath. Looking at the two lists, notice the similarities and the differences. What has been replicated from your family-of-origin in your current job, and what has changed?

Did you feel
    validated/invalidated
    empowered/disempowered

understood/misunderstood
respected/disrespected
safe/unsafe
appreciated/unappreciated
connected/disconnected
encouraged/discouraged
good enough/never good enough

Were expectations
   reasonable/unreasonable
   clear/unclear
   consistent/inconsistent

Were the boundaries
   appropriate/inappropriate

Was the environment
   cooperative/competitive
   predictable/unpredictable
   calm/chaotic
   supportive/unsupportive
   healthy/dysfunctional
   flexible/rigid
   warm/cold

2 Use the following "Strive for Five in the Workplace" assessment to evaluate the extent to which your current workplace is meeting your needs by rating from 0 (*I don't feel this at all*) to 5 (*I feel this all of the time*) each of the five major arenas that contribute to professional growth and job satisfaction. Then add up your total score.

Pride (0–5): Proud of what you do, know you do it well
Purpose (0–5): Know you affect others in positive ways, have an impact on your workplace
Productivity (0–5): Sense of accomplishment that can be tangibly measured

Protection (0–5): Physically and emotionally safe to express yourself, trust others have your back

Pleasure (0–5): Derive joy, satisfaction, and fulfillment from your work

Ideally, you want to score between 20 and 25 points. If you scored fewer points, notice those areas, and without judgment or self-criticism, think about how your score can be improved. It can be about using your voice more, setting different limits, asking for support, delegating tasks, seeking clarity about your job description, or asking for a raise. A "major factor in reducing compassion stress, especially at the end of the workday, is acquiring a sense of achievement and satisfaction" (Figley, 2002, p. 217). Sometimes it's about lowering your threshold for what's unacceptable and giving yourself permission to leave a toxic workplace that shows no promise of ever getting better.

25

STRIVING FOR BALANCE
IN YOUR LIFE

It can feel like we are walking a tightrope at times, precariously attempting to maintain the right balance between work and activities that strengthen self-soothing and self-care. Unfortunately we don't live in a culture that always supports or even values making and taking time to reenergize and regroup. Yet many books focusing on self-care and ways to avoid burnout emphasize the need for *balance* between working and play (Rothschild, 2006; Rubin & Springer, 2009; Wicks, 2008).

Rather than advocate for enough vacation or sick days, we are overworked and show up at the job when we are unwell. We often define ourselves, and others, through our job description. When meeting new people, after asking their name, we immediately ask what they do for a living. We admire professionals who dedicate their lives to their jobs, not necessarily the ones who pace themselves and spend as much time on self-care as they do helping others. And if we do find the courage to engage in self-care, the lack of societal support can evoke a feeling of embarrassment, so we don't necessarily talk about it. When no one admits to making time for self-care, it doesn't get normalized. Charles Figley (2002) also emphasized the need to let go of work by "building a firewall between ourselves and potential career-killing stress" (p. 216).

Ironically, many of us who specialize in trauma tend to unwind by going to trauma conferences, reading books about trauma, and watching movies and television programs that feature acts of violence and victimization. This level of interest is often rooted in a sincere desire to know as much as possible in order to be as helpful as possible. For other professionals who are trauma survivors, there is almost a magnetic attraction toward activities that are grounded in abuse or violence.

Whenever I give trainings on self-care to a group of mental health professionals, I ask them to identify their favorite TV stations and programs. Invariably, they admit with a combination of laughter and embarrassment that they are addicted to programs about serial killers and sexual crimes and made-for-TV movies that depict women being stalked or in some kind of peril. Although these activities are associated with downtime, these programs clearly do not offer a time-out from what these professionals are subjected to all day. All activities, both in and out of the office, revolve around victimization and the activation of the fight–flight response.

In addition, if we are in private practice, it's important to engage in recreational activities that allow us to reconnect with other people. A solo practice does have its benefits, but the price we pay is the loss of collegial interaction that can be playful, rejuvenating, supportive, and comforting. Our work role is about giving to others, and private practice doesn't allow us to reequilibrate the scales by being in receive mode from colleagues.

As we are social animals, there is an intrinsic need for affiliation and connection to others. If we can't get it in the workplace, we need to seek it out in other arenas. Therefore, it is helpful and necessary to engage in outside activities that enable us to be a part of like-minded groups. When we take regular breaks from traumatic material, it helps us reconnect with a sense of joy, serenity, consistency, predictability, and safety. This gives us a more balanced perspective about humankind and the world at large. Joyful extracurricular activities can help us better manage the challenges of our work and go a long way toward inoculating us against burnout.

Potential pitfalls

- We engage in downtime activities that are actually a perpetuation of experiences that are rooted in trauma and continue to activate fight, flight, or freeze responses in us.

- We don't search for hobbies and activities that activate our parasympathetic systems because they feel boring.
- We feel compelled to barrage ourselves with information and experiences that are trauma based in the name of improving our effectiveness at work.
- We refuse to make time for downtime because we are overly dedicated to our jobs.

THERAPIST VIGNETTE

Theresa was a seasoned clinical director who supervised a staff of crisis hotline workers. Exceptionally good at her job and highly respected by colleagues, she maintained a calm demeanor in the face of the most challenging crisis-driven scenarios. Believing she was unaffected by the intensity of her job, she worked long hours, often covering extra shifts when a staff member was sick or unavailable.

Theresa had degrees in social work and nursing, so when she wasn't working on the hotline, she volunteered at a hospital, serving as a forensic nurse in the emergency room. She interviewed victims of sexual assault and domestic violence and often testified on their behalf in court. She found the work intensely gratifying and spent many evenings and weekends in the ER. A deeply religious person, Theresa also felt committed to her church and served as a volunteer "lay counselor" to many of the parishioners when they were in crisis. Her friends frequently tried to fix her up on dates or invite her out socially, but she always turned them down, saying her plate was too full, as she had already committed to a hotline or hospital shift. Given the level of self-reported meaning and satisfaction in Theresa's life, she was truly perplexed by newly recurring headaches, stomach upset, and sleep disturbance that seemed to be more prevalent in her life.

I never actually consulted in person with Theresa. She told me her story by e-mail, after bringing her staff to a full-day training I gave on helping professionals, self-care, and burnout. She told me that the training was both a revelation and deeply disturbing, as she realized, with growing anxiety, that there was absolutely no balance in her life. "To be honest," she wrote, "I was horrified to discover that I had been kidding myself into thinking I led the ideal life. Everything I do is crisis driven, and I never understood the toll it was taking on my body. The things I do to unwind probably wind me up more. I felt like a hypocrite, as I am always pushing my staff to take better care of themselves, but I don't live that life myself."

Theresa ended by thanking me for the eye-opening experience and by vowing to find an activity or hobby that truly promoted self-care and counterbalanced the intensity of her work. She confessed that her biggest roadblock was feeling bored by mundane activities. This is often the challenge for helping professionals, especially ones who have their own trauma histories. I applauded Theresa's courage and insights and urged her to give herself permission to work on this important issue.

Putting it into practice

1   Take a large piece of paper and divide it into three equal sections by drawing two vertical lines down the page or folding it into three parts. In the center section, use markers or colored pencils to draw simple images that represent your current hobbies and recreational activities. Include the things you do alone and with other people. In the left-hand column, draw the hobbies and recreational activities that you used to do in the past. In the far right column, draw the hobbies and activities you would like to do in the future. Now review the three sections, and without judgment notice the similarities and differences. Notice the extent to which these experiences impart comfort, relaxation, competence, joy, connection to others, and lightheartedness. Take note of the things you no longer do, and spend some time thinking about why. The reasons may be quite practical. Or it may be possible that some of the activities can be reintroduced into your life. Now spend some time processing the images associated with what you'd like to do in the future. See if you can generate a list of action steps that would move you in the direction of realizing at least one of those activities.

2   On a large piece of paper, draw your version of a balanced
     scale. On one side of the scale, begin to make a list of all
     the things you do in your life—professionally and person-
     ally—that relate to trauma. On the other side of the scale,
     make a list of all the professional and personal things you do
     that have nothing to do with trauma. Use this as a visual cue
     to assess how balanced or unbalanced the scale really is and
     think about where you could add or subtract weight to make
     the scale more balanced.

26

GIVING YOURSELF PERMISSION TO GET SUPERVISION OR REFER OUT

It is important to articulate that we have the prerogative and right to not treat clients with self-destructive behaviors if it feels too upsetting or hits too close to home. In the name of altruism, we often feel compelled to take on every case that comes our way. Although that sounds noble, no one is an expert in everything, and clients deserve the best possible care. When we make decisions from only that "outward focus" by attending to clients' needs, we may lose sight of the "inward focus" that accurately assesses our comfort level and our ability to serve clients objectively, nonjudgmentally, and effectively. It is also easier to offer other treatment resources before we have forged a relationship with a prospective client.

If a client self-identifies as a "cutter" or someone who is grappling with an eating disorder or an addiction, we need to listen to and trust our internal compasses. We should ask ourselves—before signing on—whether we have the emotional, mental, and physical stamina given the current existing dynamics in our professional and personal lives. If we are in the midst of personal complications evoked by a possible life transition, health issues, marital discord, concerns about a family member, and so on, it might not be the right time to take on a challenging new case. We should also look closely at how many similar cases are already in our practice. It's equally legitimate to assess our level of interest, as well as our professional expertise, in working with that issue.

It is admittedly more complicated to refer out once we've become entrenched in a therapeutic alliance and self-destructive behaviors suddenly surface or are uncovered through our assessment process. In these cases we may feel that our insecurities or lack of expertise can be tempered by the strength of the therapeutic relationship, which inherently brings trust, honest communication, genuine caring, authenticity, and stability to the client. We can attempt to work through the challenges of self-destructive behaviors in these clients with the help of excellent supervision or consultation.

When we are seasoned practitioners, it can feel humbling to get supervision or consultation for a case involving trauma and self-destructive behaviors. Yet the sign of a wise and committed clinician is the ability to comfortably acknowledge strengths and limitations and, in the name of serving clients, to get extra support and guidance when needed.

It's worth emphasizing that the consultation we seek should be with someone who has expertise in self-destructive behaviors and an open-minded approach to assessment (moving beyond a borderline diagnosis, understanding the interplay between self-destructive acts and trauma) and treatment options (moving beyond standard safety contracts, recognizing the value of creative treatment modalities).

Getting outside guidance, wisdom, and support can provide the safety net that makes all the difference. There are some instances, however, when our comfort level, sense of safety, or lack of confidence or competence does warrant transferring clients out. When this is handled with sensitivity and reframed as giving clients an even greater opportunity to heal, it can work out positively for everyone involved. We know that clients have the right to feel comfortable and safe. Clinicians do, too.

Potential pitfalls

- We don't take into consideration the context of our personal lives before taking on additional, challenging clients.

- We don't give ourselves permission to seek out supervision or peer consultation because we are seasoned clinicians and believe we should no longer require clinical guidance.
- We are afraid to refer out a self-destructive client when we are in over our heads, because we think it makes us look incompetent or will be too upsetting for the client.
- We don't work collaboratively with other mental health and medical professionals because we think we should be able to handle it all ourselves.

THERAPIST VIGNETTE

Corey was a senior therapist in a community mental health agency. Much of his caseload involved acting-out adolescents. He seemed to have a knack with this population and always felt comfortable treating behaviors like shoplifting, sexual promiscuity, and substance abuse. His colleagues looked to him for guidance and informally ran many of their more challenging cases by him throughout the work week. Corey took great pride in his expertise and enjoyed being looked up to by the rest of the staff.

At one point, Corey began seeing a new teenaged client who was referred for her cutting behaviors. He found her quite challenging to join with but was determined to continue working with her. He tried some of the standard treatment approaches he had read about, without much success. Although it crossed his mind to get consultation, he admitted that his pride prevented it. He believed he should be able to figure out how to help her, given his years of experience as a professional.

He continued to muddle through their sessions, plagued with a growing awareness that his client was completely stuck, and he didn't know what to do about it. Although her parents insisted that she stay in therapy, after about 6 months, she was able to successfully convince them that she was getting nothing out of treatment, and they allowed her to terminate.

(continued)

(continued)

As Corey reflected back on this case, he realized he felt "kind of haunted by it" and eventually decided to process, in brief therapy, the impact this failure was having on him. In talking it through, Corey discovered just how opposed he had been to consulting with an expert in self-destructive behaviors or discussing the possibility of referring her to another staff member in the agency who could have been more helpful.

He realized that his own need to maintain an image of professional superiority and his fears about looking inadequate to his peers and to himself clouded his judgment and deprived his client of the services she most needed. This was a sobering realization for Corey, and it took some time for him to reconcile feelings of guilt and shame. However, he came out of the process with a newfound understanding that seeking consultation was not a sign of weakness. It was actually a sign of strength and a statement about a deep commitment to serving the best interests of his clients.

Putting it into practice

1   Begin to generate a list of professionals in your community who have an expertise in and work with traumatized clients and self-destructive behaviors. Be sure they subscribe to a strengths-based, depathologized approach to the issues. Start by visualizing yourself contacting one of these colleagues to request a consultation for a difficult case. Notice the thoughts and feelings that emerge when you think about reaching out for support. If you notice a feeling of resistance about getting outside support or an inner critical voice that tells you that you should be able to handle it on your own, acknowledge those feelings without judgment. See if you can access the wise part of you that knows that asking for outside help is a sign of strength, not a statement of incompetence, and allow that part to reassure you that seeking consultation or referring out is a perfectly acceptable thing to do.

27

PRACTICING WHAT
YOU PREACH

We will lose all credibility about advocating for client self-care if we don't model it ourselves in ways that are visible to our clients. This means not coming to work when we are sick and looking well rested in session because we *are* well rested. We can also offer appropriate self-disclosures about choices that promote self-care or hobbies and lifestyle choices we currently engage in that bring balance to our lives.

The powerful truth is clinicians who smell of cigarette smoke, look perpetually exhausted, or struggle with eating disordered behaviors that leave them significantly overweight or underweight communicate a subliminal message to clients that says, "Do as I say, not as I do." It also is a walking advertisement for, and condones, self-destructive behaviors and can actually be reminiscent of the confusing mixed messages that our clients received from an abusive, nonprotective, or impotent caretaker. It will evoke strong transferential responses in them, thus undermining the therapy process.

As we assist clients in their journey toward greater self-actualization and self-love, we can be authentic guides only if we have traveled that path ourselves. Although this mind-set might seem obvious, in the name of helping others, we can be oblivious to the need for self-care and personal insight. Some of us mistakenly believe that the way to achieve personal growth and healing is through our work with clients. Nothing can be further from the truth: not attending to our own unresolved issues and ignoring our physical, emotional, psychological, and spiritual needs only *compromises* our work with others.

Although it is not a popular sentiment to articulate, working with trauma survivors and their self-destructive coping strategies can be exhausting. Sitting in session with clients, holding safe space, bearing witness to their pain, and managing dual awareness as we take their emotional temperature, as well as our own, can be consuming and draining. As Goulding and Schwartz (2002) wisely described in their Internal Family Systems paradigm, whether we are conscious of it or not, as we monitor and comfort our clients' anxious, angry, despairing parts, we are simultaneously attempting to monitor and manage our own parts that countertransferentially emerge. To successfully navigate our way through a session, we need to access our own healthiest energy, affect, and cognitions. Ongoing self-care makes that possible.

The metacommunication of *our* actions reaches our clients when we practice what we preach. We are normalizing and modeling the behaviors, while giving our clients permission to try them on as well. When our actions and words are consistent and in sync, it frees clients up to focus on themselves. Their natural tendency toward caretaking and hypervigilance can be quelled in the therapeutic relationship only when clients believe they don't have to take care of us because we are taking care of ourselves.

Potential pitfalls

- We give clients the self-care message "Do as I say, not as I do."
- We neglect our own needs and in the process evoke caretaking responses from our clients that keep the spotlight on us and not them.
- We inadvertently undermine our credibility as experts in treating self-destructive behaviors when we engage in them ourselves.
- We underestimate the extent to which we serve as role models for our clients.
- We confuse our clients with mixed messages that become reminiscent of their family-of-origin dynamics.

THERAPIST VIGNETTE

Caroline was seeing me for individual therapy. She was a social worker with a thriving private practice specializing in eating disordered behaviors. She had even begun a group consortium, bringing several other clinicians into a large office complex she was renting. Although she was optimistic about her latest business venture, she was anxious about her commitment to take on such a big monthly rental payment, and as a result she was "burning it at both ends" to make sure she could meet her expenses.

The confluence of stressful clients and financial pressure took its toll, and Caroline found herself bingeing at night as a way to self-soothe and cope. In addition, her relentless schedule compromised her ability to take the time for a healthy lunch or dinner, and Caroline found herself drinking more and more coffee and eating fast-food meals in the car. By her own estimation, she had gained over 40 pounds in 2 months.

Although she expressed frustration and shame about her overeating, she didn't think about the impact it was having on her work with clients until I specifically asked about it. The question caught her by surprise: it hadn't occurred to her that her stress, preoccupation with finances, poor nutritional habits, and weight gain could impact her efficacy at work. The irony was that she, as a dedicated therapist, was very focused on encouraging her clients to engage in healthy self-care, often pointing out to them when stress impacted their lives or when they used food inappropriately.

To her credit, Caroline began to take a closer look at the dynamics within her caseload and began to see that several clients had actually been canceling more, and two clients had terminated treatment rather abruptly. Although we could not say with certainty why the withdrawal had occurred, it was important to consider the possibility that her clients were tuned in to her stress and noticed the dysfunctional ways in which she was attempting to manage it. This might have undermined her credibility, causing some of her clients to lose faith in her abilities.

(continued)

(continued)

Ultimately, Caroline's decision to alter her coping strategies should not have been based on clients' reactions, but in her case, it became an important motivating factor in her decision to start attending Overeaters Anonymous meetings, reduce her coffee consumption, and resume an exercise routine for healthy weight loss and stress management.

Putting it into practice

1   Find a comfortable place to take the following "Taking Care of Others Versus Taking Care of Myself" questionnaire. Start first with the "Others" column and rate from 0 (*not at all*) to 5 (*all of the time*) the extent to which you encourage your clients to do the things identified on the list. Then go back and reread the statements, rating the extent to which you do these things for yourself. Total your score for each column and, without judgment, notice the extent to which the scores are similar or different. The key to processing the questionnaire is to approach it without recriminations. Having an openhearted curiosity will help you to focus on areas that can be improved.

Make healthy choices in life
    Others_____   Myself_____

Give up unhealthy behaviors
    Others_____   Myself_____

Walk away from abusive relationships/situations
    Others_____   Myself_____

Work on having positive self-esteem
    Others_____   Myself_____

Be assertive to feel respected and valued in life
    Others_____   Myself_____

Take healthy risks, dream, be challenged
Others_____   Myself_____

Set boundaries/limits to feel safe in life
Others_____   Myself_____

Make personal time to unwind, relax, and regroup
Others_____   Myself_____

Distinguish between what you can and what you cannot control in life
Others_____   Myself_____

Connect with others, be a part of a community, and get support
Others_____   Myself_____

2   Once you've scored the questionnaire, choose a category under "Myself" where you scored particularly low. Write down several small action steps that you could take to begin to address the behavior.

28

STRENGTHENING
YOUR WORK

Given the challenges of working with clients with self-destructive behaviors and all of the underlying dynamics that accompany that, when we don't work from an educated and informed place, we increase the likelihood of burning out. Without realizing it, we may be spinning our wheels *and* barking up the wrong tree by placing too much energy and focus on certain aspects of treatment while simultaneously neglecting other components that would actually move our clients forward more quickly.

Despite our years of experience in the field, working with clients with self-destructive behaviors is a somewhat unique proposition. It requires an interesting combination of open-mindedness, spontaneity, and a willingness to be creative while staying grounded in sound clinical theories and evidence-based models of practice. Our willingness to stay abreast of the latest treatment paradigms that incorporate mind–body work, along with new research about trauma's impact on the brain and the dynamics of attachment and affect regulation, is a critically important part of the work.

In addition to the obvious ways in which our clients benefit, this knowledge also enhances our sense of competence and confidence. Working from this place of self-assuredness decreases our feelings of being stressed and overwhelmed. We can better endure the inevitable challenges from anxious clients who are defensive and frightened of change. We can be a beacon of strength and determination in the face of their ambivalence and constant questioning. The following are, again, some reminders of the important things to incorporate into your work with this population.

Remembering to focus on these facets of treatment will go a long way toward helping your clients in their healing journeys.

- When your clients disclose that they are engaging in self-destructive behaviors, take the time to assess for a prior history of abuse, trauma, or neglect.
- Remember that clients often hold very narrow definitions of these experiences and need to be educated about the wide range of subtle and not-so-subtle forms of abuse and neglect.
- Even when you have ruled out trauma, be open to the possibility that your clients have come with a pain narrative that is worthy of exploration. It may help to explain their need to engage in self-destructive behaviors and move you away from pathologizing diagnoses.
- Work through your initial discomfort about the behaviors when they surface and take time to assess whether you need to refer out. If you have adequate support, referring out is almost never required.
- Keep in mind the intrinsic faith your clients have in you and your abilities, evidenced by the fact that they shared something so shame based and difficult to talk about.
- Give yourself permission to get ongoing support and guidance.
- It is important to explore early attachment dynamics. Avoidant, insecure, and disorganized attachment patterns leave children bereft of the skills needed for affect regulation. As a result, much of what you are seeing can be understood as the inevitable by-product of affect dysregulation. Self-destructive behaviors become the only viable resource for self-soothing.
- Because these clients are not effective at mediating their changing emotional states, it is imperative that you teach them containment, affect regulation and safe place imagery early on in treatment, before deeper work begins.
- Depathologize the behavior by letting go of the borderline personality diagnosis and thereby shattering the glass ceiling

that limits the extent to which you believe your clients can get better. Instead of thinking "borderline," think of your clients as "trauma survivors" to engender the necessary empathy and compassion that make a therapeutic relationship possible and therapy successful.

- Explain to your clients that you have no expectation of their stopping their self-destructive behaviors before they've learned alternative strategies for coping, self-soothing, deescalating, and expressing their narratives. The decision to sublimate and eventually extinguish their behaviors is always their choice to make.

- Let go of standard safety contracts and the power struggles they evoke and offer CARESS as an alternative way to work through the urges to engage in self-destructive and punitive behaviors.

- Over time, identify all of the self-destructive behaviors your clients are engaging in, remembering that they often use multiple methods but will only reveal their least shaming behaviors unless you compassionately and nonjudgmentally explore other potential methods they may be using.

- Operate from your most adult, compassionate self when working with these clients, inviting younger, scared, or angry parts of yourself to not participate in the therapeutic process. Hold an ongoing awareness of your own internal process while simultaneously tracking your clients' cognitive, emotional, and somatic responses to the work.

- Encourage clients who cut or burn their bodies to explore the meaning that they attach to the location of the wound and the choice of their self-mutilating behavior.

- Work with and decode the metacommunication of the behavior before trying to extinguish it. Help your clients recognize that their actions are ways to creatively "tell without talking." Ask, "Whose body are you trying to hurt?" to see if they are hurting a perpetrator's body in effigy.

- Put their drinking, purging, cutting, and so on into context by exploring the circumstances and triggering events that evoked the initial urge to engage in the self-destructive behavior.

- Give clients an adequate escape clause for potential triggers to help them feel less trapped and more empowered.

- Remember to focus on the physical harbingers of dissociation so clients can begin to identify their own process and contemplate the option of choosing to stay grounded and forward rather than space out.

- Teach your clients the cycle of self-destructive behaviors and empower them with the concept of intervention sites that can help short-circuit them.

- When working with adolescents, get permission to involve parents and significant others in the treatment process to avoid colluding with the dynamic of secrecy.

- As the work unfolds, rely less on talk therapy and more on creative modalities, especially ones that activate the right brain and help clients reconnect with their bodies. Have faith in the fact that these clients are inherently creative—their coping strategies have proven that.

- Exude a sense of hope and optimism regarding your clients' abilities to recover and heal. Clients often need to borrow our ego-strength until they have their own.

- Choose to believe in the power of the therapeutic alliance and the reparative impact of attachment. Choose to believe you make a difference in your clients' lives. Accept that they have the power to change, and the decision to do so is theirs alone to make.

- Remember your efficacy as a professional is contingent on the extent to which you take care of yourself personally. And believe that, ultimately, your clients have what it takes to take care of themselves.

BIBLIOGRAPHY

All URLs were accessed on 30/07/14.

Alderman, T. (1997). *The scarred soul: Understanding and ending self-inflicted violence – A self-help guide.* Oakland, CA: New Harbinger.

Briere, J., & Gil, E. (1998). Self-mutilation in clinical and general population samples: Prevalence, correlates, and functions. *American Journal of Orthopsychiatry, 68,* 609–620.

Briere, J., & Jordan, C. E. (2009). The relationship between childhood maltreatment, intervening variables and adult psychological difficulties in women: An overview. *Journal of Trauma, Violence and Abuse, 10*(37), 375–388.

Brodsky, B. S., Cliotre, M, & Dulit, R. A. (1995). Relationship of dissociation to self-mutilation and childhood abuse in borderline personality disorder. *American Journal of Psychiatry, 152*(12), 1788–1792.

Burns, D. (1999). *Feeling good: The new mood therapy.* Stamford, CT: Morrow.

Cohen, B., Barnes, M., & Rankin, A. (1995). *Managing traumatic stress through art: Drawing from the center.* Brooklandville, MD: Sidran Press.

Conterio, K., & Lader, W. (1998). *Bodily harm.* New York: Hyperion.

Cozolino, L. (2004). *The making of a therapist: A practical guide for the inner journey.* New York: W. W. Norton.

Cozolino, L. (2006). *The neuroscience of human relationships: Attachment and the developing social brain.* New York: W. W. Norton and Company.

Crews, W. D., Bonaventura, S., & Rowe, F. B. (1993). Cessation of long-term Naltrexone therapy and self-injury: A case study. *Research in Developmental Disabilities, 14*(4), 331–340.

Cutter, D., Jaffe, J., & Segal, J. (2008). Self-injury: Types, causes and treatment. Retrieved from helpguide.org/mental/self_injury.htm

Daitch, C. (2007). *Affect regulation toolbox: Practical and effective hypnotic interventions for the over-reactive client.* New York: W. W. Norton.

Earley, J., & Weiss, B. (2010). *Self-therapy for your inner critic.* Larkspur, CA: Pattern System Books.

Emel, B. (2013). Self-Compassion: Learning to be nicer to ourselves. Retrieved from http//tinybuddha.com/blog/self-compassion

Emerson, D., & Hopper, S. (2011). *Overcoming trauma through yoga: Reclaiming your body*. Berkeley, CA: North Atlantic Books.

Favazza, A. (1996). *Bodies under siege: Self-mutilation and body modification in culture and psychiatry*. Baltimore, MD: The Johns Hopkins University Press. 2nd edition.

Ferentz, L. (2001). Self-injurious behavior. *Child Study Center Letter, 6*(2), 1–4.

Ferentz, L. (2002). Treating the self-harming client. *Psychotherapy Networker, 26*(5), 69–77.

Ferentz, L. (2011). It's not about the food. *Psychotherapy Networker, 35*(1), 40–54.

Figley, C. (1995). *Compassion fatigue: Coping with secondary traumatic stress disorder in those who treat the traumatized*. New York: Routledge.

Figley, C. (2002). *Treating compassion fatigue*. New York: Routledge.

Gerson, J., & Stanley, B. (2008). Suicidal self-injurious behavior in people with BPD. Retrieved from http://www.psychiatrictimes.com/articles/ suicidal-self-injurious-behavior-people-bpd

Gladstone, G., Parker, G., Mitchell, P., Gin, M., Wilheim, K., & Austin, M. (2004). Implications of childhood trauma for depressed women: An analysis of pathways from childhood sexual abuse to deliberate self-harm and revictimization. *American Journal of Psychiatry, 161,* 1417–1425.

Glassman, L., Weierich, M. R., Hooley, J. M., Deliberto, T. L., & Nock, M. N. (2007). Child maltreatment, non-suicidal self-injury, and the mediating role of self-criticism. *Journal of Behavioural Research and Therapy, 45*(10), 2483–2490.

Goulding, R. A., & Schwartz, R. C. (2002). *The mosaic mind*. Eugene, OR: Trailhead Publishing.

Gratz, K. L. (2003). Risk factors for and functions of deliberate self-harm: An empirical and conceptual review. *Clinical Psychology Science and Practice, 10,* 192–205.

Gratz, K. L. (2007). Targeting emotion dysregulation in the treatment of self-injury. *Journal of Clinical Psychiatry, 63,* 1091–1103.

Gratz, K., & Chapman, A. (2009). *Freedom from self-harm: Overcoming self-injury with skills from DBT and other treatments*. Oakland, CA: New Harbinger.

Haines, J., Williams, C. L., Brain, K. L., & Wilson, G. V. (1995). The psychophysiology of self-mutilation. *Journal of Abnormal Psychology, 104,* 471–489.

Haw, C., Hawton, K., Houston, K., & Townsend, E. (2001). Psychiatric and personality disorders in deliberate self-harm patients. *British Journal of Psychiatry, 178,* 48–54.

Herman, J. (1992). *Trauma and recovery*. New York: Basic Books.

Hollander, M. (2008). *Helping teens who cut*. New York: Guilford.

Huether, G. (1996). The central adaption syndrome: Psychosocial stress as a trigger for adaptive modifications of brain structure and brain function. *Progress in Neurobiology, 48,* 569–612.

Klonsky, E. D. (2007). The function of deliberate self-injury: A review of the evidence. *Clinical Psychological Review, 27,* 226–239.

Klonsky, E. D., Oltmanns, T. F., & Turkheimer, E. (2003). Deliberate self-harm in a nonclinical population: Prevalence and psychological correlates. *American Journal of Psychiatry, 160,* 1501–1508.

Levenkron, S. (1998). *Cutting: Understanding and overcoming self-mutilation.* New York: W. W. Norton.

Linehan, M. (1993). *Cognitive-behavioral treatment for borderline personality disorder.* New York: Guilford.

Linehan, M. (2000). The empirical basis of dialectical behavioral therapy: Development of new treatments vs. evaluation of existing treatments. *Clinical Psychology: Science and Practice, 7,* 113–119.

Low, G., Jones, D., & Duggan, C. (2001). The treatment of deliberate self-harm in borderline personality disorder using dialectical behavior therapy: A pilot study in a high security hospital. *Behavioural and Cognitive Psychotherapy, 29,* 85–92.

Matsakis, A. (1996). *I can't get over it: A handbook for trauma survivors.* Oakland, CA: New Harbinger.

Mikolajczak, M., Petrides, K. V., & Hurry, J. (2009). Adolescents choosing self-harm as an emotional regulation strategy: The protective role of trait emotional intelligence. *British Journal of Clinical Psychology, 48,* 181–193.

Miller, D. (1994). *Women who hurt themselves: A book of hope and understanding.* New York: Basic Books.

Najavits, L. (2001). *Seeking safety: A treatment manual for PTSD and substance abuse.* New York: Guilford.

Napier, N. (1994). *Getting through the day: Strategies for adults hurt as children.* New York: W. W. Norton.

Neff, K. (2004) Self-compassion and psychological well-being. *Constructivism in the Human Sciences, 9*(2), 27–37.

Neff, K. (2011) *Self-compassion: Stop beating yourself up and leave insecurity behind.* Stamford, CT: Morrow.

Neff, K. (2013) Why self-compassion trumps self-esteem. *Greater Good: The Science of a Meaningful Life.* Retrieved from http://greatergood.berkeley.edu/article/item/try_selfcompassion

Nixon, M. K., Cloutier, P., & Jansson, M. (2008). Non-suicidal self-harm in youth: A population-based survey. *Canadian Medical Association Journal, 178*(3), 306–312.

Nock, M., & Banaji, M. (2007). Assessment of self-injurious thoughts using a behavioral test. *American Journal of Psychiatry, 164,* 820–823.

Nock, M., & Prinstein, M. (2005). Contextual features and behavioral functions of self-mutilation among adolescents. *Journal of Abnormal Psychology, 114*(1), 140–146.

Noll, J. G., Horowitz, L. A., Bonanno, G. A., Trickett, P. K., & Putnam, F. W. (2003). Re-victimization and self-harm in females who experienced childhood sexual abuse. *Journal of Interpersonal Violence, 18,* 1452–1471.

Ogden, P., Minton, K., & Pain, C. (2006). *Trauma and the body: A sensorimotor approach to psychotherapy.* New York: W. W. Norton.

Rasmussen, D. (2011). *Cutting and more self-harm to mask emotional pain: Celebrity cutters like Christina Ricci, Angelina Jolie, Johnny Depp and more.* Webster's Digital Services.

Richardson, J. S., & Zaleski, W. (1983). Naloxone and self-mutilation. *Biological Psychiatry, 18,* 99–101.

Romans, S. E., Martin, J. L., Anderson, J. C., Herbison, G. P., & Mullen, P. E. (1995). Sexual abuse in childhood deliberate self-harm. *American Journal of Psychiatry, 152,* 1336–1342.

Ross, R. R., & McKay, H. B. (1979). *Self-mutilation.* Lexington, MA: Lexington Books.

Rothschild, B. (2002). *The body remembers: The psychophysiology of trauma and trauma treatment.* New York: W. W. Norton.

Rothschild, B. (2006). *Help for the helper: Self-care strategies for managing burnout and stress.* New York: W. W. Norton.

Rubin, A. and Springer, D. (2009). *Treatment of traumatized adults and children.* Hoboken, NJ: John Wiley and Sons.

Sachsee, U., Von der Heyde, S. and Huether, G. (2002). Stress regulation and self-mutilation. *American Journal of Psychiatry, 159,* 672–672.

Sandman, C., & Hetrick, W. (2005). Opiate mechanisms in self-injury. *Mental Retardation and Developmental Disabilities Research Reviews, 1*(2), 130–136.

Sansone, R. A., Gaither, G. A., & Songer, D. A. (2001). Self-harm behaviors and mental health care utilization among sexually abused males: A pilot study. *General Hospital Psychiatry, 23,* 97–98.

Satir, V. (1983). *Conjoint family therapy.* Palo Alto, CA: Science and Behavior Books.

Scaer, R. (2001). *The body bears the burden: Trauma, dissociation and disease.* New York: The Haworth Press.

Schiraldi, G. (2009). *The post-traumatic stress disorder sourcebook: A guide to healing, recovery and growth.* New York: McGraw-Hill.

Schore, A. (2003). *Affect dysregulation and disorders of the self.* New York: W. W. Norton.

Schwartz, R. (1997). *Internal family systems therapy.* New York: Guilford Press.

Seppala, E. (2011) Self-compassion: The secret to empowered action is not beating yourself up. *Spirituality and Health,* Sept.–Oct., 59–65.

Shapiro, L. (2008). *Stopping the pain: A workbook for teens who cut and self-injure.* Oakland, CA: Instant Help Books.

Shem, S. (1995). *The house of god.* New York: Dell Publishing.

Siegel, D. (1999). *The developing mind.* New York: Guilford Press.

Smith, B. (2008). Adolescent nonsuicidal self-injury: Evaluation and treatment. *Psychiatric Times, 25*(7), 24–30.

Strong, M. (1999). *A bright red scream: Self-mutilation and the language of pain.* New York: Penguin.

Swales, M. (2008). Pain and deliberate self-harm. *The Welcome Trust.* Retrieved from www.wellcome.ac.uk/en/pain/microsite/culture4.html

Taylor, J. B. (2006). *My stroke of insight.* New York: Penguin.

Tronick, E. (2007). *The neurobehavioral and social-emotional development of infants and children*. New York: W. W. Norton.

Turner, V. J. (2002). *Secret scars: Uncovering and understanding the addiction of self-injury*. Center City, MN: Hazelden.

Van der Kolk, B., McFarlane, A., & Weisaeth, L. (2006). *Traumatic stress: The effects of overwhelming experience on mind, body, and society*. New York: Guilford.

Van der Kolk, B. A., Perry, J. L., & Herman, J. (1991). Childhood origins of self-destructive behavior. *American Journal of Psychiatry, 148*, 1665–1671.

Vorobioff, M. (2011). EFT for emotional issues. *The International Energy Psychology Article Archive*. Retrieved from www.eft-alive.com

Wallenstein, M. B., & Nock, M. (2007). Physical exercise as a treatment for non-suicidal self-injury: Evidence from a single-case study. *American Journal of Psychiatry, 164*, 350–351.

Walsh, B. (2008). *Treating self-injury: A practical guide*. New York: Guilford.

Walsh, B., & Rosen, P. M. (1988). *Self-mutilation: Theory, research and treatment*. New York: Guilford.

Weekes, C. (1990). *Hope and help for your nerves*. New York: Signet.

Weigsheider-Hyman, J. (1999). *Women living with self-injury*. Philadelphia: Temple University Press.

Weintraub, A. (2003). *Yoga for depression: A compassionate guide to relieve suffering through yoga*. New York: Three Rivers Press.

White, T., & Schultz, S. (2000). Naltrexone treatment for a three year old boy with self-injurious behavior. *American Journal of Psychiatry, 157*(10), 1574–1580.

Whitlock, J. L., Powers, J. L., & Eckenrode, J. (2006). The virtual cutting edge: The Internet and adolescent self-injury. *Developmental Psychology, 42*(3), 1–11.

Wicks, R. (2008). *The resilient clinician*. New York: Oxford University Press.

Yates, T. (2004). The developmental psychopathology of self-injurious behavior: Compensatory regulation in posttraumatic adaption. *Clinical Psychology Review, 24*, 35–74.

Zanarini, M. C., Gunderson, J. G., & Marino, M. F. (1989). Childhood experiences of borderline patients. *Comprehensive Psychiatry, 30*, 18–25.

Zanarini, M. C., Yong, L., Frankenburg, F. R., Hennen, J., Reich, D. B., Marino, M. F., & Vujanovic, A. A. (2002). Severity of reported childhood sexual abuse and its relation to severity of borderline psychopathology and psychosocial impairment among borderline inpatients. *Journal of Nervous Mental Disorders, 190*, 381–387.

INDEX